The Eskimo Republic

To Kai.

30/10/10

#1 ♫

For John Powles, former Project Manager of the Centre for Political Song at Glasgow Caledonian University, and for Thurso Berwick.

Other books written or co-written by Ewan McVicar include
One Singer One Song
Cod Liver Oil & The Orange Juice [with Hamish Imlach]
Streets Schemes & Stages [with Mary McCabe]
Traditional Scottish Songs & Music [with Katherine Campbell]
Doh Ray Me When Ah Wis Wee
Lang Legged Beasties
One Black Isle Night

The Eskimo Republic

Scots political folk song in action 1951 to 1999

Ewan McVicar

GALLUS PUBLISHING
LINLITHGOW

First published in Great Britain in 2010 by
Gallus Publishing
84 High Street
Linlithgow
EH49 7AQ
01506 847935
ewan.mcvicar.gallus@tesco.net

This book was researched, created and published through a Writers Bursary grant in 2008 from the Scottish Arts Council, to whom full thanks are given.

Particular thanks are due to John Powles, Ian Davison, Stuart McHardy and Geordie McIntyre.

Particular thanks to Marion Blythman, Kaetzel Henderson, Janette McGinn, Meic Stephens, the families of Norman MacCaig and John MacEvoy, Ian Davison and Seylan Baxter to quote from the relevant works.
The data CD that accompanies this book can be played on a computer but NOT on an audio CD player. It holds a searchable PDF file in place of an index, 289 mp3 files of songs and data files. See the listings on pages 341-343.

ISBN 978-0-9565990-4-9
Edited, designed and brought to press by Ewan McVicar
Printed and bound in the UK by the MPG Books Group, Bodmin and King's Lynn

CONTENTS

Nations Rise That Yince Were Doon

Now fortune's wheel it is birlin roon
An nations rise that yince were doon
So it's time tae sing a rebel tune
For the Eskimo Republic

Where there is nae class, there is nae boss
Nae kings nor queens, an damn the loss
An ye get boozed up for a six months doss
In the Eskimo Republic

Scots folk song has always included a stinging dose of fervent political protest and social comment, but from 1951 on the dosage has increased and become more scouring and scourging in its intent and effect. Socialists and supporters of independence sing about living in peace with self-determination and protesting against injustice, while right wing wielders of power sing songs that seek to justify and defend their privileges.
The song 'The Eskimo Republic' was made in the 1960s by poet Morris Blythman, a extension of an idea adopted by 1961 Scottish peace protesters that the then termed Eskimos, now Inuit, have never been involved in warfare though living in several Northern countries, on both sides of the 'Cold War'. The lyric holds many of the elements that typified Scottish political folk song during the Scottish Folk Revival that began in the late 1950s and has now spread wide its influence musically and socially as its primary thrust of action loses impetus. Aspects of the Eskimo lyric include independence, republican socialism, the Scots Leid, humour, warfare, anti-nuclear weapons, enjoyment of alcohol, a vigorous tune, and applying the mirror of history to the maker's priorities. The tune Blythman selected for his song shows Scots makers' continuing reference back to and mining of older songs. 'Loch Errochside' was also used by Burns for a song about

a wandering warbling woodlark, not one of his best, and by Lady Caroline Nairne for a wooing song, 'The Lass of Gowrie'.

This book looks at Scotland's pre-1951 antecedents in political song, discusses key 1951-1999 songs, song-makers, singers and organisers, and gives many examples of the short-lived political comment and 'agit-prop' songs that were made and discarded. It investigates the period through first-hand accounts based on new interviews with the activists, and it considers the characteristics of humour, energy, and commitment that distinguish the songs, the use of older Scots song and of Scots language whether older vernacular or literary Lallans or modern urban, and the role of tunes, old, new and copyright, in the song-making.

A selection of Scottish political songs

I faught at land, I faught at sea
At hame I faught my Auntie, O
But I met the Devil and Dundee
On th' braes o' Killiecrankie, O
Killiecrankie

ଓ

Charlie Stuart came at last, sae far tae set us free
My Donald's arm was wanted then, for Scotland and for me
Their waefu fate what need I tell? Right tae the wrong did yield
My Donald and his country fell upon Culloden field
The Highland Widow's Lament

ଓ

Hark the 'Glasgow Herald' sings
English people all have wings
All the bad ones are the Scotch
Who take the Stone and leave the watch
For Kin And Country, tune Hark The Herald Angels, words W.W.

ଓ

Men and women listen to me
It's time to rise up aff yer knee
So raise the flag of Unity
And forward with the Union
If It Wisnae For the Union, tune Wark o the Weavers, words Matt McGinn

ଓ

I've been to Iraq, but now that I'm back, I wouldn't go there twice
With a name like MacHuseiney, and a dad from Azerbaijani
They'd have me doon the shredder in a trice
I'd have to go in disguise, tae gie them ma Eski expertise
Iraq 'N' Bac, tune The Lancashire Toreador, words Ukes Against Nukes

The Scots trait of engaging in robust and at times irreverent political discussion and action periodically expresses itself in song. These songs stimulate and support action, articulate the issues and principles espoused, particularise, sloganise and at times sentimentalise. One period of song-based action, the Jacobite song aftermath of the 1745 Rising, led to the egalitarian songs of Burns.

Another, the 1951 poetic expressions of pleasure at the Lifting of the Stone of Destiny, resulted in a sequence of song-supported actions on the issues of independence and republicanism, freedom from nuclear weaponry, opposition to the Poll Tax and the First Gulf War, and other linked causes, exemplified in the 'Eskimo Republic' concept of a Scottish nation of peace and equality.

The term Scottish Political Song is a

More Scottish political songs

O the Thistle o Scotland was famous of old
Wi its toorie sae snod and its bristles sae bauld
Tis the Badge o my Country, it's aye dear tae me
And thocht o them baith brings the licht tae ma ee
The Thistle of Scotland, As sung by Willie Main

Lang afore the Poles and Rumanians
The Czechoslovaks or Bulgarians
We led the workers tae victoree
We up and nationalised the Govan Ferree
The Labour Provost, tune The White Cockade, words Iain Nicolson

To the Lords of Convention twas Claverhouse spoke
"Ere the King's crown go down there are crowns to be broke
So let each cavalier who loves honour and me
Let him follow the bonnets o Bonnie Dundee"
Bonny Dundee, tune The Band at a Distance, words Sir Walter Scott

Wee Prince Chairlie's a lucky laddie
He's got a daddy and a mammy
Disna see the approachin rammy
Lucky wee Prince Chairlie
Wee Prince Chairlie, tune O Ro Se, words Thurso Berwick

So while our anger burns for those oppressed
By Uncle Sam, John Bull and all the rest
Remember in these Islands
In the Lowlands and the Highlands
There are nations that we only hold in jest
Workers of the World, tune and words Jim McLean

loose one, which can encompass protest, political comment, social comment, social history and narrative that supports a political stance. Some characteristic elements are that it is ephemeral, lyric based, exploitative of tunes, and uses humour as a weapon.
Ingredients of political song can be the urging of action against social and political injustice, approval for and support of warfare both internal and international, appeals for peace or for defence of the status quo, the joys of drink, the lessons of history, the concerns and complaints of labour, radicalism, socialism, republicanism, independence - all expressed through the medium of sung poetry in support of political and social action. Much Scottish political song is ephemeral. Nearly all political song is ephemeral, living only while it has direct and immediate relevance and is being sung by the creator individual and the surrounding group who identify with and adopt the song. But then the same kind of active life limitation is true of nearly all poetry ever published. Consider how little of the work of even the great poets is still read for other than academic purposes. As always, Robert Burns is our touchstone. Look through a collection of his work, and identify how many pieces, or rather how few, you recognise. And the effusions of our many lesser poets, neatly bound at the maker's expense, are to be found in cosy rows in the reference sections of our libraries. Open one up, and smell the must.
Scottish political song is lyric based and exploitative of existing tunes. Political song is very much a matter of lyric content. New tunes are seldom employed. Up until very recent times, in both the Scots and the Gaelic traditions, the creation of Scottish song has been the creation of lyrics. Neither Robert Burns nor Hamish Henderson composed a single tune, though they and many others trawled deeply for the airs, marches and dance tunes they used, and they then freely amended melody, tempo and rhythmic feel. On occasion parodies or new songs are written using the tune of a song of political comment that had itself employed an air created for other purposes. 'Parody' does not necessarily mean the employment of humour, but Scots political song uses humour, satiric or broad or sly or subtle, more often than English or Irish political song does.

Examination of Scottish political song begins with the old anonymous ballads that tell of battles and strife between the Scots and English, or internally in the Borders and the Highlands. Then comes the welter of songs occasioned by James 7th and 2nd being ejected from the British throne, and the successive attempts to restore the Stuart dynasty.
Once there was little chance of the Stuarts making it back onto the British throne a great manufactory of Jacobite songs arose. James Hogg was perhaps the finest and most prolific collector and creator of such, while Lady Caroline Nairne created some new songs and skilfully softened and emasculated some of the old songs.

Burns also collected and published and sometimes polished old songs, which were then labelled his wholecloth creations by some of his worshippers. His own political songmaking began with Jacobite songs, he moved on in the 1790s to hackpenny election ballads and to the expression of republican sentiments, then in order to avoid deportation to Australia's rocky shores he had to recant in public song. But though he wrote, "*Who will not sing 'God Save The King' shall hang as high as the steeple,*" he followed that with, "*But while we sing 'God Save The King' we'll ne'er forget THE PEOPLE!*"

The developing radicalism of Thomas Muir and the United Scotsmen, through the 1820

17th and 18th Century Scottish political songs

Arise now my country and hail reformation
Arise and demand now the rights of our nation
Behold your oppressors shall meet the desolation
That marked the brave victims on Dark Bonnymuir
Dark Bonnymuir, 1820s broadside

☙

Carle, an' the King come
Carle, an' the King come
Thou shalt dance and I shall sing
Carle, an' the King come
17th Century song

☙

An somebodie were come again
Then somebodie maun cross the main
And every man shall hae his ain
Carle, an the King come
18th Century Jacobite version

☙

Sawney, now the king's come
Kneel and kiss his gracious ---
Sawney, now the king's come
Tune traditional

Radical War and the organising of industrial labour can be fitfully traced through songs of the time.
Surprisingly little political Scots song from Chartist times can be found. Indeed, except for the radical weaver poets and occasional broadside protests about urban working conditions, the field is fairly unfruitful pretty well up to and past World War One. True, 'The Red Flag' was set to a Scots Jacobite tune, 'The White Cockade', by Irishman James Connell in 1889 – years later the lyric was shifted to the ponderous German tune 'Tannenbaum'.
The Spanish Civil War brought songs like Alex McDaid's proud song for the International Brigade, 'Jarama Valley', and Ewan MacColl's reworking of the Peninsular War lament for 'Jamie Foyers'.
Some of the Ballads of World War Two were collected together and published pseudonymously by Hamish Henderson, who had a hand in the creation of some of the best. Henderson's 'John Maclean March' in 1948 was a political song of poetic weight that heralded the Scottish Folk Revival of the 50s and 60s.
As well as songs that explicitly protest, demand or criticise, Scotland has a fine heritage of social comment songs. Themes include criticism of bad employers and poor working conditions, complaints about the excesses and abuses of privilege of the powerful, complaints about unemployment, support for trade unionism, social organisation and teetotalism, and songs about army life.
The collection 'Radical Renfrew', works of the Radical weaver poets of Renfrewshire edited by Tom Leonard, is presented as poetry, but the lyrics are often set to specified

A Radical 19th Century song

Glass after glass we'd often pass
And make the rafters ring
With roaring toasts for Radicals
And songs that traitors sing
We gave the Queen, but drank the toast
That laughed that she might be
And pray'd that she might ne'er have peace
Till Britons all were free
And thus we ranted to the crowd
With pleasant wordy show
In the days when we were Radicals
A short time ago

In the Days When We Were Radicals,
tune In the Days When We Went Gypsying,
words Edward Polin, from 'Radical Renfrew'

traditional tunes. There is a rich seam of Scottish coalminers' songs; a few of the best lyrics were made by Fife's Joe Corrie. Mary Brooksbank's songs of work in the Dundee jute mills are still celebrated and sung. The earlier Bothy Ballads of the North-East are almost invariably crisp and direct in their complaints about grasping and unfair farmers. Are they political songs?

Songs can live on as accounts of social history and supportive narrative, after they have outlived their function as protest or comment on current conditions. Such lyrics tend to have an extra spark of poetry, graphic example or energy, and be utilised for the complaint of, "And they're just like that still!" Further, at social gatherings of politically active groups the performance with audience participation of such 'non-current' songs functions as an expression of shared social identity, history and values.

There is a string of such Scots songs, from 'Such A Parcel Of Rogues In A Nation' to 'Maggie's Waddin', from 'Wee Magic Stane' to 'Maggie's Pit Ponies', from 'Jamie Foyers' to 'Don't You Go My Son'. When first made they were trenchant comment, now they are sung as nostalgic narrative.

Is political song only a product of the left? Of course not. The Jacobites were hardly leftwingers, and Hogg printed a couple of dozen Whig anti-Jacobite ditties. For each bothy ballad that belabours the farmers there is a sylvan ballad on the joys of country life and a sentimental ditty

Protests ancient and modern

Fareweel to aa our Scottish fame
Fareweel our ancient glory
Fareweel ev'n to the Scottish name
Sae famed in martial story
Now Sark rins over Solway Sands
And Tweed rins to the ocean
To mark where England's province stands
Such a parcel of rogues in a nation

Such A Parcel Of Rogues, Robert Burns

Sing a song o tax an woe
Empty pooches in a row
The Chancellor's collectin dough
Aa for Maggie's Waddin

Silk an satin, gold lame
Tony weirs a lum hat tae
Ma suit's in the pawn, sae whit'll ah dae
At the Royal Waddin?

Maggie's Waddin, Tune Mhairi's Wedding, words Jim MacLean

advising peace, harmony and social drunkenness.
True, the songs that are badges of the Right are often less politically or socially explicit. Is 'Keep Right On To The End Of The Road', sung by Harry Lauder to support the WW1 troops, not a political song? Is 'It's A Long Way To Tipperary'? Is 'Flower Of Scotland' left wing? Or 'Erin Go Bragh'?
What song which comments critically on the working life and the social viewpoint of people is not political song in some sense? How about the viciously anti-Catholic or anti-Protestant (and the viciously racist) songs which disfigure football terraces?
When considering political songs I will consider where and when they were sung, the makers, disseminators, performers, documentors and preservers of them, and the printed and recorded sources available to me.
I have in working on this book developed my own working terms, limits and exclusions. They are intended to be instructive rather than prescriptive. Here are some.
Protest usually includes open support for some specific group's position, whether political grouping, group of people met together to march or talk, work group or category. Protest song can be action lyric or illustrative lyric, dealing with the here and now rather than in retrospection.
In more general political song the lyric can be action-based, illustrative, retrospective or supportive.
The protest action lyric is an 'agit-prop' simple lyric protesting re the effects or consequences of current action or the position of government or powerful figures, including demands for alternative action. More general action-based lyrics suggest as well as demand alternative action positions, and articulate positions re wider issues.
The protest illustrative lyric has narrative accounts of events and people, and is employed to illustrate issues and support the need for preferred options and actions. More general illustrative lyrics are accounts of events, actions, situations and consequences that are considered and used by wider groupings of politically committed or

like minded people or groups as illustrative of their identity, critical position, or recommended alternative actions or values.
Retrospective lyrics tell of past historical events or beliefs or values, expressing what the writer believes to be the political and protest positions and responses of that time, in archaic or modern language, for the purpose of supporting and urging action to change attitudes, values and actions in the writer's own time.
Supportive lyrics are accounts of events or prescriptive statements that are not allied to any specific group, but can be used by a group or individual as an example statement that articulates an element of one's political stance, as a support and justification for one's stance and actions, in helping justify the need for actions, or as a social entertainment used at the end of political meetings or in concerts supporting political or social causes or campaigns.
Themes of identity and the need for action run through this topic. Also, richness of Scots language, both poetic and urban, is important for reinforcing one's sense of identity when in confrontation with a ruling elite and media who increasingly do not employ these. But always there is conflict in song as in politics. The Whigs and the Tories, the Radicals and the anti-Democrats, the Conservatives and the Socialists, all express confrontation and comment through songs.
There is a problem of structure and sequence when discussing political song. A historical sequence based on datable events rather than dates of composition might begin with 'Scots Wha Hae', as its stated topic is the Battle of Bannockburn in 1314, or since there is said to be written evidence of use rather than oral tradition only, one could begin with the tune's use as a march by the Scots soldiers of Joan of Arc in 1429. A sequence based on political themes intended by Burns would place 'Scots Wha Hae' in the late 18th Century, and a sequence based on who used the song politically and why would have to consider Scottish groupings and political actions from the time of the song's making, through quotations appearing on banners in the 19th Century, right up till yesterday.
One could trace 'Scots Wha Hae' through its appearances in print, from its first anonymous publication in London's Morning Chronicle

on 19th May 1794 through many dozens of poetry and song collections, and consider what lyric company it is given by editors and why.

Non-Scots comment on the dual importance of sung and printed versions of Scottish songs. In 'Folk Song In England' A L Lloyd says, "No doubt, the influence of printed collections has been greater on Scottish singers than on English, because Scottish collections have been abundant over a longer period, and have circulated widely in a land where villagers, crofters and farm-hands have long been busy readers."

In 1951 American folklorist Alan Lomax commented: "The Scots have the liveliest folk tradition of the British Isles, and paradoxically, it is also the most bookish.... Everywhere in Scotland I collected songs of written or literary origin from country singers; at the same time I constantly encountered learned Scotsmen who knew traditional versions of the great folk songs."

This book considers not only Scots political songs sung in Scotland, but links with political songs of Ireland, the USA, England and other lands. While my major focus is on songs newly minted and used politically in the period from 1951 on, I also give accounts of the types of earlier songs that were drawn on in the Revival – warfare and strife, old ballads, songs of national and local politics, and songs of work and unemployment and poverty – particularly those songs that entered into the shared sung repertoire in the Scots Folk Song Revival.

'Revival' suggests rescue from near death, used for want of a word that communicated the ideas of discovery, phoenix-like renewal and revitalisation. In political song-making, the new grows from the old.

When an Eskimo sings an Eski sang
He gies it the real auld Eski twang
An his favourite wan is 'I belang
Tae the Eskimo Republic'

It's Time To Sing A Rebel Tune

The Dean was in his braw nichtgoon
A cauldrife morn his doup aroon
When herried was the Stane o Scone
That gied him Geordie-Lowrie

Noo Geordie-Lowrie's no for me
Nae gladness in ma Deanery
I've tint the Stane o Destiny
It gies me Geordie-Lowrie

Auld Scotia's hert is heech aboon
Sair pitten-oot is England's Croun
As muckle as yon cheil de Bohun
Whan he got Geordie-Lowrie

Geordie-Lowrie, tune Muckin o Geordie's Byre, words Tom Law

The Return to Scotland of the Stane of Scone at Christmas 1950 caused greetin in Westminster Abbey but was greeted with delight in Scotland. Half the best poets in Scotland wrote songs to praise the act, to assert Scotland's rights and to ridicule the Scotland Yard searchers. The role of poet Morris Blythman was central and crucial at this time, as were the regular ceilidhs run by the Bo'ness Rebels Literary Society, a loose confederation of left wing political activists and writers whose joint aim was an independent Scotland.

The atmosphere at the Rebels' Hogmanay ceilidh of the 29th December 1950 was supercharged. Four days earlier the Stone of Scone had been prized out from the Westminster Abbey throne by four unknown young Scots and taken to a secret location somewhere in Scotland. The local newspaper, the 'Bo'ness Journal', reported that the ceilidh "was dominated by one topic – the Stone of Destiny and where was it? When Calum Campbell arrived (with a bandaged hand) along with Dr McIntyre and other well-known Scots Nationalists and it was known that at least one detective was present, the atmosphere, to say the least, became charged with expectancy."

Oliver Brown gave a "brilliantly witty speech". "He hoped that the 'Scone Stone' would form the foundation of a modern progressive Scotland."

The programme included "spirited piping – a worthy effort", "violin selections movingly interpreted" and songs in Scots and Gaelic.

This ceilidh also featured the first reported Bo'ness appearance of Morris Blythman, who would be one of the key creators of the highly influential series of 'Bo'ness Rebels Ceilidh Song Books'. Blythman wrote under the nom-de-plume Thurso Berwick, chosen to represent the length and breadth of Scotland. The 'Bo'ness Journal' said "The ceilidh moved to its climax when the chairman called on Thurso Berwick, the well known Lallans poet, to do his piece in 'Poets Corner'.

The first Sang O The Stane

The Stane the Stane the muckle Stane, the Stane worth half a croun
Whit's aa the steer aboot the Stane, this offa Stane-o-Scone?

Fa's taen it this time? Fa's taen it nou?
The Dean that hed it yon time hesna got it nou

The polis say it's Lang-neb Nell an Tousie-heidit Tam
A keelie pair frae Glesca toun that dinna care a damn

I ken it wasna Stalin, man, it wasna Mao-tze-Tung
But did MacDiarmid tak the Stane tae croun hissel at Scone?

The Muckle Stane O Scone, tune Ball of Kirriemuir, words Thurso Berwick.

Other verses ask if the reiving culprits were an intoxicated 'Reid-nose Rudolph Reindeer'; 'Santie Claus' who had 'sclimmed doun by the lum'; or 'Guid King Wenceslas' seeking 'the Front Page'?

"This recitation of the humorous poem 'The Muckle Stane o Scone' was the highlight of the whole evening, and was of a highly amusing nature." After the speeches, "Robin Adair and his Band played as if inspired" for country dancing, and the evening "was concluded with the singing of 'Auld Lang Syne' and the Scottish National Anthem 'Scots Wha Hae'." *The Bo'ness Journal*

The Stane had been removed from Westminster Abbey and returned to Scotland by a team of four led by Ian Hamilton on Xmas Eve, 1950. But they were not the only ones to have the idea, which was being widely urged by poet Christopher Grieve, who wrote under the name Hugh MacDiarmid. Rob Gibson says that the idea of getting the Stone was talked about back in the 1930s.

SNP activist Hugh MacDonald

O, the Dean o Westminster wis a powerful man
He held aa the strings o the state in his hand
But wi aa this great business it flustered him nane
Till some rogues ran away wi his wee magic stane
Wi a toora li oora li oora li ay

Noo the Stane had great powers that could dae such a thing
But without it, it seemed, we'd be wantin a King
So he caa'd in the polis an gave this decree
"Go an hunt out the Stone and return it to me"

So the polis went beetle'n up tae the North
They huntit the Clyde an they huntit the Forth
But the wild folk up yonder juist kiddit them aa
For they didnae believe it wis magic at all

Noo the Provost o Glesca, Sir Victor by name
Was awfy pit oot whan he heard o the Stane
So he offered the statues that staun in the square
That the high churches' masons might mak a few mair

When the Dean o Westminster wi this was acquaint
He sent fur Sir Victor and made him a saint
"Noo it's nae use you sending your statues doon here"
Said the Dean "but you've given me a right good idea"

So he quarried a stane o the very same stuff
An he dressed it aa up till it looked like enough
Then he sent for the press and announced that the stane
Had been found and returned to Westminster again

When the reivers found oot what Westminster had done
They went aboot diggin up stanes by the ton
And fur each wan they feenished they entered the claim
That this was the true and original stane

Noo the cream o the joke still remains tae be telt
Fur the bloke that wis turning them aff on the belt
At the peak o production wis so sorely pressed
That the real yin got bunged in alang wi the rest

So if ever you come on a stane wi a ring,
Jist sit yersel doon and appoint yersel King,
Fur there's nane wud be able to challenge yir claim
That you'd croont yersel King on the Destiny Stane

The Wee Magic Stane, tune Villikins, words John McEvoy

explains. "Exactly a week before it was lifted from Westminster Abbey, I was deputed to recruit a group of guys. Four of us were in Central Station, waiting for a driver to take us south, he was from Elmbank Street office. He arrived at last. "Oh, ah cannae make it" - a load of guff. We were going to go down and take the Stone. I got the idea originally from Chris Grieve, he'd passed the idea on, it was being generally discussed that we should bring the Stone to Scotland, to be a focal point, that it was our property and symbol."

Jean McGillveray, wife of SNP organiser Angus McGillveray, says the Stane was passed from place to place and hidden. Several times it was transported in her husband Angus's van, and their daughter Janice's sledge used to move it. Broken off bits of the Stane were given to and are still treasured by various people. The author's dentist has a relative who holds a piece of the Stane, passed down in her family.

Morris Blythman later wrote about the response of the Scottish people to the Lifting. "For the first time in generations, Scotland had asserted herself in an active way.

The Scots gaed doun to Westminster,
And danced awa wi the stane, man,
"Ower lang ye've bade in alien bield;
We're come tae tak ye hame, man."

The stane's awa, the stane's awa
The stane's awa frae the aibbey;
And the Reverend Dean cam on the air,
And begoud to griet like a baby.
The Stane's Awa, tune: The Deil's Awa, words AT

"This was a departure from the passive whining about what England was doing to us and a real blow for freedom. Above all, it was an action with which virtually every Scot could identify. It was England's turn to do the whining – and the Scots treated it all as a marvellous joke." *Morris Blythman*

"Sorley MacLean's widow tells that when Sorley heard the news about the Stane, he was jumping round the room, whooping and screaming." *Rob Gibson*

"Within days – just like the chapmen and balladeers of days gone by – Scots were writing quite independently at all levels about this great event. One song above all others has lasted from that period, 'The

Wee Magic Stane.' Its success is probably due to the ballad, story-telling technique employed. Here was a song for the layman, however far removed he was from the actual events, and how he liked it."
Morris Blythman

The song was made by a Rebel Ceilidh regular, John McEvoy. Shortly afterwards he emigrated to Canada, soon moved to the USA, and retired back to Scotland in 1989. His step-son Colin Ward says that 'The Wee Magic Stane' was the only political song McEvoy wrote. "Other than ditties to amuse his friends from time to time, which are now lost, I only know of two other songs he tried to write about his experiences in Canada. To his great frustration he was unable to complete either."

Morris Blythman's wife Marion thinks that John McEvoy's example, and the excitement both the Blythmans had felt on discovering a living tradition of ballad singing while on a working trip to Aberdeenshire, led Morris to change his 'Muckle Stane' poem into a song, using the tune of a favourite bawdy song, 'The Ball of Kirriemuir'.

Finding that other poets like Norman MacCaig had also written songs, Blythman gathered together lyrics, cajoled more poets, and engineered the creation of a booklet of fifteen anonymous pieces, set to popular Scots tunes.

More Stane Sangs

There wis a wee Super o Scotland Yaird
Barraty-parraty, cocatou!
He cam up ti Glesca – He wisna feared!
Barraty-parraty
Gie him ti Charity!
Niver fund clarity,
Niver a clue!

Superintendent Thomas Barrat, Requiem I, tune Wee Cooper o Fife, words Thurso Berwick

☙

O, Sherlock Holmes is deid lang syne
In some forgotten garret
Bit aa o youse hae heard the news
O Superintendant Barrat.

He cam up here in Janiveer,
The day it was a Monday:
He crossed the Border deep in snaw
An wished ti Hell he hadnae!

Requiem II, Tune Barbara Allen, tune Thurso Berwick

"The 'Sangs Of The Stane' booklet was Morris's idea, because he thought it was iconic, the stealing of the Stone of Destiny, and it was one of the first times that people in Scotland had a right good laugh at the Establishment. The Scots were thumbing their nose at them, and Morris thought that should be noted. Morris wrote 'The Muckle Stane o Scone' – a narrative poem. He was pals with John MacEvoy who wrote 'The Wee Magic Stane', and Morris thought it would be a good idea to have a song-book. It was he who got Hugh MacDiarmid and people like that to write poems and songs about the Stone. The songbook was basically his idea and he didn't want people thinking they were making money out of it, so he wouldn't put the writers' names on it. He never put his own name on it and he never claimed copyright on anything. No!" *Marion Blythman*
The omission of writers' names also obscured the fact that Blythman had written half of the 14 songs himself. Pencilled notes on the National Library of Scotland copy identify the others as H Ramsay, WW, Sydney Goodsir Smith, Norman MacCaig, AT, Tom Law, and John McEvoy. Hugh McDiarmid wrote an introductory poem.
Issue 32 of the 'Chapman' literature magazine in 1982 was 'In Memoriam Thurso Berwick". In her editorial Joy Hendry says of Blythman, "Part of the motivation in writing these was, he wryly remarked, to keep up the morale of the 'culprits', but the 'Sangs o the Stane' did much more than that: they captured the spirit of Scottish resistance at the time, partly because of their use of Scottish folklore traditions with Scottish humour and political attitudes. These songs truly were of the people, easily incorporated into the vernacular tradition."
Among his 'Sangs' were two that derided the first Stone-seeking Scotland Yard detective, Superintendent Barratt, and another for his successor, Detective Inspector McGrath. Hendry notes that when the latter was reported to be travelling north, and was shortly due to arrive at Glasgow Central Station, Morris and eight friends decided to welcome him with song. Bystanders stopped to listen, and probably to join in the choruses. "Officialdom, however, were unable to view this spectacle as a group of people having a peaceful singsong, and for

reasons best known to themselves, interpreted this as a potential riot, an ugly mob of demonstrators, diverted the train and cleared the station." *Joy Hendry*

Marion Blythman says, "We were slightly nutty, young and wild. When we heard [in April 1951] that the Stane had been left in Arbroath Abbey to be handed over, we dashed to the Abbey and were there all night making a protest. I fell asleep at school next day."

The Blythmans and Hugh MacDonald heard that the Stone had been found in Arbroath Abbey. Hugh MacDonald remembers, "The police were going to transport it back south. I had inside connections, and heard details. I got on to Morris, we took Stane songbooks and a large Saltire and went down to Central Station. It was an England Scotland game, so the station was mobbed, Morris was singing the songs and selling the books, and I was holding up the banner. Suddenly two policemen came and said, 'Get that flag down'. I said, 'If ye care to take it - try it'. 'Shift that flag!' An altercation struck out, with the Scotland supporters on our side, and I saw a helmet going up. Morris said, 'Let's get out of this.' We ran out of the station, unscrewing the flagstaff as we ran, and up to the SNP office at Elmbank Street, and got the caretaker to take the flag in. 'Just dropping this off.' Next morning SNP officialdom was not pleased. 'When I get hold of these bastards'." *Hugh MacDonald*

Morris Blythman later wrote a furious song condemning prominent nationalist John McCormick for colluding in

A Stane Sang

A chiel cam doun tae London toun
An nicked awa wi the stane, man
A lassie cried oot, " I'll gie ye a haun
For it's ill tae dae it alane, man"

A chiel's awa, a chiel's awa
A chiel's awa wi the stane, man
A lad an a lass made His Worship an ass
An nicked awa wi the stane, man

They had nae lorry tae carry it hame
Nae steamer or airyplane, man
For – here's a baur – in a wee Ford caur
They nicked awa wi the stane, man

There's spies in Biggar, and spies in Perth
In Bo'ness and Dunblane man
They're speirin but an they're speirin ben
But Scotland's holdin its ain, man

Stane Sang, tune Deil's Awa,
words Norman MacCaig

the handing over of the Stane, dubbing him John McCorbie.
By 13th April 1951 the booklet 'Sangs o the Stane' was available, price 6d, from Bo'ness newsagents H & M Oliver. The 'Bo'ness Journal' commented that "The booklet has a special significance to Bo'ness folks who attend Rebels Ceilidhs as most of the authors are honorary members of that club". Several were regular performers there, "and Bo'ness itself has been immortalised in a song to the tune 'The Deil's awa wi the Exciseman' by Norman MacCaig".
Norman MacCaig's son Ewen says that his father "was basically apolitical most of his life, though to some extent a nationalist fellow traveller. But support for any Party would have been unthinkable at any time and the rise of the SNP since that time would not have been a source of satisfaction. At the time of the Bo'ness ceilidhs, he was a friend of Willie Kellock, politically naive (as he ever after remained) and susceptible to persuasion. I know he was not ashamed of this poem [*The Stane Sang*] at the time because he used to sing it, but probably would have shrunk from it in later life, partly because any form of political alignment became obnoxious to him, and partly because of the poetic quality (or absence thereof)."
Local bank manager Willie Kellock was the key motivator and initiator in Bo'ness. He organised the ceilidhs, found the guest speakers and performers, wrote the lengthy local newspaper's accounts of the ceilidhs complete with the key points of speeches, and motivated and supported activists. Jean McGillveray says "Willie Kellock was full of fun. The songs were important, they sang about a past era we didn't know."
The Bo'ness ceilidhs began in January 1948 with a Burns Supper in the Coffee House organised by the newly-formed Rebel Literary Club [renamed the Rebel Literary Society in mid 1951]. Every few months for the next six years another ceilidh was organised, usually in Bo'ness Masonic Temple or Bridgeness Miner's Welfare. The concert segment would begin with piping, and feature a mixture of visitors and local artistes, Gaelic song intermingling with Scots song and verse.
Speeches were made by prominent literary or political guests including Wendy Wood and Oliver Brown. Hugh MacDiarmid visited several

times to speak 'in his own forthright manner' and deliver 'highly intellectual discourse'. A basket tea was provided after the speeches and songs, and hostesses were reminded to bring supper cloths and teaspoons. Then there was a dance. In tandem with the ceilidhs were annual Burns Suppers.

"We went to all the Bo'ness Rebels events. I think it started with Willie Kellock getting in touch with us. He was in the Bank in Bo'ness. He was the funniest wee lugubrious character. He had this absolutely clear idea in his head for an independent Scotland and he thought the way to do it was through the Bo'ness Rebels and the ceilidhs. I don't know that the ceilidhs had any particular purpose other than to get people together and promote the ideas. But they were always on a Friday evening and we used to get there about seven or eight. They went on right through the night, nobody went to bed, there is a famous photograph with Morris and Hugh MacDiarmid and others, that was taken in the morning after we'd all been up all night!

"Charlie Auld had the Lea-Rig Bar and sometimes we started in the Bar, but the ceilidhs were actually held in Willie Kellock's house. At that time he was living with his mother and she wasn't necessarily for the ceilidhs. Willie was always saying "Oh, my mother'll no like this!" and going on and doing it anyway.

Bo'ness Rebels Song Book songs

Bo'ness is a terminus
The Lea Rig is a Bar
The landlord's name is Chairlie Auld
O, come fae near and far

To the Lea Rig we will go, will go
To the Lea Rig we will go

The Lea Rig, tune To The Begging, words Willie Kellock and Thurso Berwick

☙

On the banks of the roses
My love and I sat down
When I brought out my fiddle
To play my love a tune
In the middle of the tune she cried and she sighed
"Oh Johnny, lovely Johnny, won't you leave me"

The Banks Of The Roses, traditional, as sung by Norman MacCaig

"Willie Kellock had a great admiration for Hugh MacDiarmid. Willie Kellock was the guy – and when he and Morris got together, it was like a marriage of twin minds because Morris had the songs and Willie had the place, and it went from there. Sometimes they were quite outrageous, terrible great fights, drunken brawls. The famous fight was at a Burns Supper. It hit the press because Norman MacCaig started shouting about Hugh MacDiarmid and it caused a real rammy. That was MacDiarmid's way of operating – he was never going to be agreeing with anybody. The best thing I heard about him was when everybody was leaving the Communist Party. He had left because he was a Nationalist, but when everybody else was leaving – he rejoined! Entirely Scottish, you know." *Marion Blythman*

Billy Wolfe became a parliamentary candidate in the local by-election, and later Chairman of the SNP. He recalls, "Willy Kellock of Bo'ness was a great nationalist and a great propagandist, and very thrawn too. He wrote all the newspaper accounts of the ceilidhs. The Bo'ness ceilidhs were sometimes riotous. There was a fight between MacDiarmid and MacCaig, they had to get the polis in. Those two didn't come off the same loom.

"I became a disciple of Willy Kellock and Charlie Auld - he was a great ideas man. Kinneil pit was still open at that time, so the basic culture of a mining community was still prevalent. A wonderful place. Bo'ness was basically a working class society, but they had an opera society, a wonderful brass or silver band, a pipe band, a fitba team, Scouts and Guides and BB, Women's Guild. Absolutely hoaching with activities, everybody knew everybody else.

"After the by-election I stood in we had a ceilidh in the Town Hall, and I said 'I now ken what the SNP stands for - independence for Scotland and a parliament for Bo'ness.'" *Billy Wolfe*

Angus McGillveray wrote in 1994 that "The Bo'ness Ceilidh was always a source of wonder to me; how Willie Kellock managed to get all those talented people from everywhere, from Brass Bands to Mod Gold Medalists, from the Fianna na h'Alba to the much respected Patriotic orators Oliver Brown, Robert Blair Wilkie, Wendy Wood, Hugh MacDiarmid, Hamish Henderson of the School of Scottish Studies, Norman MacCaig, Seumas MacNeill the Principal of the College of Piping, Thurso Berwick and many many others.

"It was great to feel your blood rekindling in your veins by songs from MacGregor Kennedy and the Inverscotia Singers or an old haunting Gaelic air by Dolina MacLennan [Dolina herself says she never sang at the Ceilidhs, only at Bo'ness Burns Suppers], the rousing 'Stirling Brig' by Hugh MacDonald, puirt a beul from Kitty MacLeod or a laugh when John McEvoy sang his 'Wee Magic Stane' - they made everyone present proud to be a Scot." *Angus McGillveray*

Poet Norman MacCaig was a regular performer, but as a singer. His rendition of the traditional ballad 'The Wee Toon Clerk' was particularly admired, and he also would deliver 'Kissin's No Sin' and the 'Bonnie Banks of the Roses'.

Ceilidhs happened not only in Bo'ness. By June 1950 two new clubs in the Rebels mould were being welcomed in the local Bo'ness newspaper – the Thistle Society of Glasgow, and the Heckleburnie Club. Heckleburnie is a Scots euphemism for Hell. The author has found no clues as to where the club met. There were house ceilidhs in Glasgow and elsewhere, and evening campfire singing as young city Scots took to the hills and moors at weekends - the second song book produced by the Rebels was of 'Patriot Songs for Camp & Ceilidh'. The contents of the first song book, the 1953 'Rebels Ceilidh Song Book' show that Irish 'rebel' songs were an important element in the Rebels repertoire

Hugh MacDonald says, "The song books were promoting Scotland, independence and revolution. We were aware that the situation was growing, and more needed to be done. There were weekly ceilidhs at Pitt St, the Fianna premises, with some good and some bad singers. Song was always involved. Scots and Gaelic song, and learning Gaelic in the Fianna, helping to promote Scotland.

"The Fianna was Socialist, Republican and Communist. A co-operative approach rather than a single political party. It wasn't SNP, but the whole beginnings of Scotland - who we are and where we should go. I joined in 1944, aged 14 and a half. I joined the drumming section. On Tuesday and Thursday nights there were fifty odds attending. John McEvoy brought friends, poets and writers, to the Fianna, Calum Kennedy, lads from Scalpay, Tiree."Willie Kellock set up the Clann

Alba, modelled on the Irish Fianna, in Glasgow. The Piping College is an offshoot of Fianna. Willie came out of the army, became a bank manager in South Side Glasgow, then in Bo'ness. Bus loads went from Glasgow to the Ceilidhs. Bo'ness was the most important place in Scotland re culture at the time. There were Burns Suppers run by the Burns Society as well as ceilidhs by the Rebels." *Hugh MacDonald*

In her paper for the RSAMD, 'Hillwalkers, Long Distance Melodeon Players and Gangrels', musician Seylan Baxter says the Fianna na h'Alba was formed in around 1940 by Harry Miller and Drummy Henderson. "It had certain similarities to the Fianna Erin in Ireland, not least the name, but was very much a loose association of young people with a belief in Scotland and a desire for a change in the current order." Out of it came the College of Piping, formed out of chanter classes taken by Seamus MacNeill and the Inverscotia Singers, one of whom was Baxter's father Jim.

A grouping within the Fianna were the Inverscotia Nomads. They caught the bus out of Glasgow, and went hill walking and stravaiging together. They all wore ex-army WW1 kilts, and member Jimmy Jennett commented, "When you got on the bus at Killermont Street it was like embarking for France in 1914, every bloody regiment in Scotland was there." Jennett composed a valedictory 'The Soldier's Road' for the Nomads, that says while they were walking,

Bo'ness Rebels Song Book songs

Ye loyal MacDonalds awaken awaken
Why sleep ye sae soundly in face of the foe?
The clouds pass away and the dawn it is breaking
But when shall awaken the sons of Glencoe?

The Sons of Glencoe, as sung by MacGregor Kennedy

ꟹ

Oh the green hills are calling me to shoulder up my pack
Along the track, where the air is fresh and free
Where torrents leap and play, I go today

For the calling of the hills I hear
From the birds so near, from the distant deer
As I swing along with eager stride
Up the rugged mountain side

Green Hills, tune Green Hills of Tyrol, as sung by the Inverscotia Singers

Randolph, Rab, Roy and Terry would sing, Seamus would lilt canntaireachd and Big Dave play the moothie.

An offshoot of the Nomads was the Singers. "This was not just simple ceilidh singing. Songs were well rehearsed and arranged in three and four part harmonies. The Inverscotia Singers recorded an LP, 'Angus's Ceilidh'. Angus McGillveray had put up the money and organised the LP, which was recorded in one day. The Singers were engaged for a week at Jimmy Logan's Glasgow Metropole, and went to Moscow with Calum Kennedy." *Seylan Baxter*

It's fa took it this time? And fa's got it nou?
The yane that had it last time canna get it nou.

Meanwhile The Times does thunder, and the ither jackals yap,
And the polis o the kingdom bizz round in a fearful flap.

Fowr and twenty sextons wi fowr and twenty shools,
They werena owre anxious to be shiftan Grannie's mools.

Brass-handles, coffin-lids and urns, were scattered aa about,
The deid sat up, they thocht it was the Resurrection Toot.

There was howkin in the cloisters, howkin in the crypt,
They coudna see the Stane, for aa the bogles round them skipt.

They dug and delved the yerdin-grund, and plouter't amang the banes,
And sure enuff it was nae bluff – They fand a feck o stanes!

And ilka 'humourless' Scot i the land lauchs loud in ilka toun,
And bides the time whan the Stane comes hame til its richtfu seat at Scone.

Ballad O The Reivin O The Stane, tune Ball of Kirriemuir, words Sydney Goodsir Smith

The 1951 People's Festival Ceilidh

I gaed up to Alford
For to get a fee,
I fell in wi' Jamie Broon,
And wi' him I did agree
The Guise o Tough

꧁

I hae seen the Hairst o Rettie
Aye, and twa-three on the throne
Ah've heard for sax or seven weeks
The hairsters girn and groan
But a covie Willie Rae
In a monthie and a day
Gart aa the jolly hairster lads
Gae singin doon the brae
The Hairst o Rettie

On Friday 31st August 1951 a ceilidh was held in Oddfellow's Hall in Central Edinburgh, part of the first Edinburgh People's Festival. Festival and ceilidh sprang from a political purpose. The songs sung and tunes played, the way the songs were sung, and the points made in the spoken introductions, exemplified many of the elements of the coming Folk Revival in Scotland. The ceilidh was organised by the second of the three Scottish architects of the Revival, Hamish Henderson.

Three of the five key figures whose work created and shaped the Revival, Scots Hamish Henderson and Norman Buchan and American Alan Lomax were at the centre of the ceilidh action; a fourth, Englishman of Scots parentage Ewan MacColl, arrived in time for the after-ceilidh dance. The fifth key person, Scot Morris Blythman, missed this People's Festival ceilidh, but not the following ones.

The concert became legendary because it alerted astonished city folk to the living continuing richness of Scotland's traditional song heritage. The 1951 Edinburgh People's Festival Ceilidh was a key event that heralded, generated and vitalised the Scottish Folk Revival of the 1960s.

"As I went into the Oddfellows Hall the bloody place was packed, feet were going, and it was Jimmy MacBeath singing 'The Gallant Forty-Twa'. Hamish had assembled these people. Jessie Murray sang 'Skippin' Barfit Through The Heather'; ... Flora MacNeil was singing 'The Silver Whistle [An Fhideag Airgid]' - beautiful! I'd never heard anything like this. John Strachan was singing about forty verses of a ballad... An amazing night for people who'd never heard them before! It swept me off my feet completely." *Norman Buchan*

"What made this inaugural People's Festival ceilidh so important was the fact that this was the first time such a masterly group of authentic traditional musicians and ballad-singers from rural Scotland had sung together to a city audience; the result was a veritable cultural explosion, for a number of the 'folk' virtuosi of the future were present in the audience." *Hamish Henderson*

"The beauty of the evening was probably due to the fact that the Gaelic and Lallans singers were operating in the true folk tradition, singing music that was unscored and also, if I may use the word, untitivated. Though the ceilidh was public it remained intimate owing to the smallness of the hall." *Neil MacCallum*

American folklorist Alan Lomax of the Library of Congress was there to record the ceilidh. Lomax had come to Scotland in June 1951 expecting to "give Scotland a modest corner on the [World Library] album titled English Folk Songs." The astonishing harvest that he garnered in Highland and Lowland Scotland in 1951 is still being distilled and bottled.

1951 People's Festival Ceilidh song
As I was waakin doon yon hill
It was then a summer evening,
It was there I spied a bonnie lass
Skippin barfit through the heather

O but she was neatly dressed,
She neither needed hat nor feather,
She was the queen amang them aa
Skippin barfit through the heather
Skippin Barfit Throu The Heather

He donated copies of the 25 hours of recordings to the University of Edinburgh, to become the cornerstone of the sound archives of the School of Scottish Studies. Hamish Henderson was his guide for much of the trip.

Lomax had already met and collected songs from singer, songwriter, actor and playwright Ewan MacColl. He and director Joan Littlewood were the 'leading figures' of Theatre Workshop. MacColl had in turn met Hamish Henderson through Theatre Workshop's visits to Edinburgh. At the time MacColl was known for his theatrical work, and his long term musical partner Peggy Seeger had not yet come to Britain.

The official Edinburgh Festival began in 1947, and Theatre Workshop was there that year to help initiate the Fringe. The 1945 Labour government, radical in much of its social planning, created the Edinburgh International Festival by enlisting what Hamish Henderson called "the Edimbourgeoisie... the city's arty elite and effete middle class, to organise the party and draw up the invitations. They remain firmly in charge to this day, self-elected critics and guardians of taste and morality."

In 1951 the Edinburgh Labour Festival Committee was established to organise a People's Festival. The aims were "to initiate action designed to bring the Edinburgh Festival closer to the people, to serve the cause of international understanding and goodwill." Committee participants included the

1951 People's Festival Ceilidh songs
Translations from Gaelic

As I awoke early in the morning Great was my joy and merriment
On hearing that the Prince is coming
To the land of Clanranald
You are the best of all rulers
May you come back in good health
If the crown was placed on you
Your friends would be joyful

From Oran Eile Don Phrionsa (Another Song to the Prince)

Alas, young Charles Stewart
Your cause has left me desolate
You took from me everything I had
In a war on your behalf
It is not sheep or cattle that I mourn but my spouse
Since the day I was left alone, with nothing in the world but my shift

From Mo Rùn Geal Òg (My Fair Young Love)

Trade Unions' Council, the Miners' Union, the Labour party and the Communist Party. Cultural groups, independent arts organisations and individual arts activists became involved. Theatre companies were invited to participate. Henderson credits the renowned innovative theatre director Joan Littlewood with some of the impetus for the People's Festival, and in 'Joan's Book' she gives a vivid and exciting account of various People's Festival events, but sadly none of her dates or descriptions tally with other accounts, or newspaper reports of the time. She has perhaps conflated and over-dramatised various Edinburgh Festival-time events.

Theatre Workshop brought MacColl's play 'Uranium 235', 'A modern morality play for the atomic era'. Theatre Workshop was so popular it stayed on till 15th September, performing MacColl's ballad opera 'Johnny Noble' as well as 'Uranium 235', which was later described on TW posters as 'the sensational success of the '51 Edinburgh Festival'.

In some accounts the People's Festival ceilidh arose from a need to support financially Theatre Workshop's visit. Poet and arch stirrer of the cultural pot Hugh MacDiarmid wrote to Henderson, 12/7/51, "Will you still be in Edinburgh when Theatre Workshop are there? I hope so. I'll be through then too. Since the short season they have in Edinburgh will not leave them with any dough after defraying their expenses it has been requested that they also have a number of ceilidhs and if you are on the spot you might help to organise these... Alan Lomax will take part and I understand Flora MacNeil and Calum Johnston have also agreed." Hamish Henderson says when this letter came he had already been put in charge of the Ceilidh.

Janey Buchan (later Labour MEP for Glasgow) and Norman Buchan, at that time a schoolteacher of English, later organiser of the 1953 People's Festival, then Labour MP and Shadow Minister for the Arts, were both heavily involved in the creation of the Festival. Janey later said "You look back and wonder how did you summon up the physical energy to do what we did? We didn't have a car among the lot of us, we did it all on tram and bus, and on our two feet."

The week of events was a great success. Poetry readings, art exhibitions, plays and concerts. Although the People's Festival was planned as a counterweight to the International Festival's inattention to Scots culture, in 1951 there was in fact Scottish music in the official Festival. The Scotsman newspaper featured days of continuing debate about the chaos of the Pipers' March down Princes Street that had initiated the official 1951 Festival. In the Freemason's Hall there were two evenings of the Music of Scotland. Performers included two who had already been recorded by Lomax - Jimmy Shand playing accordion, and John Mearns singing Bothy Ballads 'with endearing gusto'.

In the People's Festival programme Hamish Henderson wrote "In Scotland ... there is still an incomparable treasure of folk song and folk music... The main purpose of this Ceilidh will be to present Scottish folk song as it should be sung. The singers will all without exception be men and women who have learned these splendid songs by word of mouth in their own childhood, and who give them in the traditional manner. This fact alone will make the People's Festival Ceilidh an absolutely unique thing in the cultural history of Edinburgh." And so it proved to be.

Friday night in the Oddfellows Hall arrived.

1951 People's Festival Ceilidh songs

There was a troop o' Irish Dragoons
Cam a-marchin' doon through Fyvie, O
An their captain's fa'n in love wi' a very bonnie lass
An' her name it was ca'd pretty Peggy, O
The Bonny Lass O Fyvie

☙

Johnnie rose up in the May morning,
Called for water to wash his hands,
Says "Gae lowse tae me ma twa grey dogs
That lie bound in iron bands,
That lie bound in iron bands."
Johnnie O Braidislie

☙

Fare ye weel ye dungeons dark and strang
Farewell, fareweel tae ye,
MacPherson's time will no be lang
On yonder gallows tree
MacPherson's Rant

☙

As I cam in by Turra market,
Turra market for tae fee,
It's I fell in wi' a wealthy fairmer,
The Barnyards o Delgaty.
Barnyards o Delgaty

Theatre Workshop's stage lights troubled the singers. There was a calm enough beginning. John Burgess says that a few douce Edinburgh dames walked out early on. The poster "looked conservative" but their prim sensibilities were soon threatened by the honest gruff voice of Jimmy MacBeath.

The atmosphere became so supercharged that the listener to the CD recording of the Concert half expects sparks to shoot out of the speakers, the applause and cheering was so loud and prolonged that Lomax turned off his recorder between songs to conserve tape, thereby losing the start of some pieces.

Three elements were combined – Gaelic song, piping, and North-East Scots song. Three older performers aged 57 to 76, three younger ones aged 16 to 21.

"This was an amazing, indeed epoch-making folk-song concert which brought together some of the 'greats' of the traditional folk-scene: outstanding tradition-bearers from the Gaelic-speaking Hebrides, and ballad-singers from Aberdeenshire, heartland of the great Scots ballad tradition.

"The Barra singers Flora MacNeil and Calum Johnston presented Hebridean folk-song, stripped of its Kennedy Fraser mummy-wrappings. Jimmy MacBeath sang 'Come A' ye Tramps and Hawkers' for the first time on any stage (as opposed to the reeling road, or the booths of Porter Fair). John Burgess, master piper, played us marches, jigs, strathspeys and reels with all the expertise of Auld Nick at Kirk Alloway. John Strachan, the Fyvie farmer, and Jessie Murray, the Buckie fishwife, sang versions of classic ballads such as 'Johnnie o' Braidislie' (Child 114) and 'Lord Thomas and Fair Ellen' (Child 73) which convinced even the most

1951 People's Festival Ceilidh song

I'll gyang tae the ale hoose an look for my Jimmy
The day is far spent an the night's comin on
Ye're sittin there drinkin and leave me lamentin
So rise up, my Jimmy, an come awa hame

Nae mind o the bairnies, they're aa at hame greetin
Nae meal in the barrel tae ful their wee wames
The Ale Hoose

sceptical that a noble oral tradition was still with us." *Hamish Henderson*

After the 'official' ceilidh had finished, the whole company moved to St Columba's Church hall in Johnstone Terrace, where they were joined by Ewan MacColl and Isla Cameron, their Theatre Workshop show having finished. Hugh MacDiarmid was there, and part of 'A Drunk Man Looks at the Thistle' was spoken during the evening. Hamish Henderson wrote that "All over Auld Reekie the ceilidh was continuing. In a sense, it is continuing still."

Norman Buchan's highly influential efforts to support and educate young urban singers were inspired by that night. "Looking back, I know that though the evening was devastatingly new to me, it really shouldn't have been. Although I grew up in the Orkney islands, my folk came from the North East coast. The Revival didn't really start that night at the Festival Ceilidh. Things were going on, it's just that we didn't know about it. There were still ballad singers going around, there were still professional entertainers like G S Morris and John Mearns singing bothy ballads. They were even beginning to appear on records. But no-one said to us, "Look, these things matter. They matter for you in the cities. You should listen to this and learn."

Communist Party organiser Martin Milligan's comments show the politically committed motivation that drove aspects of the People's Festival. "The leading role the Communist Party can play in the defence and development of British culture was made evident at the conference by the quality of the contributions by its spokesmen there." Seventeen organisations had backed the first Festival. The 1952 Festival had the backing of fifty organisations, and was a triumph, running for three weeks.However, the involvement of the Communist Party in those days of the gathering ice storm that became the Cold War caused unease to the Labour party members involved in the Festival. The Festival was proscribed by the STUC as a 'Communist Front'. This was a shattering blow to the many people involved in its success and the 1954 festival was the last.

A particular richness of the 1951 Lomax recording is the preservation of Hamish Henderson's legendary manner of presenting song and music – warm and inclusive, enthusiastic yet wry, knowledgeable but not always fully accurate, delighted at what he had found to share with others.

"Hamish's extempore performances were, as far as I am concerned, one of the most memorable aspects of those early People's Festivals (forerunners of the Fringe). By day one encountered him on the streets and squares of Edinburgh, generally accompanied by one or two of his discoveries, Jimmy MacBeath, Frank Steele, or Jeannie Robertson, or he would be bent over a hypnotised acquaintance lilting his latest 'find'. At night he could be found presiding over the ceilidh which generally began at 11pm and finished at two or three in the morning. There must be hundreds of Edinburgh folk who heard their first traditional song at those splendid affairs." *Ewan MacColl*

The 1951 performers were chosen by Henderson for their excellence. 17 year old piper John D Burgess had in 1950, in his first appearance aged 16, won Gold Medals for his playing in piobaireachd competitions in Oban and Inverness. Gaelic singer and piper Calum Johnston was born on the Outer Hebridean isle of Barra. He worked as a draughtsman in Edinburgh, retired to Barra. Johnston died suddenly in 1973 while piping the coffin of novelist Sir Compton Mackenzie to its grave in violent weather. Jimmy MacBeath was born in the Buchan fishing village of Portsoy. For most of his life Jimmy footslogged the roads of Scotland and beyond, earning pennies from street singing and shillings from casual labour, living in 'model' public lodging houses. In the 1960s Jimmy began to be recorded commercially and to sing in folk clubs and festivals.

Gaelic singer Flora MacNeil was also born on Barra. When she moved to work in Edinburgh in 1947, "She was already a most accomplished traditional singer, with a repertoire more varied and more extensive than anyone else of her age." *Dr John Macinnes*

Jessie Murray aged 70 came with her Portknockie niece Blanche Wood aged 18. Jessie Murray was a fishwife living in the North-East port of Buckie, and would have trudged from door to door, a little lady dressed all in black, a basket of fish or shellfish on her back. "I always remember Jessie Murray, and she came forward and gave a little curtsey to the audience. And she sang 'Skippin Barfit Through The Heather', and of course these were songs you had never heard, and clearly the whole audience had never heard either." *Janey Buchan*

John Strachan was born and died on the Aberdeenshire farm of Crichie near Fyvie. A wealthy farmer, Hamish Henderson wrote that Strachan "took a kindly paternalistic interest in the welfare of his fee'd men", and was a highly knowledgeable champion of the songs of farm life and old ballads.

Janey Buchan pointed out an irony. "When John Strachan, who was himself a wealthy farmer, sang two lines and said, 'The fermer I am wi the noo, He's wealthy but he's mean', that summed up every employer people like me ever had in their life. But he could sing that and maybe not see the irony of himself singing it."

Though there were no songs of politics in the 1951 ceilidh, many of the songs and tunes had a general political context – of warfare and strife, of sexual and social conflict, and of unfair work conditions.

Among the warfare and strife songs was a sequence of Gaelic Jacobite songs. First came two celebrating the coming of Bonny Prince Charlie - 'Oran Eile Don Phrionnsa' (Another Song for the Prince and 'An Fhìdeag Airgid' (The Silver Whistle) - then one lamenting what his coming had wrought, 'My Fair Young Love' (Mo Rùn Geal Òg).

Piper John Burgess played 'Blue Bonnets Over The Border', a tune fashioned in the 1740s, for which Sir Walter Scott wrote a lyric based on an old Cavalier song.

'Blue Bonnets' is a metaphor for the Scots marching men, who are going 'over the border' into England seeking a fight.

John Strachan essayed 'The Bonny Lass O Fyvie', a martial Aberdeenshire song of death for love, hardly known in 1951, but since massively popular in Scotland in 'sing-along-a-tartan' style. Bob Dylan recorded an American version, 'Pretty

1951 People's Festival Ceilidh song
You may taalk aboot your First Royal Scottish Fusiliers,
Your Aiberdeen Mileesha, an your dandy volunteers,
Yer Seaforths in their stickit kilts, yer Gordons big and braw.
Gae bring tae me the tartan o the gallant Forty Twa.
The Gallant Forty Twa

Peggy-O'. MacBeath's 'The Gallant Forty Twa' is a lighthearted theatrical song, which lists Scots regiments but gives the palm to the 42nd Highland Regiment, the Black Watch. In all, four songs about heroic villains were sung. All four songs became very popular in the 1960s folk song Revival.

Sexual politics were addressed as usual by men seeking with varying degrees of success to undress women. Jessie Murray sang a Scotland-located version of the widely-known ballad 'Barbara Allen', in which Barbara's rather feeble lover dies for love when she rejects him. Some versions justify Barbara's apparent heartlessness in the matter by explaining her swain had spoken slightingly of her in the alehouse. Murray also gave another ballad of love's confusions that is sung throughout the English-speaking world, 'Lord Thomas and Fair Ellen' which has two murders and a suicide with an apparent element of racial prejudice. Blanche Wood sang 'I'm a Young Bonnie Lassie' of faithful love, and 'Portnockie Road' of betrayed love.

1951 People's Festival Ceilidh song
In Scotland I was born and bred,
In Scotland I was dwellin.
I fell in love with a pretty fair maid,
And her name was Barbara Allen.

Near the end of the concert Jessie Murray sang a ballad that enchanted Norman Buchan. "The place was electric, and I was surprised because on the stage was a tiny old lady, less than five feet, dressed in black, fisherwife dressed, and she was chanting out a song called 'Jamie Raeburn'. Now, I'd never heard that song before, but I did know what it was. I knew it was a street ballad from a century and a half or maybe two centuries ago. It was a street ballad that people had sold about a transportation, but I had absolutely no idea that people still sang a song like that. In fact, during the rest of that evening every preconception I had was swept out of existence, and indeed if any man had a Damascus, that was me."

1951 People's Festival Ceilidh song
I know you're a Pat by the cut of your hair,
But you all turn Scotchmen as soon's you come here,
You have left your own country for breaking the law,
We are seizing all stragglers from Erin go Bragh.
Erin Go Bragh

John Strachan sang a fine account of noble deer poacher Johnnie O Braidislie's fight with the King's gamekeepers, and another of how Duncan Campbell of Argyll is addressed by an Edinburgh policeman as 'Erin Go Bragh' (meaning Ireland Forever). Campbell fights the policeman, and escapes North. Jimmy MacBeath sang of Scotland's Robin Hood, James MacPherson.

Jessie Murray also sang the social comment song 'The Ale Hoose', a small morality lesson on the evils of the Demon Drink, reminding us of the strength and manipulative vehemence of the Temperance Movement in the 19th Century. The transcript of this song in the School of Scottish Studies archives is annotated, "This hodden-grey tear-jerker is a find – can't trace it in any of the earlier collections."

The evening began with two Aberdeenshire Bothy Ballad songs of farm life, the work and personalities. The final two songs were the only ones with an explicitly political dimension sung in the evening.

The last song was Robert Burns' 'Scots Wha Hae' considered by many to be Scotland's own National Anthem. Just before it, Henderson and a Mrs Budge sang his composition 'The John Maclean March', written for and sung at the John Maclean Memorial Meeting in St Andrew's Hall in Glasgow, 1948, and later called by Morris Blythman "the first swallow of the Revival". John MacLean was the great hero of Scottish socialism, 'martyred' for his opposition to World War One, a fiery orator, writer and organiser.

Forward tae Glasgie Green we'll march in good order:
Will grips his banner weel (that boy isna blate).
Ay there, man, that's Johnnie noo - that's him there, the bonnie fechter,
Lenin's his fiere, lad, an' Liebknecht's his mate.

Tak' tent when he's speakin', for they'll mind what he said here
In Glasgie our city - and the haill world beside.
Och hey, lad, the scarlet's bonnie: here's tae ye Hielan' Shony
Great John Maclean has come hame tae the Clyde!
Great John Maclean has come hame tae the Clyde!

The John Maclean March, tune The Bloody Fields of Flanders, words Hamish Henderson

Freedom's Sword - Songs of Warfare And Strife

Scots, wha hae wi' Wallace bled,
Scots, wham Bruce has aften led,
Welcome to your gory bed,
Or to Victorie.
Now's the day, and now's the hour;
See the front o' battle lour;
See approach prood EDWARD'S power,
Chains and slaverie!

Wha would be a traitor knave?
Wha can fill a coward's grave?
Wha sae base as be a slave?
Let him turn and flee!
Wha for Scotland's King and Law,
Freedom's sword would strongly draw,
FREE-MAN stand, or FREE-MAN fa',
Let him follow me!

By Oppression's woes and pains!
By your Sons in servile chains!
We will drain our dearest veins,
But they shall be free!
Lay the proud Usurper low!
Tyrants fall in every foe!
Liberty's in every blow!
Let us Do - or Die!

Scots Wha Hae, tune Hey Tutti Taiti, words Robert Burns

Songs of fights, large and small, have always been prominent in the repertoire of Scotland. Are warfare and strife the outcomes of failed politics, or are politicians in the long term as bloody and bloody-minded as are soldiers? Do Scots glory too much in their songs of battles just and unjust, betrayal, injustice and atrocity? In earlier days political debate was on the lines of 'My sword's longer than your sword, that shows I am right'. The songmakers decide who won the fight, and lament the cost in lives smashed. They also re-light old contests as candles to illuminate problems and lessons for the present day. In the last century Scots songmakers have begun to advance the startling notion that peace is of itself a good thing.

The 1314 Battle of Bannockburn was later celebrated repeatedly in song. Robert Burns' enduring anthem, 'Scots Wha Hae', is about the battle, but also about the political Scotland of his time. Robert Burns wrote this lyric as what "one might suppose to be [King Robert The Bruce's] address to his heroic followers on that eventful morning" of 24 June 1314, when the Scots routed the army of King Edward II of England and regained their independence.

He used the tune 'Hey Tutti Taitie', of which he wrote "There is a tradition, which I have met with in many places of Scotland, that it was Robert Bruce's March at the battle of Bannockburn". The Town Council of Orleans in France accept this story, saying the tune, 'Le Marche des Soldats de R. Bruce', was played by the Scots soldiers fighting with Joan of Arc's army when she entered Orleans on 29th April 1429.

Hey tuttie taiti
How tuttie taiti
Hey tutti taiti
Wha's fu noo?
Hey Tuttie

Writer Hector MacMillan says of Burns' lyric that "the basic form was thought out and a first draft put together" when in 1793 Burns and fellow Dumfries radical John Syme were on holiday touring the Galloway coast, at exactly the time arch-radical Thomas Muir was expected to land on that coast from Ireland. "Muir was arrested 30 miles away, and 'Scots Wha Hae' completed in the same or following week."

Several other Bannockburn songs were made by Scots poets. The latest well known song to refer to the loser of the Bannockburn fight,

Edward II, is Roy Williamson's song, 'Flower of Scotland', another candidate for a Scottish national anthem.

A lyric in the first Rebels Songbook tells of the 1411 Battle of Harlaw between the Lord of the Isles and the Earl of Mar. This ballad was made popular in the 1950s through the singing of traveller Jeannie Robertson of Aberdeen, and awards victory to the North East fighters. The title of the song is listed in the 1550 Complaynt of Scotland as 'the battel of the hayrlau', but scholars consider Robertson's text to be much later.

There have always been Scottish songs that protested about war, as there have ever been Scottish songs that celebrated soldiery and battle. Stirling Brig, Bannockburn, Otterburn, Harlaw, Flodden, Cromdale, Killiecrankie, Prestonpans, Falkirk, Culloden - the songs mix elements of admiration and glorification with lament, sober reporting, biased misreporting, and occasional humour. Are Scots songs that tell of past battles and armed clashes historical or political? They are seldom fully 'historically accurate' in the historian's sense. But accounts of history illuminate the present knowledge, values and belief of the writer as much as they shine a lantern on the past.

Songs of warfare

It fell about the Lammas tide
When the muir-men win their hay,
The doughty Douglas bound him to ride
Into England, to drive a prey.

The Battle of Otterbourne, traditional

CS

Ay, I cam near an near eneuch, an I their numbers saw;
There wis forty-thousand Hielanmen a-marchin ti Harlaw.

CS

Now as we rode on an further on, an in aboot Harlaw,
It's there we met the Hielanmen, sic strikes ye never saw.

The Battle of Harlaw, traditional

CS

I've heard the lilting at our yowe-milking,
Lasses a-lilting before the dawn of day;
But now they are moaning on ilka green loaning
The Flowers of the Forest are a' wede away.

The Flowers of The Forest, about the Battle of Flodden, tune traditional, words Miss Jean Elliot of Minto

Most Scottish songs about battles and strife were made long after the events, and the makers' current beliefs and allegiances shine through the texts. Most of the songs ever made, political or other, only lived on the page or were sung once or twice. Most of those that were performed three or more times also died soon after they were created, and much of the rump lasted only while the maker breathed. Why were the songs written? Some or most through antiquarian interest, 'stirring of the blood in the veins', the poet's urge to explore a gripping topic. Many songs so created were then used to support the singer's patriotic sense of emotional identity.

A very few of those songs are kept alive by singers who have learned them aurally, others are on occasion lifted from print and put into sung circulation. The motivation to sing them comes sometimes through antiquarian interest, sometimes there is a specific local relevance of the event or the maker, sometimes because of the high drama of the tale and how it is told, sometimes because the performer and listeners appreciate some higher poetic value in the text.

High o'er the waving broom, in chivalry and grace
Shone England's radiant spear and plume, by Stirling's rocky base
And stretching far beneath the view, the bloody Saxon banners flew
When, like a torrent rushing, oh God, from left and right the flame
Of Scottish Swords like lightning came, those English legions crushing
Stirling Brig, writer not known

But another spur to the preservation of a song as a live thing is its continuing or reawakened relevance to current political events or preoccupations. Songs of strife support a sense of national identity, and raise issues of social rights and justice.

Historical songs are very susceptible to adoption by political causes and groupings. Many of them can be sung with a sense of ownership by Whig and Tory, Left and Right, who can find elements of their own core values exemplified in the songs.

The songs considered here have resulted from international and national violent confrontations that have involved Scots bloodshed, with more attention paid to those songs that were still sung or were resuscitated in the second half of the Twentieth Century, especially where such songs were performed in a political or social comment context, rather than as light or heavy entertainment.

A song of Borders strife
To seik het water beneath cauld ice,
Surely it is a greit follie –
I have asked grace at a graceless face,
But there is nane for my men and me!
Johnnie Armstrong's Goodnight, traditional

The first song in the 1950s Bo'ness Rebels songbook, 'Patriot Songs For Camp and Ceilidh', is the oldest in setting, the tongue-mangling account of William Wallace's victory at Stirling Brig in 1297 that entranced Hugh MacDonald in the 1940s. "When I was 16 I went on the walk for Bannockburn. On the way back, when I passed the Wallace Tavern I heard a voice ringing out from the pub, singing 'Stirling Brig'. I didn't drink, but I stopped to listen. The singer was a member of the William Wallace Lodge, they were colliers, they carried the William Wallace banner."
It was the only warfare song from the Ceilidh Songbooks not to enter the Folk Revival repertoire. Various other songs of North East battles and clan-based strife became prominent in the Revival – 'The Haughs o Cromdale', 'The Baron of Brackley', 'The Burning of Auchindoun', 'Bonny George Campbell' - while nearly all the ballads of Borders feuds and fights and cattle lifting so lovingly

Songs of Warfare
I met a man wi tartan trews,
An spiered at him fit wis the news,
Says he, the Hielan Army rues,
That e'er it focht at Cromdale.

But it's this the Great Montrose did say,
John Hielanman shaw me the way,
For I maun o'er the Hills the day,
Tae view the Haughs o Cromdale.
The Haughs o Cromdale, traditional

Cope sent a challenge frae Dunbar,
Saying "Charlie meet me an ye daur,
An' I'll learn ye the art o war,
If ye'll meet me in the morning."

O Hey! Johnnie Cope, are ye waukin' yet?
Or are your drums a-beating yet?
If ye were waukin' I wad wait,
Tae gang tae the coals in the morning.
Hey Johnnie Cope, tune traditional, words Adam Skirving

collected and annotated by Sir Walter Scott in his 'Minstrelsy of the Scottish Border', faded from singing memory.

Scott included many other ballads kent far and wide in Scotland, and his pioneering work subsequently led many to lump all old ballads together as 'Border Ballads'. Scott's songs that do tell of strife across the Border or inter-clan clashes in the Debatable Lands comment on natural justice and the misuse of political power, injustice, revenge, complaint and daring deeds. Few of them are now sung in the Borders or elsewhere in Scotland, though 'Johnnie Armstrong's Goodnight' has stayed in memory because of its account of King James V's dastardly 1530 betrayal of a promise of safe conduct.

The greatest outpouring of retrospective lyrics about battles and their contexts arose from the series of Jacobite Risings, which some called Rebellions, from Killiecrankie in 1689 to Culloden in 1746.

William Donaldson says, "Most of them purport to be contemporary with the events they describe, and some were explicitly presented as such by their writers, and the same is true of the overwhelming majority of what the songbooks of Scotland contain under the heading 'Jacobite Songs'. Is there anything, then, to prevent the conclusion that they are fakes, brilliant fakes perhaps, but fakes notwithstanding?" Donaldson concludes that there is of course more to the story than this, and that "the struggle for the rights and liberties of the [Scottish] nation... merged with 'the Matter of Prince Charlie', to produce a new national consciousness and transform the Scottish identity."

There were of course songs made at the time of the Risings, particularly in Gaelic, as given in Anne Lorne Gillies' 'Gaelic Songs of Scotland' and J L Campbell's 'Gaelic Songs of the Forty-Five'. 'Hey Johnnie Cope' was written at the time of Prestonpans, the tune of 'Old Killiecrankie' eventually attracted several sets of lyrics, and Donaldson gives various early broadside Jacobite lyrics.

The major creators of retrospective Jacobite songs were Robert Burns, James Hogg and Lady Nairne. Sir Walter Scott contributed only 'Bonny Dundee'. Some commentators suggest Burns began as a Jacobite supporter, and progressed to become a radical. Others point out he kept writing or rewriting Jacobite lyrics while penning modern revolutionary lyrics. Jim McLean comments that "Burns was a democrat and a romantic Jacobite at the same time. That is very Scottish, we hold contradictions."

Cam ye o'er frae France?
Cam ye doun by Lunnon?
Saw ye Geordie Whelps
And his bonny woman?
Were ye at the place
Ca'd the Kittle Housie?
Saw ye Geordie's grace
Riding on a goosie?
Cam Ye Ower Frae France,
Words James Hogg

Burns' Jacobite songs include 'Awa Whigs Awa', 'The White Cockade', 'It Was Aa For Our Rightful King', 'Charlie He's My Darling' – and 'Ye Jacobites By Name', though some authorities assert it is an earlier song, possibly reworked by him.

Twenty years after Burns died, James Hogg published his 'Jacobite Relics of Scotland' collection, songs both pro and anti Jacobite. Donaldson considers Hogg the creator of at the very least 'Donald Macgillavry', 'Cam Ye O'er Frae France', 'Will Ye Go Tae Sheriffmuir', 'The Piper O Dundee' and 'Come O'er The Stream Charlie'.

Lady Caroline Nairne disapproved of much of Burns's work, and "deeply lamented that one endowed with so much genius should have composed verses which tended to inflame the passions." She softened and "purified the national minstrelsy" of older Jacobite songs, and created new ones under her pen name of Mrs Bogan of Bogan. For example she rewrote 'Charlie Is My Darling', and wrote 'The Hundred Pipers', and 'Will Ye No Come Back Again?'

The best known Jacobite song was written in the 1880s by an

Versions of Charlie Is My Darling
As Charlie he cam up the gate
His face shone like the day
I grat to see the lad come back
That had been lang away

Out-owre yon moory mountain
And down yon craigy glen
Of naething else our lasses sing
But Charlie and his men
By James Hogg

☙

As he came marching up the street
The pipes play'd loud and clear
And aa the folk came running out
To meet the Chevalier

They've left their bonny Hieland hills
Thir wives and bairnies dear
To draw the sword for Scotland's lord
The young Chevalier
By Lady Nairne

Englishman, Sir Harold Boulton. He used the tune of a Gaelic rowing song, an iorram, for 'The Skye Boat Song'. When the lyric was given in the Bo'ness 'Patriot Songs' booklet, they changed the last line from "*Charlie will come again*" *to* "*Scotland will rise again*".

There are many other more modern creators or revisers of Jacobite songs. 'King Fareweel' occurs on a late 19th Century broadside as 'Charlie Stuart and his Tartan Plaidie', and also in the 'Greig Duncan Folk Song Collection'. In the 1960s, singer and songwriter Andy Hunter developed and rewrote 'King Fareweel' from a short sung version.

Songwriter Jim McLean's retrospective 'Massacre of Glencoe', *"Cruel is the snow that sweeps Glencoe"* is widely popular, as are Brian MacNeill's Flora MacDonald song called 'Strong Women Rule Us All', and Ronnie Browne's 'Roses of Prince Charlie'.

Some Jacobite songs were protest songs of the time, but many more were either later right wing romantic Tory songs, or disguised assertions about Scotland's place in the United Kingdom. Geordie McIntyre comments, "Most Jacobite songs were written later, when it was safer to write them. I've never heard anyone singing a Whig song, though there are plenty of them. We love a loser. I said to [Glasgow singer with the Whistlebinkies group] Mick Broderick 'You're a bizarre guy, like a lot of the rest of us you're a left wing Jacobite Marxist Socialist Conservative Presbyterian.'

"How many people who sing Jacobite songs know the slightest thing about the Stuart monarchy? People who are republicans sing Jacobite songs. I think they are singing about an ideal of somebody who was popular, singing about something good that might have happened, though Bonny Prince Charlie was not universally popular in Scotland. And of course people can be attracted to the tune and the language, and images are brilliant in some of the songs. We sing them now for different reasons, sometimes from a basis of ignorance." *Geordie McIntyre*

After the '45, tartan and kilts were banned, except in the British army. The song topics move, opposition to the British Government turns into praise for the foreign exploits and valour of our gallant Jocks.

Another song made popular through the singing of Jeannie Robertson is 'Twa Recruitin Sergeants', a Scots language version of the widely sung Napoleonic Wars song *'Over the hill and across the main, to Flanders, Portugal and Spain'*.

The advent of the Crimean War brings on a small flock of humorous 'Here Come The Russians' broadsides. 'The Russian In Glasgow' begins, *"The Russian is coming, oh dear oh dear"*. 'The Finishing Stroke' will be given him by the Yeomanry, and the Volunteer forces are also praised in 'The Camlachie Militia'. 'The British Lion And The Russian Bear' is to the tune of 'The King Of The Cannibal Isles'. Another new broadside is also named 'The Russians Are Coming'.

Broadside songs that praised the daring Scottish soldiery included 'The Scotch Brigade', 'We'll Hae Nane But Highland Bonnets Here', and 'Lads That Were Reared Among The Heather'.

Other broadside lyrics made fun of army life, like 'The Gallant Forty Twa' which was sung with high vigour by Jimmy MacBeath in the People's Festival Ceilidh, and broadside ballad 'Sodger Jock'.

Says oor sairgent jist the day, "Jock! Ye'll sune be gaun awa
Oot tae Indy for tae fecht the Blackymoors"
But I'll tak my rifle heft, and I'll paste them richt and left
An I'll dimple in their goblets wi the cloors
Sodger Jock, A Comic Song, dated Saturday, May 22, 1886

The last line could be translated as "I'll bash in their cooking pans with blows", where 'pans' means heads.

Weaver David Shaw of Forfar, who wrote 'The Wark O The Weavers', made another such 'comic' song, 'The Forfar Sodger'. In the 1960s folk clubs several less chucklesome verses were omitted, like the following.

The bluid cam bockin thro my hose, and when I couldna gang,sir
I toom'd my gun among my foes, and syne sat doon an sang, sir

At 'Scots wha hae wi Wallace bled', an 'Up wi Maggie Dick' sir
But sune wi cauld my woundit leg, it grew stiff's a stick, sir

These verses come from Robert Ford's 1904 'Vagabond Songs and Ballads of Scotland'. Other soldierly songs included there are the old lyric of 'Jamie Foyers', 'The Plains of Waterloo', 'Corunna's Lovely Shore', 'The Bonny Lass of Fyvie', 'Bannocks of Bearmeal', 'The Kilties in the Crimea', 'The Heights of Alma', and a Jacobite lyric for 'The Bonny Banks of Loch Lomond'.
When World War One began, an alliance of socialists and pacifists objected. Some went to prison.

Oh Calton Gaol! Oh Calton Gaol!
Sae sombre, grim and grey,
Within thy wa's were gallant hearts
Held captive mony a day.
For they refused to bend the knee
To tyrants' cruel sway;
The stand remembered aye shall be
They made for Liberty.
Calton Jail, tune Rowan Tree, words Robert Stewart,
from 'Prison Rhymes'.

Two retrospective songs that query the value of the sacrifice of the WW1 Flanders warriors were made by Scots emigrant to Australia Eric Bogle, 'The Green Fields of France' (also known as 'Willie McBride') and 'The Band Played Waltzing Matilda'. Both songs were recorded by the Irish group The Fureys and Davy Arthur, and were very successful in the Irish Hit Parade, so subsequently Bogle has been claimed as an Irish songwriter.
These songs illustrate two of the problems of considering why songs are labelled 'political'. First, the songs are critical of the way the First World War was prosecuted, no-one in the last 80 years has argued in favour of how that war was waged, so where is the political dissention? Second, a sense of ownership over the songs is felt by left wingers who

are pacifists, but they are sung with equal fervour and a sense of ownership not only by people in the Scottish National Party and the Scottish Labour Party, but also by Scottish Tories. Bogle has of course made other songs about more recent matters that are politically explicit, and he views his WW1 songs as generally anti-war. The inter-party popularity of these songs reminds us that no politician makes statements in favour of waging war, it is always someone else who starts or forces the fight, and they are reluctantly obliged to respond.

Most songs of the time of World War One were pro that War. An American songwriter, Alfred Bryan, covered his bets by using the same tune and lyric approach in both directions – his 1914 song 'I Didn't Raise My Son To Be A Soldier', was in 1917 rewritten by him as 'I'm Glad My Son Grew Up To Be A Soldier'. In the 1970s Scots singer Hamish Imlach had only one verse of the antiwar version and wanted to use the song, so got more verses written so he could perform it. Neither Eric Bogle nor Hamish Imlach wanted to change attitudes or promote new action re WW1, but both wanted to use the example of that War to promote the principle of peaceful resolution of differences.

Post war fury at betrayed promises led to such bitter jibes as:

After the war was over, after the Slaves had bled,
After the dead were buried, after the prayers were said,
Many a Slave was saying, "Good God, what was it for?"
Many a mother was weeping after the war.

After The War, tune After The Ball, words Comrade Tom (Anderson)

☙

Aprés la guerre fini, heroes they said we'd be
Skimming the milk in the land of the Free, aprés la guerre fini

Aprés la guerre fini, first fruits of victory
We got our medals and wooden legs free, aprés la guerre fini

Aprés la guerre fini, no homes for such as we

Without a deposit and bank guarantee, aprės la guerre fini

Aprės la guerre fini, no jobs for one in three
"Take it or leave it" the bosses decree, aprės la guerre fini

Aprės la guerre fini, we're on the U.A.B.
Helping build guns with the tax on the tea, aprės la guerre fini
Aprės La Guerre Fini, Tune Under The Bridges Of Paris, From People's Parodies

There have always been soldiers' squibs, parodies and rewritten verses. The Theatre Workshop show 'Oh What A Lovely War' was made up of such. Ronnie Clark of Glasgow recalls his father singing the following, one of many verses for 'Bless Em All'.

Ah ye'll go, ah ye'll go, ah ye'll go
Whether ye like it or no
Wee baggy troosers wi seams up the side
Hauns in yer pockets wi nuthin inside

World War Two produced many such soldiers' songs. Hamish Henderson collected some together in a volume, Ballads of World War II, published by the 'Lili Marlene Club'. They included songs of his own making like 'The 51st Highland Division's Farewell To Sicily', better known as 'Banks O Sicily' – "*Nae Jock will mourn the kyles o ye*". Another that he developed from "a Ballad which was circulating among the '8th Army scroungers'" in Italy was 'D-Day Dodgers', of which he claimed authorship of five of the eight verses. Both these songs have been much sung in the Folk Revival. A song made by Henderson which was dropped from the sung repertoire expressed wartime admiration for the Red Army's resistance to Hitler, and its leader.

O Hitler's a non-smoker and Churchill smokes cigars
And they're both as keen as mustard on imperialistic wars

But your Uncle Joe's a worker and a very decent chap
Because he smokes a pipe and wears a taxi driver's cap

Ian Davison has made a WW2 song, to the tune of 'John Anderson' in march time, about the 1941 'Clydebank Blitz'. It begins

The moon was on the river, and a chill was on the town
The children in their siren suits were told to cuddle down
And in from off the North Sea, across the eastern shores
With shining lochs to lead them on, the waves of bombers roared

Clydebank, London, Coventry and Dresden
Hamburg, Tokyo, Hiroshima, Nagasaki

It ends with

Night-shift workers found the place their families had been
They saw the shattered tenements, and spaces in between
They saw the miners digging, and they knew what it was for
It's babies on the front line now, and that's a modern war

Peacetime soldiering also produced small songs. In revolution-torn Aden in 1965 an ex-Indian army man sang the author a piece that combines Hindi words, a combination of condescending attitude and recognition of rights outraged re the Indian servants that even non-commissioned men had, and an older final joke line of 'Baboo English'.

Sixteen annas one rupee, seventeen annas one buckshee
Sixteen years you love my daughter, now you're bound for the Blighty, Sahib
Hope the boat that carries you over sinks to the bottom of the briny, Sahib
Sergeant Major very fine fellow, Queen Victoria very fine king

Current Scots songwriters in no way thought of as politically active have made current or retrospective songs. John Martyn's 'Don't You Go My Son' and Billy Connolly's 'Sergeant Where's Mine?' are both quiet laments. Martyn's song speaks for all mothers. 'Sergeant Where's Mine?' is a neat and affecting comment on puzzled beleaguered squaddies in Northern Ireland, set to the same pipe tune, 'Farewell To The Creeks', which Hamish Henderson utilised for 'Farewell To Sicily' and Bob Dylan reworked for 'The Times They Are A-Changin'.
Other makers have created songs about Dunkirk, Aden, Northern Ireland, Libya and Iraq. The Lanarkshire Songwriters Group and New Makars Trust in 2006 created a whole CD of new songs about the Victoria Cross medal winners of Lanarkshire.
Are the Scots more war-obsessed through song than the English? No. Karl Dallas's 'Cruel Wars' volume of soldiers' songs has 12 traditional songs that are Scots, 25 that are English, 14 Irish, and 32 that are National rather than from one part of Great Britain, plus 15 songs of newer mint.

As I cam in by Fiddich Side on a May mornin
I spied Willie Mackintosh an oor afore the dawnin
Turn again, turn again, turn again, I bid ye
If ye burn Auchendoun, Huntley he will heid ye
Heid me or hang me, that shall never grieve me
I'll burn Auchendoun tho the life leave me

As I cam in by Fiddich Side on a May mornin
Auchendoun was in a bleeze an oor afore the dawnin
Crawin, crawin, for aa your crouse crawin
Ye brunt your crop an tint yer wings an oor afore the dawnin
The Burnin o Auchendoun, traditional

Scotland Hasnae Got A Queen

O, Scotland hesna got a King
And hesna got a Queen
Ye canna hae the saicint Liz
Whan the first yin's never been

Nae Liz the Twa, nae Lillabet the Wan
Nae Liz will ever dae
We'll mak oor land republican
In a Scottish breakaway

Her man's cried the Duke o Edinbury
He's wan o they kiltie Greeks
O dinna blaw ma kilts awa
Cos Lizzie wears the breeks
Coronation Coronach, tune The Sash, words Thurso Berwick

The song-making impulse and sense of celebration of nationhood given new life by the 'Lifting o the Stane', led to renewed interest in old Scots songs and the creation of new songs supporting Scottish independence that applauded acts of resistance to authority, and worked to support a developing sense of shared identity and aspiration. The ubiquitous 'Rebels Ceilidh Songbook' was then the essential source of political songs.

Marion Blythman, wife of Morris Blythman who wrote under the name Thurso Berwick, says, "When they were blowing up pillarboxes because of the Elizabeth the Second inscription, Morris wrote 'Nae Liz the Twa, Nae Lillabet the Wan' in response to that. Some people say Hamish was the bomber, but naw! That wasn't Hamish's style! When Morris wrote 'Sky High Joe' we knew that whoever was doing it had got the dynamite from the Carron Iron Works. '*I want it for a special job, I want the real Mackay.*'

"Morris always said the Orangemen had the best tunes. The first time the BBC wanted me to ask Morris about broadcasting, I said they'd have to play the 'Coronation Coronach'. 'Oh' says the woman, 'They'll not like that – it's the tune to 'The Sash'.' I told her to forget it! Morris wasn't an Orangeman. My mother got his politics right, she put her finger on it once. 'You two would be all right in the Morris Blythman Party.' He liked the Orangemen's tunes, and he wasn't anti-Catholic, but the whole magic, mystic nature of the Catholic Church was anathema to Morris. I would say he was philosophically against the darkness of the Catholic Church, the way the people didn't really know what was going on, all the stuff about faith. But he wasn't anti-Catholic, and his friend Hugh MacDonald kept on being a sort of Catholic, I think." *Marion Blythman*

Blythman himself wrote that the 1952 announcement that the new Queen, Elizabeth, was to be styled The Second, though there had never been a first Queen Elizabeth of Great Britain, "sparked off a wave of anti-Royalist songs, and the 'National Weekly' published many of them. We also pushed them by singing everywhere and anywhere we could. People were shocked by this sort of thing. The Scots then had been brainwashed into a complete fear of and respect for authority."

Blythman used shock tactics. "In the early days of the anti-Royalist songs I was put out of the Scottish Youth Hostels Association's annual meeting, was put out of Scottish National Party meetings, frowned upon everywhere. Nowadays they are common parlance."

The Edinburgh People's Festival was 'proscribed as a Communist Front' and killed off in 1954, but the Bo'ness Ceilidhs continued to thrive. New political songs responding to events had a place where they could be sung and celebrated. In the same year as the demise of the People's Festival a chapbook style booklet of song lyrics was published, 'The Rebels Ceilidh Song Book'. The 35 songs mix old and new Ceilidh favourites in Scots and Gaelic. The cover, by Bo'ness art teacher Jimmy Dewar, packs together references to songs and personalities. In one example, a Scots terrier harasses the policeman in pursuit of the couple running away with the Stane. The terrier's teeth are the initials HH for Hamish Henderson. Henderson's connection with the 1953 newly formed School of Scottish Studies within Edinburgh University gave him at last a secure base to develop his collecting and documenting work on Scottish traditional song and story.

The 'Rebels' booklet seems to have been assembled and edited jointly by Morris Blythman, Willie Kellock and Angus McGillveray. In 1994 McGillveray wrote that the Ceilidh Song Book was published in 1951, and the Introduction to Song Book No 2 in 1965 gave the publication date of Book 1 as 1951/2.

However, unless there was a first edition of which no copies have been traced, and which omits several songs in the edition that was widely distributed, the correct date is late 1954 or 1955. Three songs in what appears to be the first edition of the Song Book tell of the February 1953 blowing up by 'Sky High Joe' of pillar boxes that bore the EIIR symbol. Another song details aspects of the November 1953 trial of four seditious young members of the Scottish Republican Army.

The 1954 Rebels' St Andrew's Nicht Ceilidh of 27th November 1954 in Bridgeness Welfare Hall helps us get closer to the correct date of the first edition of the Song Book. The Bo'ness newspaper report tells of the singing that night of the 'new ballad The Lea-Rig', written as 'a hansel sang' for the birthday night of the Bo'ness pub that had received its licence in November 1953.

Bo'ness Rebels song

O, Tam Dalyell cam sookin in
He's a frightfully decent chap
"I've fotch my Saft Soap Bottle, Heah!
Would you like a tiny drap?"

Sydney Smith wis mair nor there
His elbows moved sae free
Ye'd swore it wis the links o Forth
Gaun doon tae meet the sea

Twas Berwick-Kellock rimed this song
An they were warst av a'
Yer whisky's blunt, it willna write
Juist hand me doon a saw

The Lea-Rig, tune To The Begging We Will Go, words Morris Blythman and Willie Kellock

"The November 1954 Ceilidh programme ended with the singing of that new Bo'ness ballad 'The Lea-Rig', which was composed jointly by Thurso Berwick, the Glasgow poet, and William Kellock." It was sung by John McEvoy and Enoch Kent, accompanied on guitar by Josh McRae, and "great enthusiasm swelled the chorus, 'To the Lea-Rig we will go'." The band was Alisdair Hunter's Ceilidh Band, and among the many other artistes were Ian M'Rae (Josh McRae) and his Glasgow College of Art Guitarists, and Hamish Henderson.

Bo'ness Rebels Song Book song
O, Sky-High Joe is on the go
Some gelignite tae buy
So he gangs tae the Carron Iron Works
For tae get a guid supply

When the Pillar Box sees Sky-High Joe
It blanches deadly pale
"Staun back, staun back, wi yuir hair sae black
Ah dinnae want your air-mail"

But when ye're postin Valentines
Wi a yaird o fizzin fuse
Ye hinnae ony time tae be polite
Ye've an awfy lot tae lose
Tune The Overgate, words Thurso Berwick

Twenty verses from the October 1954 'The Lea-Rig' are included in the 'Song Book'. The song is a Rabelasian account of excessive alcohol consumption, cut down 'for safety's sake' from the original sixty verses of 'mainly social characters in Bo'ness. Many of the verses describing local personalities of the past and present are omitted." *Willie Kellock*
Charlie Auld had built the new Lea-Rig pub alongside his licensed grocer premises in Dean Road.
The pub became the famed venue for more frequent smaller scale ceilidhs.
Harry Constable remembers that "on a Monday and a Friday night we would meet in the Lea-Rig lounge. It wasn't a concert ceilidh, it was almost like a debating society. We had people from the Labour Party,

Bo'ness Rebels Song Book songs
An were ye up in Embro, Jock
An were ye quate an douce?
Ir were ye packan gelignite
Aa roun St Andro's Hoose?

Ah gaed tae the High Coort Pantomime
The law wis daean a play
They hed fowr fellies in the dock
They cried the S.R.A.
Sky-High Pantomime, tune Harlaw, words Thurso Berwick

communists, left wing socialists, nationalists, it was remarkable. But not only left wingers. Discussions took place, and I believe a lot of people learned a lot. I think the Rebels Literary Society helped people to gain knowledge. It wasn't just core politics, it was about passion, and patriotism, and people like Clydesider John Maclean and Irish rebel James Connolly. I went to a Gaelic class when I was quite young, and I met Willie Kellock and Charlie Auld there, and ended up joining the Literary Club. I was the first Treasurer they had had in a while."

There was of course much singing too, and most of the Song Book songs have some political element. The three songs about the blowing up of EIIR pillarboxes by 'Sky High Joe' give few clues to his identity, other than he had 'hair sae black' and was a 'big black-coated chiel'. Hamish Henderson's biographer, Timothy Neat, is confident that Henderson was 'Sky High Joe', but the hair colour is wrong, and others I interviewed do not agree, feeling such violent action did not chime with his personality. I was told that black-haired piper Seamus MacNeill was suspected, and that "people always joked, 'Don't give Seamus any letters to post'." Whoever lit the fuses, the campaign was effective, and pillar boxes in Scotland bore no royal initials until in 2008 a box transplanted from the South was spotted on an industrial estate in Linlithgow.

The title of another song, 'Sky-High Pantomime', suggests it too was about pillar boxes, but it tells of the four students accused of being part of the Scottish Republican Army, plotting to blow up St Andrew's House, the base of the government's Scottish Office. The song 'Grieves Galorum' celebrates the 1952 prison sentence given conscientious objector Michael Grieve, son of Hugh MacDiarmid. Grieve was not the only Scot to be incarcerated for refusing to 'fight for an English queen', songwriter Jim McLean did likewise.

Hamish Henderson contributed to the Song Book two songs from WW2 days, the very famous 'D-Day Dodgers' and, anonymously, 'The Taxi Driver's Hat'. His 'John Maclean March' is included, and under the pseudonym Seamus Mor his 1948 'Ballad of the Men of Knoydart', one of two songs of Highlanders reclaiming land. The furiously vituperative tone of Henderson's attack on English landlord

Lord Brocket shows why his own name is not attached to the lyric. The other, Blythman's 'Ballad of Balelone' tells in more wryly humorous style of a 1952 'land raid'.
Norman Buchan's 'The Happy Blunderer' expressed worry about the defeated Germans being allowed to reform an army. Iain Nicolson's 'The Labour Provost' addressed a more local issue, the former Labour Party left wingers who shunted themselves right-wards when they got into political power as Glasgow councillors.

When I was young and fu o fire
Tae smash the Tories was my firm desire
But noo I'm auld I hae mair sense
I just blame the lot on Providence

I am a man o' high degree
Lord Provost o' this great cittee
The workers want a world tae gain
But I'm content wi' my badge and chain
The Labour Provost, tune The White Cockade, words Iain Nicolson

Four Gaelic songs are included without translation in the Song Book - Foghnan na h-Alba (The Badge of Scotland), 'Mhic Iarla Nam Bratach Bana' about the white banners of an earl's son as his fine birlinn sails, the dance-accompanying port a beul 'S Ann an Bhoidhich', and 'Tiugainn do Scalpaidh' in which bard John Morrison praises his Hebridean island home of Scalpay.
Four songs came from the older political struggles of Ireland. In discussion with me Harry Constable emphasised the importance of Irish rebel songs in the Bo'ness movement, and the political example of James Connolly. "The Irish songs were important, but they did it by the gun, we do it by the ballot box. Dominic Behan's song 'The Patriot Game', that tells how James Connolly was '*shot in a chair, his wounds from the battle all bleeding and bare'*. The cause of freedom can be fought for in different ways. Ireland has been a sad country, all the way down the line from Brian Boru." *Harry Constable*

The 'Rebels Ceilidh Song Book', like the ceilidhs, was not a narrow party political product. Willie Kellock's introduction says "This book is Labour, it is Nationalist, it is Tory in the original sense of the word – it is a Rebel Song Book uniting the varieties of Scottish Rebels to the realisation that what's wrong with the world is wrong here and now in Scotland."

In April 1955 the Linlithgowshire Journal reported about this first Song Book that it not only had "become popular in Scotland, but it is beginning to be known overseas." They explained that Russian poet Marshak, attending an International Burns Festival, was presented with a copy. "He was so impressed that he asked for copies to take back home with him for presentation to the Moscow University Library." Marshak went on to translate several Rebels songs into Russian.

The first 'Rebels Ceilidh Song Book' was distributed throughout Scotland, and young singers seized hungrily on it to learn songs. Contexts in which to hear the songs were developing. As well as the Heckleburnie Club and Thistle Society, in 1954 Blythman adopted the London model of a Ballads and Blues Club developed by Ewan MacColl and A L Lloyd, and started such a club for the boys of the all-male Glasgow secondary school where he taught French, Allan Glen's Academy. He brought traditional singers like Aberdonian diva Jeannie Robertson to the Club, and to the ceilidhs in his and his wife Marion's home in Balgrayhill.

In an appreciation of Blythman published in 'The Scotsman', singer Jimmie Macgregor wrote, "Through these vastly enjoyable, and always crowded house parties, Morris, by a process of illustration, propaganda, encouragement, education and sometimes downright bullying won us all away from the commercial music of the time, and introduced us to the traditions of our own country."

Now her sister Meg had a bonnie pair o legs
But she didnae want a German or a Greek
Peter Townsend wis her choice, but he didnae suit the boys
So they selt him up the creek

O, it's here's tae the Lion, tae the bonnie Rampant Lion
An a lang stretch ti its paw
Gie a Hampden roar, an we're oot the door
Ta-Ta to Chairlie's Maw

Coronation Coronach, tune The Sash, words Thurso Berwick

Troublesome Men And Troubled Women – Big Ballads

A lassie was milkin her father's kye,
When a gentleman on horseback, he cam ridin by.
A gentleman on horseback, he cam ridin by,
He was the laird o the Dainty Dounby.

"Lassie, oh lassie, fit wid ye gie,
If I wis tae lie ae nicht wi ye?"
"Tae lie ae nicht that will never never dee,
Though you're laird o the Dainty Dounby."

He's catched her by the middle sae sma,
He's laid her doon whaur the grass grew lang.
It wis a lang lang time or he raised her up again
Sayin "Ye're lady o the Dainty Dounby."
The Laird o the Dainty Dounby

The old Scots songs tell stories not only of battle, but also of sexual conflict and the abuse of women by the powerful, and of heroes and villains and heroic villains. They say much about the pleasures of alcohol, and just a little about the dangers of drinking.

At the end of the 19th Century an American scholar, Francis J Child, collected together, analysed and annotated and codified with identification numbers 'The English and Scottish Popular Ballads'. In 1994 Scottish scholar Emily Lyle edited a collection of 83 'Scottish Ballads' and ballad versions. Some of these were Scots versions of songs also sung elsewhere, many have or seem to have originated in Scotland. These narrative songs are of warfare, strife, love, jealousy, trickery, incest, magic, witchcraft, tragedy, betrayal, loyalty, injustice, seduction, rape, would-be rapers fooled, prejudice, murder, fair fights and more.

Singers refer to them as 'the big ballads'. They have been sung and learned aurally for centuries, and collected together in print and studied over the last 200 years. They are key among the traditional song gems of Scotland. Many were printed on broadsides alongside the new compositions of catchpenny balladeers, and in parlour songbooks alongside the songs of Scotland's national poets.

Hamish Henderson, and other Revival collectors like Peter Shepheard and Geordie McIntyre, collected and shared versions of these ballads as they were still sung by John Strachan, Jessie Murray, Duncan Williamson, the Stewart families of Blairgowrie and Fettercairn, Jeannie Robertson, Jimmy MacBeath, Davie Stewart and many more.

Norman Buchan, Morris Blythman, Ewan MacColl and Alan Lomax put them into accessible non-academic print and onto recordings, and incited young singers to engage with them and sing them.

A Ballad

There was four and twenty lairds and lords
Stood at the gates o Drum o
But nane o them put his hand to his hat
To welcome the shepherd's daughter in o

The Laird O Drum

I have in Chapter 4 listed many 'big ballads' on the topics of warfare and strife. Other ballads address issues of sexual politics. Many of the ballads that were taken up and were and are sung in the Revival tell tales of aspiration and the misuse of superior power. 'The Laird O The Dainty Dounby' tells of the rape by the laird of a tenant's daughter. When she becomes pregnant and he decides to marry her, her parents dance for joy. There are other similar ballads, but on occasion the girl pursues her rapist and gets justice, or else outwits the assailant and laughs at him.

'The Laird O Drum' tells of class prejudice. The laird marries a farm girl and his 'gentlemen' will not raise their hats to her. In 'Lord Thomas and Fair Eleanor' there is possible racial prejudice, his parents make him marry the Brown Girl because she has land, his beloved is killed by the Brown Girl, he kills the killer and commits suicide.

'The Gaberlunzie Man' asks shelter as a beggar, seduces the daughter of the house and runs off with her. He proves to be a noble man, or even the King. In 'The Gypsy Laddies' a gypsy seduces and tempts away the lord's wife, for which he and his brothers are hanged.

For bearing (and in some versions killing) a child by 'the highest Stuart of all', Mary Hamilton of 'The Queen's Four Maries' is executed, lamenting her actions and fate. No punishment seems to fall on the man. This ballad has a tangled skein of historical source elements that link the courts of Scotland and Russia.

As well as the men behaving abominably towards women, there are politically touched ballads of heroic or tragic men, and of heroic villains. Sea captain 'Sir Patrick Spens' is sent to Norroway to bring home a princess, and the ship founders with all hands. 'Young Beichan' sails to Turkey for adventure but is imprisoned, freed with magic by the gaoler's daughter, and marries her at last.

'Johnnie o Braidislie' and 'Hughie the Graeme' go poaching. Johnnie fights off the King's Foresters, but Hughie is hanged. The King sends the Earl of Huntly to arrest 'The Bonny Earl of Moray', Huntly kills him instead. Hardly any of the 'big ballads' have comic elements, but giant 'Lang Johnny More' who lives on the top of Bennachie goes seeking work in London, is to be hanged for falling in love with the princess, and is

Ballads

The Laird o Hume is a huntin gaen
Through the woods and the mountains fleein
And he has ta'en Hughie the Graeme
For stealin o the bishop's mare

He has taen Hughie the Graeme
Led him doon through Carlisle toon
The lads and the lassies stood on the walls
Cryin "Hughie the Graeme must not gae doon"
Hughie The Graeme

The reprieve was comin ower the Brig o Banff
Tae set MacPherson free
But they pit the clock a quarter afore
And hanged him frae the tree
MacPherson's Rant

Ye hielans and ye lowlans, whaur hae ye been?
They hae slain the Earl o Moray, and laid him on the green
The Earl o Moray

rescued by his giant uncles.
Some ballads sung by People's Festival Ceilidh singers appeared on broadsides but not in the Child collection. Jimmy MacBeath not only sang but told the detailed story of how outlaw and fiddler James MacPherson was captured by trickery, unfairly tried and condemned, and cheated of a retrial by the laird in 1700 in the town of Banff. Robert Burns rewrote this ballad, and Scotland's traditional fiddlers still play the air as 'MacPherson's Rant'.
Glasgow baker 'Jamie Raeburn' was unfairly sentenced to transportation for theft. Duncan Campbell, aka 'Erin Go Bragh', clearly was an active sympathiser with Irish political aspirations, who escaped from the Edinburgh bobbie and 'sailed for the North'. His story reminds us that Scottish support for political rights in Ireland was no new thing. He is of a clan identified with Protestant support of the Crown, yet has the look, manner and actions of a Fenian rebel against English rule, and his blackthorn stick identifies him with Ireland.
Seeded through this book are references to songs that tell of the pleasures of social drinking with people with whom one agrees politically, or why people should drink and forget about politics. Most of Scotland's folk clubs were run in the back rooms or lounges of pubs, so it is not surprising that temperance songs were less present. Jessie Murray's 'The Ale House' was little sung in the Revival, but another warning of the social evils of drink, 'Nancy Whisky', was a firm favourite, sung rousingly in the pubs where the message of the song was missed.
Of the big ballads I have named, only 'Sir Patrick Spens' did not enter the repertoire of Scots Revival singers.

O laith, laith were oor gweed Scots Lords, to wat their coal-black shoon
But lang ere a' the Play wis dune they wat their hats aboon

Half ower, half ower to Aberdour, where the sea's sae wide and deep
It's there lies young Sir Patrick Spens wi' the Scots Lairds at his feet

Patriot Songs

Come along, come along, let us foot it out together
Come along, come along, be it fair or stormy weather
With the hills of home before us and the purple of the heather
Let us sing in happy chorus
Come along, come along
Uist Tramping Song, as sung by Margaret Kellock

In the later 1950s the third of the architects of the Scots Folk Song Revival came to the fore. Norman Buchan spoke, organised, formed the Reivers group, wrote and published. Scots folk performers began to appear on television, and another influential lyric booklet appeared, Patriot Songs.

Ian Davison remembers, "I met Norman Buchan, when he gave a lecture [in 1957] in a ward meeting of the Labour Party in the Partick Burgh Hall.

Lyrics from Patriot Songs song book
One Hogmanay, at Glesca Fair
There was me, masel and sev'ral mair
We aa went aff tae hae a tear
And spend the nicht in Rothesay o
We wandered through the Broomielaw
Through wind and rain and sleet and snaw
And at forty meenits aifter twa
We got the length o Rothesay o
The Day We Went To Rothesay O, as sung by John McEvoy

ꟹ

There lived three brothers in merry Scotland
In merry Scotland there were three
And they did cast lots which of them should turn robber, turn robber, turn robber
Who should turn robber all on the salt sea
Henry Martin, traditional

ꟹ

Young Michael Grieve they've latten oot
Tan-tee-ree-orum
He wadna wear thir Karkee suit
He widna mak thir quorum
Thir bobbies taen him aff tae jile
Barlinnie, Saughton, aa in style
They'll cry mair kilties up it's true
But no if Scotland rises noo
Grieves Galorum, tune Soutar's Feast, words Thurso Berwick

He had a connection with the school I was at, his son was there, and he gave a famous lecture there that is often referred to, as influential for a lot of later folksingers. The key moment at the ward meeting, a debating point, was when he invited us to look around the room, and said, "Do you notice that there's anything missing in this room?" The thing missing was electric plug points.

"He was saying that the normal expectation of political and community groups is that you meet and people talk at you, and you talk back at them. It's all talk. They don't think that you might want to play a track from a record, or show a picture that you've painted. There's no concept of culture in the politics. He was quite tight with the Weskers, who were pushing this down south, trying to organise theatre groups, and write left wing plays. Which my father and mother had done with amateur and semi professional groups long before that, but in a more old fashioned way.

"It was Norman Buchan who made me realise that others were thinking the same thing, that politics was bloody boring, the way it was conducted, and it had to become more cultural. The power of the press, there ought to be not just left wing newspapers. There should be left wing magazines that were more entertaining than newspapers.

"The Buchans were keen to promote song, and drama, and everything." *Ian Davison*

The Buchans gave support, encouragement and songs to young singers like Archie Fisher and the author, and ran influential folk concerts in Rutherglen. Buchan began a song column in the 'Weekly Scotsman', each week bringing to hungry youngsters the tune and lyric of an old song. He also began a folk song Ballads Club in the school where he taught, Rutherglen Academy; among his pupils who became Revival singers were Gordeanna McCulloch and Ann Neilson, who tells about the early days of the club in Chapter

From Patriot Songs song book

By Clyde's bonny banks as I sadly did wander
Among the pit heaps as evening drew nigh
I spied a fair maiden all dressed in deep mourning
A weeping and wailing with many a sigh

The Blantyre Explosion, as sung by Rena Swankie

18. The club was initially run by Buchan alone, then jointly by him and Ian Davison, then by Davison alone, then by Davison and Adam McNaughtan, and then by McNaughtan on his own.

Skiffle music had put guitars in the hands of young Britain. In January 1956 Lonnie Donegan and his Skiffle Group first entered the Hit Parade with 'Rock Island Line'. Skiffle groups mushroomed around the land, singing a mixture of traditional American folk songs, blues and country songs in unison and strumming strings with a minimum of finesse and much enthusiasm. Donegan introduced songs of Woody Guthrie, and enthusiasts trailed Donegan's US sources back home through recordings and printed sources, while also beginning to realise the wealth of traditional Scots song around them, and working out how to accompany songs with more than rhythmic chording. Alan Lomax and Ewan MacColl fed the kindling fire with recordings and BBC broadcasts.

A Glasgow song popular in concerts

Oh, good morning til youse Glasgow boys, I'm glad to see youse well
For I'm just as self conceited as any tongue can tell.
Oh, I've got a situation, or-a-be-gob a fancy job,
I can whisper I've the weekly wage of eighteen bob.
It's a twelve-month now come Easter since I left Glenory town
Along with my brother Barney for to mow the harvest down,
Ah, but now I wear a garnsey and around my waist a belt
For I'm gaffer o'er the boys that makes the hot asphalt.

Hot Asphalt

Pioneer performers on Scotland's broadcast media were the Reivers group - Moyna Flanigan, Enoch Kent, Josh McRae, Rena Swankie, all playing guitars.

They were resident folk singers on Scottish Television's 'Jigtime' programme. Norman Buchan was instrumental in obtaining this exposure and getting the four solo singers to present themselves as a group. On British national BBC TV, the 'Tonight' early evening programme featured two Scots duos. Robin Hall and Jimmy Macgregor, who were proteges of Morris Blythman, and brothers Rory and Alex McEwan. Sister and brother Ray and Archie Fisher sang on a local STV tea time television news programme.

Down in London Ewan MacColl and others were developing the concept of a folk club, then termed Ballads and Blues. MacColl came to Glasgow for a late 1950s Ballads and Blues concert in the Iona Community, where Josh McRae was cheered on by the local crowd but reportedly quietly dismissed by MacColl as a tartan cowboy. Out on the stairs Archie Fisher was getting instrumental tips from American Ralph Rinzler.

The Reivers disbanded after two years. The dangers of accepting what reference books assert is highlighted by what 'The Great Scots Musicography' has to say about the group, that the members were Macrae, Norman Buchan "and – it was thought - Ewan MacColl". Flanagan had left earlier, then Kent emigrated to Canada, and Josh McRae became a solo singer again, and his several recordings had some chart success. He was a key member of the Glasgow Eskimos.

"Josh and Morris [Blythman] were twin souls, absolutely. They just complemented each other. Josh was not a songwriter, but he was a great interpreter of songs. He sang all the songs that Morris wrote and publicised them. And sometimes got punched on the jaw for it!" *Marion Blythman*

From 'The Rhyming Reasoner'
B. and K. were travellers, the greatest ever seen
They travelled up to Windsor to see the Duke and Queen
The Duke now sells the 'Worker' every day along the Mall
And the Queen is Party Organiser in the servants' hall
The Comrades' One-Day School, tune: The Darkies' Sunday School

ꕥ

They passed a resolution tae gie the rebels hell
An' exorcised 'The Reasoner' wi' candle, book and bell
Then up spake John an' Edward, wi a voice as bold as brass
"We don't want your resolution, you can throw it in the grass"
The Ballad O 'The Reasoner', tune: The Ball of Kirriemuir

An initial political motivation for encouraging young people to investigate and adopt aspects of their own song culture had come in part from ex-members of the Communist Party. These had first taken an interest for ideological reasons of supporting indigenous culture rather than 'commercial American pap', but were seduced by the songs and music.

Along-side, or separately from the developing enthusiasm for traditional song, poets plied their wordskills to pound home political points. There is an ongoing tradition of creating topical political lyrics using popular tunes of the day or traditional airs, well shown in two 1956 cyclostyled issues of 'The Rhyming Reasoner, A Journal of Indiscretion, edited by W. McGonagall, Elysian Fields, N.' Mr McGonagall roundly lambasts his Communist Party comrades by first name or initial and bastes Party personalities, policies and actions from the inside, telling "Marxist stories that you've never heard before".

Around 1958 another chapbook-like booklet of song lyrics was published, dateable by the Preface mentions of the Reivers and skiffle music. Published by the Bo'ness Rebels Literary Society, 'Patriot Songs for Camp and Ceilidh' offers the lyrics of "35 ceilidh songs: Scots bothy ballads, industrial songs, patriotic and battle songs, songs of the sea and of our working loons, Irish songs and songs of bonnie lassies."

From Patriot Songs song book
An as I cam in by Achendoun
Just a little wee bit frae the toon
Intae the Hielans I was bound
Tae view the Haughs o' Cromdale
The Haughs o' Cromdale, traditional

Why Camp? In the Preface, Hugh MacDonald writes that Scots and Irish songs learned from his parents "like a rudder and a fair wind" steered him into Fianna na-h-Alba (the League of Young Scots). "There a new world opened up. Around the Fianna campfires the history of our country, denied me at school, came sharply into focus in the songs we sang at the weekends." *Hugh Campbell*

At the time troupes of young city folk like the Nomads of Chapter 2, a few toting guitars or other

From Patriot Songs song book
'Twas at the great convention that my father wore it last,
When 40,000 Orangemen assembled in Belfast;
We gathered to show those rebels all so resolute and cool
That Ould Ulster rules her own degree, we shall not have Home Rule.
The Sash My Father Wore, traditional

instruments, caught buses out to the countryside on a Friday after their work or school, hiked and camped or stayed in youth hostels or bothies, and returned refreshed on Sunday night.

The 'Patriot Songs' booklet bears no names of editors, but was surely the joint work of Willie Kellock and Morris Blythman. Many others are also named and thanked for help, and most of the songs are marked 'as sung by' a particular performer. The song list mixes old and new, traditional gems and Kennedy Fraser confections.

A few of the lyrics are modern political songs. 'The Scottish Volunteers' and 'Johnnie Destinie-O' are both Thurso Berwick products, late 'Sangs o the Stane'.

From Patriot Songs song book

O Stuart was a Commissar in High Saint Andra's Hoose
But a tinkle on the telephone frae Lizzie's made him douce
'Gae tak a sea-trip Jimmy lad, tae speir ma friens oot-bye
Tak lollies fur the Auld Wives and lie-cake fur the Kye'

Whitehall, Blackhall, everybody come
Join the Rocket-Racketeers and let them have their fun
Bring your Dumpy levels and Theodolites galore
If there's nae room on the Machar - juist tak ower the Croft next door!

Bally Rocket, tune Johnson's Motor Car or The Darkies' Sunday School, words Uilleam Beag

In the first verse Blythman nails his heroes' names to the mast, *"Wallace, Muir and John Maclean, An him the yin that taen the stane"*. Later on Blythman calls for the Fiery Cross to raise Scotland and resist conscription for foreign wars, *"No a single Jock is gaen, To fecht a fecht that's no oor ain"*.

Uilleam Beag's 'The Ballad of Bally Rocket' makes fierce fun at length of the siting of a rocket testing range on South Uist, and the determined resistance, naming supporters and opponents of the plan. Some less immediate political songs are also there. 'Erin Go Bragh', 'Scots Wha Hae', the patriotic bragging of 'The Thistle of Scotland', and the overwrought 'The Sons of Glencoe'.

Four of the 'Patriot Songs' are Irish, and three of these are political. Two 'Patriot Songs' are in Gaelic. Others are derived through the manipulations of Anglifiers from Gaelic song. One is that odd hybrid,

the 'Skye Boat Song', words by late 19th Century Englishman Sir Harold Boulton, tune from a Gaelic rowing air.
The other songs are 'traditional' or national in nature. There are a couple about alcohol, with one interloper from American country music and one US reworking of an old ballad of Scots piracy.
The booklet finishes with 'Auld Lang Syne', another song with multiple parentage.
Robert Burns wrote to George Thomson "The air is but mediocre; but the following song, the old song of the olden times, and which has never been in print, nor even in manuscript, until I took it down from an old man's singing; is enough to recommend any air."
The tune usually sung at New Year is not Burns' 'mediocre' one, but another called 'The Miller's Wedding', which was substituted when the song was printed in 'The Scots Musical Museum'. In the 1990s Scots folk singers began with great pleasure to sing the song to the original tune Burns had found lacking in quality.
Though Burns says the song had never been in print, in 1711 a ballad, 'Old Lang Syne' had been printed with substantially the same first verse and chorus, and other basic elements of the lyric have been traced in print and in various manuscripts, for example the following.

Should auld acquantence be forgot
And never thought upon
The flames of love extinguished
And freely past and gone?
Is thy kind heart now grown so cold
In that loving breast of thine
That thou canst never once reflect
On old-lang-syne
Probably written by Sir Robert Ayton (1570-1638)

Lay Your Disputes Aa Aside – Songs Of National Politics

Here's a health to them that's awa,
Here's a health to them that's awa!
And wha winna wish luck to our cause,
May never guid luck be their fa'!

May Liberty meet wi success!
May Prudence protect her frae evil.
May Tyrants and tyranny tine i' the mist,
And wander their way to the devil!

Here's freedom tae them that wad read,
Here's freedom tae them that wad write,
There's nane ever feared that the truth should be heard,
But they whom the truth would indite.

Here's friends on baith sides o the firth,
And friends on baith sides o the Tweed;
And wha wad betray old Albion's right,
May he never eat of her bread.

Songs about aspects of national political issues and movements are often at the time deeply contentious, but after the uproar and heat of political fervour has died to embers the best of the songs live on, sometimes as educational tools, sometimes as nostalgic reminders, and often as historical examples to illustrate present concerns and support present political positions.

The above sixteen lines are drawn from the forty in Robert Burns's 1792 lyric, 'Here's A Health To Them That's Awa'.

Other parts of the lyric say "*It's guid to support Caledonia's cause and bide by the buff and the blue*", and offer *"a health to Charlie, the chief o' the clan*", *to "Tammie the Norlan' laddie, That lives at the lug o' the Law*", to Maitland and Wycombe, and to "Chieftain M'Leod". The song supports the Whig 'Buff and Blue' cause, rather than the White Rose of Tory Jacobitism. Charlie was Charles James Fox, the other names are prominent Scots Whigs of the time that we feel little desire to know more about. However, into a jovial partisan and personally specific drinking song Burns weaves toasts that in other contexts of the time might have been considered highly seditious, and address general issues and principles. As does a favourite political song, Hogg's 'Both

What's the spring, breathing jasmine and rose
What's the summer with all its gay train
Or the splendour of autumn to those
Who've bartered their freedom for gain?

Let the love of our King's sacred rights
To the love of our people succeed
Let friendship and honour unite
And flourish on both sides the Tweed
Both Sides The Tweed, Words James Hogg

Jacobite song lyrics
A Highland lad my love was born
The Lowland laws he held in scorn
But he still was faithful to his clan
My gallant braw John Highlandman
Robert Burns

Pibroch o Donuil Dhu, pibroch o Donuil Dhu
Wake thy wild voice anew, summon Clan Conuil
Come away, come away, hark to the summons
Come in your war array, gentles and commons
Pibroch O Donuil Dhu, words Sir Walter Scott

It's owre the border awa awa
It's owre the border awa awa
We'll on and we'll march to Carlisle Ha
Wi its yetts, its castles an aa an aa
Wi A Hundred Pipers, words Lady Nairne

Come gies a sang, Montgomery cried
An lay your disputes aa aside
What nonsense is't for folks tae chide
For what's been done a fore them
Let Whig an Tory aa agree
Tae drop their whigmigmorum
Tae spend this nicht wi mirth and glee
An cheerful sing alang wi me
The Reel o Tullochgorum
Tullochgorum, words Rev John Skinner

Sides The Tweed'.

Present day singer Dick Gaughan has created a fine new melody for this lyric, and slightly amended the words. Gaughan's alteration of the text from "*our King's sacred rights*" to "*our land's sacred rights*" shifts the song from right-wing to left-wing.

Burn's lyric strongly pre-echoes Hogg's, and the title of the specified tune, 'Here's a Health to Them That's Awa', suggests he may have drawn on an older song again.

Most political songs that are specific to time, place and person do not last long in the mouth of singers. The exceptions are marked by simplicity of lyric and vigour of tune and narrative, or by fine poetry and sweet melody, but they live on shorn of context.

1950s Scottish schoolchildren in their music classes sang Scots political songs of warfare and violence lustily, but had and were offered no notion of the political or social context these songs were made in. Ten of the thirty lyrics in the 1958 'Scottish Orpheus School Song Book, Book One', have strong political content. Six of them are Jacobite songs, whose lyricists include Burns, Hogg, Nairne and Skirving, with two traditional songs. Sir Walter Scott contributes a song of Highland summons to war, and Bonny Dundee's flourishing exit from Edinburgh. The other two political songs tell of clan-related murders. The Orpheus songs were selected from a national song repertoire that would seem to have been codified and considered the acceptable settled corpus of Scottish Songs in later Victorian times, and continue to appear in hefty volumes graced by piano accompaniments.

A typical earlier music book, the 1870s 'The Songs of Scotland', has 151 songs, of which 21 are political. Fourteen of these are Jacobite, five are accounts of other

A broadside ballad
Sons of Scotia raise your voice
With shouts of exultation
The Bill is past, we have at last
Free trade throughout the nation

Russell and Brougham, Althorp and Hume
Laboured both late and early
The Champion Grey has won the day
Now he has beaten them fairly
Reform Song, for Scottish Reform Act 1832, no tune named

historical violence, one is 'Tullochgorum' which advocates dancing rather than political dispute, and the other song is 'Scots Wha Hae'.
'The Songs of Scotland', and the mound of other such collections, differ from each other largely in the detail of the 'new symphonies and accompaniments' in each volume, the piano arrangements to be used for their performance. The singers at the Bo'ness and Edinburgh ceilidhs had learned their song tunes aurally, and sang them from memory and unaccompanied.
Versions of the lyrics of many of the ceilidh songs can however be traced in older broadsheets and in song collections. In some songbooks the music is given, but more often a tune is named to which the song is to be sung. And some songs appeared first in newspapers. Some of Burns' most intensely political songs were dangerous to his personal liberty, so were printed anonymously in the news-sheets of the time, and scholars still debate his authorship of a few.
Some songbooks are collections with the maker named when known, others are the work of individual writers who typically paid for the printing of their volumes and told the reader their name or pseudonym in large letters. Broadsides hardly ever named the lyric maker.
In 'Sons of Scotia, Raise Your Voice' Peter Freshwater tells how broadsides printed on one side of a single sheet of paper were hawked through the streets by ballad-singers. These sang or droned out the lyrics to the named tune or a selected known one. "The printed broadside was the

A broadside ballad
Hey, great Duke, are you waking yet?
Have you heard your dead drum beating yet?
Tho going to Heaven, we aa wad wait
To see you hanged some morning

The Pats are kicking up a row
The Scotsman says, "What's aa this now?"
John Bull cries "I'll not bear't I vow
I'll hang him up some morning"

Make ready, Wellington, in haste
To lose your head or be displaced
As all your mercy we did taste
When we sought reform yon morning
The Tyrant's Fall, tune Johnnie Cope, words Mrs Kennedy, 1832

principle vehicle of publishing current information in the streets until newspapers became affordable by all but the very poorest."
After that point, song lyrics topical and old were still most cheaply bought on broadsheets. The songs of current events were not created by poets but by catchpenny rhymesters who 'knew what the people wanted'. If there was space on the page, reprints and unattributed lifts from other broadside makers were added. We find much topical comment, left and right wing, in songs in broadside collections, and in the cheap little chapbooks which usually gave prose accounts and stories, but sometimes included songs.
The ephemeral nature of much political song means that the broadside is a natural location for it. Freshwater discusses in particular broadside ballads of the early 19th Century, but the medium is far older. For example, a contemporary broadside cheers on the 1705 Darien Scheme that ruined Scotland.

Come rouse up your heads, come rouse up anon
Think of the wisdom of old Solomon
And heartily join with our own Paterson
To fetch home Indian treasures

The 1707 Act of Union roused songmakers. One song lamented "*O Caledon! O Caledon! How wretched is thy Fate.*" Author Hector McMillan says that the best known song about the Union, 'Sic a Parcel of Rogues', was "written by Robert Burns from an older work dating from the 1707 Union of Parliaments, it seems likely this reworking was at very least informed by current efforts being made to turn Scotland, politically and linguistically, into North Britain."
A 1713 broadside, 'Samson's Foxes', lambasts both Catholics and Covenanters.

From the Roman whore or Geneva slut
The one dawbed with paint, the other with smut
From the Beast's horned head, or his cloven foot, libera etc

From Rome's old darkness or Geneva's new blaze
Which lead men from heaven quite different ways
From excluding from thence by decrees or by keys, libera etc

The Jacobite Risings raised a torrent of songs at the time, and the stream still runs. 'God Save The King' was an earlier 18th Century royalist song.

In the garb of old Gaul, with the fire of old Rome
From the heath-covered mountains of Scotia we come
Where the Romans endeavoured our country to gain
But our ancestors fought, and they fought not in vain

Quebec and Cape Breton, the pride of old France
In their troups fondly boasted till we did advance
But when our claymores they saw us produce
Their courage did fail, and they sued for a truce
In The Garb Of Old Gaul, music General John Reid, words Lt General Sir Henry Erskine (The 'garb' is a reference to the kilt)

It won renewed life in the theatres of a London panicked by the 1745 Rising, when the notorious "*rebellious Scots to crush*" verse appeared. The 1788 Edinburgh song collection 'Calliope or the Vocal Enchantress', that the editor says includes "every popular and fashionable song, whether English, Scots or Irish" has only one Jacobite song, 'Lewis Gordon'. Jacobite songs were then quite out of fashion, to be brought back into the singing repertoire by the collecting work and new songs of Burns and Hogg. Among various Calliope songs on the joys of international warfare are the Scots songs 'Deil Tak The War' and two lyrics for 'The Garb of Old Gaul', one made in 1748 by General Sir Henry Erskine as a recruiting song against the French, and another

Does haughty Gaul invasion threat?
Then let the loons beware, Sir!
There's wooden walls upon our seas
And volunteers on shore, Sir!
The Nith shall run to Corsincon
And Criffel sink in Solway,
Ere we permit a foreign foe
On British ground to rally!

Who will not sing God Save the King
Shall hang as high's the steeple;
But while we sing God Save the King,
We'll ne'er forget the People!
Does Haughty Gaul Invasion Threat? tune Push About the Jorum, words Robert Burns

later lyric that adds in the Spanish as enemies. Several of the Scots songs urge political peace, promoting boozing instead.
'Tullochgorum', 'Every Man Take his Glass', 'When Once the Gods' and 'John of Badenyon'. The latter rejects the ideas of John Wilkes and Parson Horne. Another song in the collection 'The Vicar of Bray', approves of repeated trimming of one's coat of allegiance. It is English but was still sung in Scottish 1950s schools.
We can trace how Robert Burns develops his political lyrics - retrospective Jacobitism, Heron election ballad squibs supporting his favoured local candidates for office, Masonic minstrelsy, revolutionary songs re both internal and international politics, and the 1795 internationalism of 'A Man's A Man', ' inspired by the French Revolution and Tom Paine's 'Rights of Man'. Is he obliged to then trim his coat, and retreat from the threat of transportation along with Thomas Muir, by writing '*Does haughty Gaul invasion threat?*
Burns' radical songs are counterbalanced by the anti-democratic songs of Glasgow's William Campbell. A manuscript collection of these in Glasgow's Mitchell Library shows how horrified the powerful and well-to-do were at the prospect of the rule of the common people. Campbell also uses the 'Garb of Old Gaul' tune, for

We'll boldly fight like heroes bright, for honour and applause
And defy the frantic democrats to alter our laws
Shall we barter those gifts from our sires handed down
For the whims of the madman, the freaks of the clown
And ignobly yield up to the frenzy of P-ne
What our ancestors spent their best blood to obtain

Another, sneering at the courage of the Parisians, he labels as 'Translation of a Song Sung in the National Convention In Praise of the Sans Culottes', and he adds new verses to 'The King's Anthem'.

Know frantic democrates
Scotia your frenzy hates
Scorns your vile noise

Tell your apostle Paine
All his great blustering's vain
Freedom's mild gentle rein (sic)
Britain enjoys

Campbell also gives us two songs in praise of locally recruited Volunteers. One says "*Discord shrinks to nothing when she views the Glasgow Volunteers*". The other, to the tune of 'The British Grenadiers', is even more complimentary.

No rotten hearted democrats among our band appears
Such wretches shun the presence of the Paisley Volunteers

As for foreign foes,

Whene'er their tribe eludes our Tars, and on our coast appears
They'll find their first opposers in the Paisley Volunteers

Campbell was not alone, many Anti-Jacobin songs and novels were published, spearheaded by Edmund Burke's 1791 attack on the French Revolution. "Along with its natural protectors and guardians, learning will be cast into the mire, and trodden down under the hooves of a swinish multitude."
Balladeers responded. One song, to the tune 'Maggie Lauder', was entitled 'Swinish Gruntings'.

What! Shall a base deceitful crew
Supported by our labours,
Gainsay our wills - wage wicked war,
With our good Apeish neighbours?
Forbid it, Heaven! Forbid it, Earth!
Ye Grunters brave, forbid it!
Nor yet your haughty rulers tell,
With your consent they did it;
Come rouse, &c.

From bloody fields our brethren's ghosts,
Starting in dread succession,
Their wounds displaying, shriek aloud,
"We've paid for our transgression.
O! sheath the instruments of death,
Forbear the strife inglorious,
Sweet Liberty inspires the Apes
Their arms will shine victorious.

Paine counter-attacked Burke with 'The Rights of Man', and battle was joined. In 1793 the Scots radical hero Thomas Muir of Huntershill was sentenced to 14 years' transportation for sedition. Burns would have been in real danger of accompanying him if he had had no powerful friends at court. As is usual in wartime, it became ever more dangerous to seek to publish radical ditties. There are rumours, mentioned in 'The People's Past', of radical songs of the 1790s United Scotsmen, but the trail is cold.
Right wing lyrics of the time are easier to locate. James Hogg's 1811 collection 'The Forest Minstrel' has 22 National Songs by various hands that praise King, Country and William Pitt (*O Willy was a wanton wag, The Blythest lad that e'er I saw*). There are also a few Jacobite ditties, and a truly dreadful lay by Thomas Montgomery in praise of the Scots at Bannockburn, set to 'Hey Tutti Taitie'.

Wide o'er Bannock's heathy wold, Scotland's deathful banners roll'd
And spread their wings of sprinkled gold to the purpling east

The editors of the 1820 'Union Imperial Song-Book, containing a selection of the most popular Scotish (sic) English and Irish Songs', printed in Edinburgh for G. Clark, Aberdeen, say "The editors having no political purposes to serve, do not wish to let any bias of this nature appear". They excuse their inclusion of "some of the best of the old Jacobite songs, at this distance of time, the interest which they once excited has now but little connection with party feelings." These songs are now safely Tory, and are accompanied by a clutch of Unionist pieces, two of them songs by Walter Scott. One of these praises Pitt, his royal Master, and Wellington. The other celebrates the Allies' victory over Napoleon.

For a' that, and a' that
Guns, guillotines, and a' that
The fleur-de-lis, that lost her right
Is queen again for a' that

His last two verses threaten the cowardly Americans, "*Ye yankie loun, beware your crown, The kame's in hand to claw that*".
In the same year of 1820, the skirmish at Bonnymuir between a small band of armed weavers and local Kilsyth Yeomanry that was dubbed The Radical War resulted in the political martyrdom for the crime of armed insurrection of Hardie, Baird and Wilson, who were then repeatedly celebrated in broadsheet ballads.

As evening dashed on the western ocean
Caledonia stood perch'd on the waves of the Clyde
Her arms wide extended she raised with devotion -
"My poor bleeding country" she vehemently cried
"Arise up my country and hail reformation
Arise and demand now the rights of our nation
Behold your oppressors shall meet the desolation
That marked the brave victims on dark Bonnymuir"
Dark Bonnymuir

Alexander Rodger, the radical Glasgow weaver poet of the 1820s, was scathingly anti-royalist. In 1822 George IV visited Edinburgh. Sir Walter Scott for the occasion recalled a royalist song perhaps as old as the 17th Century Commonweath, 'Carle, An The King Come', when "*thou shalt dance and I shall sing*". Sir Walter wrote a long congratulatory poem called 'Carle, Now The King's Come', based on the older song, and then was furious when Sandy Rodger weighed in with,

Sawney, now the king's come
Sawney, now the king's come
Kneel and kiss his gracious --
Sawney, now the king's come

Tell him he is great and good
And come o Scottish royal blood
To yer hunkers, lick his fud
Sawney, now the king's come

Rodger was the "most prolific bard for radicalism in the first decades of the 19th century, he was himself imprisoned in Glasgow Tolbooth during the 1820 Rising, during which incarceration he and his comrades bawled themselves hoarse with 'Scots Wha Hae', though possibly not, as was said, just to annoy the screws." *Robert Ford*
Ford says he also sang "at the top of his lungs his own political compositions. These, highly spiced as they were by the awful radicalism of the time, gave his jailors 'fits'".
He was not the only radical weaver poet. Present day Glasgow poet Tom Leonard combed through slim leather-bound volumes of locally published poetry in Paisley Library to assemble the book 'Radical Renfrew'. Many of the earlier pieces are intended to be sung, and marked with the tunes to be used. Leonard's topics include Unemployment, Trade Unions and Co-operation, Anti-Ruling Class, Parliamentary Representation, Republicanism and Feminism, though none of these sections are as large as the ones on Alcohol, Religion, and Nature and the Country.
'The Deluge of Carnage ', to the tune 'Jamie, the Glory and Pride of the Dee', was sung in an 1822 soiree to celebrate the release from jail of Orator Hunt.

For kings have resolved that in Europe for ever
The tocsin of freedom shall sound again never
But power shall be law, and the flaming sword sever
'Twixt man and the path to fair liberty's tree

'The Hour of Retribution's Nigh' is more grimly hopeful.

And Liberty two blasts has blown
That still in Europe's ears do ring
And at the third, each tottering throne
Shall hold a man, or Chosen King

Scots songs of the 1840s Chartists or the Suffragettes are far to seek. They surely sang, but what? General National songs of struggle and protest of course, but where did the Scots radical streak of song go? Was this a fallow period, or just less recorded?
Songs from outwith Scotland were sung. The Suffragettes had 'The March of the Women', trade unionists had "*Hold the fort for we are coming, Union men be strong*". Frenchman Eugene Pottier's 'The Internationale' and Irishman Jim Connell's 'The Red Flag' were anthems that were sung with religious fervour at political and protest meetings and marches. The latter, written to support an 1889 London Dock Strike, was set by the writer to a jaunty Scots Jacobite tune, 'The White Cockade'. Years later the lyric was transferred to the lugubrious traditional German tune 'Tannenbaum'.

The workers flag is deepest red, It shrouded oft our martyred dead
And ere their limbs grew stiff and cold, Their life's blood dyed its every fold
Then raise the standard banner high, Within its shade we'll live and die
Though cowards flinch and traitors sneer, We'll keep the Red Flag flying here

In John Broom's 1973 biography of John Maclean the 'Red Flag' is the only song named. It was sung periodically to 'punctuate' a 1915 speech by then Minister of Munitions David Lloyd George in Glasgow's St Andrew's Halls as he struggled to be heard and "defend the dilution of labour policy... the introduction of female unskilled labour into the factories in order to free the men for military service". When in1916 Maclean was sentenced for speeches considered seditious, his wife and friends stood up in court and "sang the 'Red Flag' lustily."

A lonely Scots contribution to anthems of struggle was made by James Connolly, shot for his Citizen's Army's part in the 1916 Easter Dublin Rising, who was an Edinburgh Scot of Irish parentage. He had been a union organiser in the USA, and a songwriter. He wrote this defiant 'Rebel Song' lyric.

Come workers, sing a rebel song, a song of love and hate
Of love unto the lowly and of hatred to the great
The great who trod our fathers down, who steal our children's bread
Whose hand of greed is stretched to rob the living and the dead
Then sing our rebel song as we proudly sweep along
To end the age-long tyranny that makes for human tears
Our march is nearer done with each setting of the sun
And the tyrant's might is passing with the passing of the years

In the aftermath of World War One came Socialist Sunday School songs, dreich stuff indeed, and at times appalling. Contemplate a child whose father was killed on the Somme being invited by Tom Anderson, a comrade of John Maclean, to sing this.

My father was a soldier, a great big fat soldier
My father was a soldier in the King's Army

My father was a Tory, a stupid ugly Tory

My father was a Christian, a meek and mild good Christian

My father loved his Captain, his class-made lovely Captain

My father went to Heaven to play a harp in Heaven
My father went to Heaven from the King's Army

An occasional squib is placed under a Scots politician. Jimmie Maxton, a darling of the left in the 1920s, gets attacked by a songmaker further left than himself, to the tune of 'The King's Horses'.

Jimmie Maxton and the I.L.P, they want a 'living wage' for you and me
Jimmie Maxton and the I.L.P
But when your wages meet attacks, and when your boss the Government backs
Where's Jimmie Maxton and all his men?

"We don't want a fight today, and we point out a better way
You arbitrate, and halve your pay, we'll make a speech protesting in the House next day
It's our sad duty, now and then, to call out the cops to down working men
Jimmie Maxton and all his men"

The work of left wing lyric writers began to emerge in print, more often as poetry than as song, and often their writing focused on trades and employment. I mention elsewhere in this book songs by Comrade Tom Anderson, miner and playwright Joe Corrie, factory worker and poet Mary Brooksbank, trade unionist Josh Shaw, and poet Helen Fullarton. There were many others whose work appeared in flyaway leaflets. In 1941 'Popular Variants of Auld Scots Sangs, edited by M. P. Ramsay' were published by Scotland United and sold for 3d. The tune of 'Bonny Dundee' is used for the following.

To the Lords and Commons in Westminster Ha'
That thought they ruled Scotland sae snugly and a'

The folk o' the North they had something to say
And it's "Scots maun guide Scotland in Scotland's ain way"

To the tune of 'A Hundred Pipers' Ramsay says we'll "*gie the English a blaw, Ayont the Border awa*". Some Scots' conscientious resistance to WWII conscription is celebrated in

A Glesca lad my love was born
The English law he held in scorn
For he kept his faith wi' Scotland true
And wadna fecht for the red, white and blue

After his poetry and songs created in and of World War Two, Hamish Henderson wrote a song later referred to by Morris Blythman as "the first swallow of the [Folk] Revival". Henderson's 1948 'John Maclean March' was written quickly for the 25th anniversary of the death of that hero of the left, and set to a WW1 pipe tune.

The haill citie's quiet noo, it kens that he's restin'
At hame wi' his Glasgie freens, their fame and their pride!
The red will be worn, my lads, an' Scotland will march again
Noo great John Maclean has come hame tae the Clyde

"Political songs tell us a bit about the history. Maclean, the Dominie, he held the Clyde for a long time as a socialist and a nationalist. He also believed in freedom. Some of these political songs are beautiful, some of them are love songs as well." *Harry Constable.*
In the same year of 1948 Henderson penned, to an Irish Rebel tune, another song on the issue of land ownership and use which also became staple fare of the Revival. Seven war-returning crofters from Knoydart repossessed untended land.

'Twas down by the farm of Scottas Lord Brocket walked one day
And he saw a sight that worried him far more than he could say
For the Seven Men of Knoydart were doing what they'd planned

They had staked their claims and were digging their drains on Brocket's Private Land

'You bloody Reds,' Lord Brocket yelled, 'Wot's this you're doing 'ere?
It doesn't pay, as you'll find today, to insult an English peer
You're only Scottish halfwits but I'll make you understand
You Highland swine, these hills are mine, this is all Lord Brocket's land'

During the Folk Revival songs lambasting national and international politicians were easily found. Morris Blythman wrote 'John MacCorbie', lambasting Nationalist "wee black sleekit nyaff" John McCormick, for allegedly first sending Ian Hamilton to "snitch the Stane", then when *"McCorbie and his privateers were threatened wi the nick"* handing the Stane over to Sunday Express reporters Hector MacNeill and John Gordon, and being paid "*twa thoosan doon for the Stane o Scone, an mind, that's just the start*".
One of the verses of 'Boomerang' tells of when Labour politician Hugh Gaitskill had used the word 'peanuts' about CND, and had then come to address a 1960 Labour rally in Glasgow's Queen's Park, when he was 'shelled' with peanuts by protestors.
Matt McGinn then set about Harold Wilson.

I'm the boy to please them and I'm the boy to tease them
My silver tongue will please them and I'll tell you what I'll do
I'll tie their arms, I'll tie their legs, I'll tie their spirits too
Then I'll kick them in the teeth like the Tories never could do

Jim McLean picked up the molar theme when he made a song to support the Upper Clyde Shipbuilders work-in, attacking PM Edward Heath as 'Head Teeth'. In the 1980s the SCND Buskers made many lyrics featuring Maggie Thatcher and Ronnie Reagan, and then lyrics were updated to replace Thatcher with Major and Reagan with Bush. Most lately Ukes Against Nukes have used the tune of the old 'Nigger

Minstrel' song 'Jump Jim Crow' for 'Oh! Bama, Oh! Bama', complete with careful arrangement instructions on what the kazoo should play. These show that the apparently rather chaotic approach to performance is carefully worked out.

Oh! Bama, Oh! Bama, you no mean dude
Got the pockets o the trousers emptied oot
Yur cat-walk strut and yur dimpled tie
And four and twenty blackberries baked in the sky.
With manufacture in terminal decline
How do ya, how do ya look so fine?
If I knew yur secret I would mak it mine
Put some in ma dinner to ease the pain.
Kazoo plays American Patrol

To end the song Ukes Against Nukes specify the following.

"TUNE: Zip-a-de-doo-dah, Zip-a-dee-day, Bobb B Soxx & the Blue Jeans
Zip-a-de-doo-dah, Zip-a-dee-day. Life, old chum, is a cabaret.
Plenty O' bamas; shortage of grain.
Plenty of doo-dah all down the drains.
Kazoo plays American Patrol then Wedding March (Mendlessohn)"

Songs sympathising with politicians were thinner on the ground. One MSP, Cathie Peattie, told her fellow member of Linlithgow community song group Sangschule, Linda McVicar, how Cathie's daughter was complaining that she was seeing much less of her mother now. Cathie felt there should be a song beginning *"Ma maw's an MSP*'. Linda wrote a song as a present to Cathie, who responded by singing it in Parliamentary shows and on a 2007 BBC Radio Scotland programme, and tells in Chapter 18 how she sings the song and teaches it to children when visiting schools to talk about her parliamentary work.

Ma maw's an MSP, she's too late to get the tea

Frozen dinners on a tray, they don't get my vote any day
Ma maw's an MSP

Ma maw's an MSP, hame's not what it used tae be
Robbers take one look and run, they think the job's already done
Ma maw's an MSP

Ma maw's an MSP, she doesnae care for me
She's oot makin Scottish laws, ah huvny got a change a drawers
Ma maw's an MSP

Ma maw's an MSP, she's keen on democracy
It's "You dae this and you dae that, ah huvnae time tae feed the cat"
Ma maw's an MSP

Ma maw's an MSP, aye too late to get the tea
Mince and tatties, soup an stew, I think I can remember you
Ma maw's an MSP
Ma Maw's An MSP, tune Ma Maw's A Millionaire aka Let's All Go Down The Strand, words Linda McVicar

Unholy Doings At The Holy Loch

O ye canny spend a dollar when ye're deid,
O ye canny spend a dollar when ye're deid;
Singin Ding ... Dong ... Dollar; everybody holler
Ye canny spend a dollar when ye're deid.

O the Yanks have juist drapt anchor in Dunoon
An they've had their civic welcome fae the toon,
As they cam up the measured mile, Bonny Mary o Argyll
Wis wearin spangled drawers ablow her goun.

O the Clyde is sure tae prosper noo they're here
For they're chargin wan and tenpence for a beer
An when they want a taxi, they shove it up their ... jersey
An charge them thirty bob tae Sandbank Pier

An the publicans will aa be daein swell
For it's juist the thing that's sure tae ring the bell
O the dollars they will jingle, they'll be no a lassie single,
Even though they'll maybe blow us aa tae hell

Ding Dong Dollar, tune Comin Round the Mountain, words Glasgow Song Guild

The entry of American nuclear submarines into the Holy Loch near Glasgow resulted in mass protest demonstrations. The growing strength of Central Belt Scottish song creation and confidence in performance resulted in a body of songs that articulated the issues, and a group of singers who supported and heartened the marchers. The concept of the peaceful republican Glasgow Eskimo was born, and documented in another Rebels Ceilidh Song Book.

In 1961 what Morris Blythman called 'the first real singing campaign ever undertaken in Scotland' developed a workshopped 'agit-prop' song format for demonstrations so precise and succinct that in some songs every line and a half - since that may be all the observer hears as the march sweeps past - makes a key point in unambiguous and enjoyable language. The lyrics crackle with energy and wit.
The jaunty determined 'agit-prop' songs became needed when in Spring, 1961, the US Navy nuclear supply ship Proteus "sailed up the Clyde with her Polaris missiles and sparked off a wave of demonstrations and songs which were to make headlines all over the world in the months ahead. By train and bus, in rattle-trap lorries , by hitch of thumb, the motley anti-Polaris crew made for Dunoon and the Holy Loch area at every available opportunity. And also at every available opportunity the hard core sang their protests on station platforms, on quaysides, on the march; from improvised platforms, through hastily-assembled loud-speaker systems, from floating craft of all shapes and sizes; sitting down, standing up; to the police, at the police; but most of all at the extremely ruffled Americans." *Morris Blythman*
A March 1962 article in the Economist commented, "The CND remains a minority movement on Clydeside, but it certainly has all the best songs. The songs are not classics: they are not likely to survive as the best of the Jacobite ones, the last occasion on which there was such an outpouring of the music. But they do have the first essentials of virility and emotion, they are mostly satirical, and they have much in common with the industrial-coalfield work songs that evolved naturally from the Gaelic and Lowland culture. Within two months of [the American supply ship] the Proteus's arrival the first anti-Polaris songbook was published in Glasgow (five editions in the past eight months). This was directly in the Scottish tradition of cheap chapbooks sold at country fairs." *The Economist*
The Economist's Glasgow Correspondent's strong linking of the songs with 'coal field work songs' does not convince. The influences were 'a haill clanjamfrie'. Morris Blythman explained in the sleevenotes of the 1962 US Folkways LP Ding Dong Dollar.

"Everything was thrown into the pot: the missionaries first to give it the bite, army ballads from World War II, football songs, Orange songs, Fenian Songs, Child ballads, street songs, children's songs, bothy ballads, blues, skiffle, Australian bush ballads, calypso..." Blythman's exuberant continuing list of 'genial eclecticism' includes elements not obviously present in the anti-Polaris songs, but his ingredients are a checklist of the major influences that shaped the 1960s Scottish Folk Revival – song types, song makers and singers, and subjects. "... MacColl and Lomax, Ives and Leadbelly, songs about the Stone of Destiny, Dominic Behan, S.R.A. songs, I.R.A. songs, Guthrie and Houston, pantomime and vaudeville, Billy Graham, Scottish Land League songs, Gaelic songs and mouth music, Wobbly songs, spirituals, mountaineering and hiking ballads, Elliot and

Ding Dong Dollar songs
He had some Scotch and scoosh
Then he went back aboard
He turned his key – then whoosh
And o Lawdy Lawd
He said "I'm so embarrassed
We'll no be goin tae Paris
For I've launched the first Polaris
Thru bein a drunken sod"
The Misguided Missile and the Misguided Miss, tune and words John Mack

ɞ

O, we'll blaw the yahoo Yankees oot the Clyde
We'll blaw the yahoo Yankees oot the Clyde
Get yuir twa-twa-zero an pick them aff the pier-o
We'll blaw the yahoo Yankees oot the Clyde

For we dinnae gie a docken or a damn
For the sons of Uncle Psychopathic Sam
Every day they get absurder wi their fancy ways o murder
An we're gaun tae mak them tak it on the lam
Twa-Twa-Zero, tune Canny Shove Yer Grannie, words Thurso Berwick

ɞ

The U.S.A are giean subs away, giean subs away, giean sub away
The U.S.A are giean subs away but we dinnae want Polaris

Tell the Yanks tae drap them doon the stanks

The Cooncil o Dunoon, they want their hauf-a-croon

Tak the haill damn show up the River Alamo
We Dinnae Want Polaris, tune Three Craws, words Jim McLean

Seeger, mock-precenting, the Royal Family, Roddy McMillan, and Matt McGinn."

Blythman explains that this stewpot resulted in "a new metropolitan folk-song corpus" with dozens of songmakers, a breaking of the Orange-Fenian monopoly on rebel songs, and a "structure of ceilidh, concert, soiree, melee, jazz club, folk club, and youth hostel" where the songs could be heard.

The songs were carried into the streets and on the mass demos by the makers and singers. "Acting as an independent unit, they supported demonstrations called by the DA Committee, the CND Committees, the Glasgow and District Trades Council and the English and Scottish Committees of 100. They became known as the Anti-Polaris Singers and were accepted with pride and affection by demonstrators and organisers as their own establishment singers. No-one told them what to sing, where to sing or how to sing it. They kept to the main theme of Anti-Polaris, uniting and binding the many disparate organisations into one body. And to this body they gave heart, voice and laughter.

They were BBC'd, STV'd, televised, NBC'd, broadcast, telecast, free-lanced and pirated, AFN'd, Radio Moscowed, translated, interpreted and given in evidence in court."

Morris Blythman

Blythman had reapplied one element of the 'Sangs o The Stane' era, when he had

It's up the Clyde comes Lanin, a super-duper Yank,
But doon a damn sight quicker, when we cowpt him doon the stank,
Up tae the neck in sludge and sewage fairly stops yuir swank,
We are the Glesca Eskimos.

Hullo! Hullo! we are the Eskimos,
Hullo! hullo! the Glesca Eskimos.
We'll gaff that nyaff ca'd Lanin
We'll spear him whaur he blows,
We are the Glesca Eskimos.

We've been in many a rammy, lads, we've been in many a tear
We've sortit oot this kind afore, we'll sort them onywhere
O, get yuir harpoon ready – he's comin up for air
We are the Glesca Eskimos

Glesga Eskimos, Tune: Marching Through Georgia

pioneered the idea of 'demonstration singing' in Glasgow Central Station.

Some of the songs were short, punchy, with deliberately repetitive sloganising: The titles give the message: 'We Dinna Want Polaris', 'I Shall Not Be Moved', 'Get Yer Twa Twa Zero', 'Ye'll No Sit Here', 'We're Off to the Camp in the Country', 'Ban Polaris – Hallelujah', 'K-K-Kennedy', A Letter to Uncle Jack'. (The word 'slogan' is itself Gaelic, meaning a war cry!) This 'agit-prop' approach was developed further later in the '60s in SNP campaigning songs.

Other peace songs used choruses that rammed the message home, but the verses had more detail and bite. 'Ding Dong Dollar', 'The Glasgow Eskimos', 'Boomerang', 'Paper Hankies', 'The High Road to Gourock', 'As I cam by Sandbank', 'Oor Een Are on the Target', 'The Rampant Lion', 'Cheap-Jack the Millionaire', 'Sit Brothers Sit', 'Gie the Man a Transfer', 'Lanin the Berserk Commander'.

Not for the march, but for associated events, were longer narrative songs. 'The Misguided Missile and the Misguided Miss', 'The Polis o Argyll', 'Hi Jimmy Tyrie', 'The Young C.N.D.', 'What a Friend We Have in Gaitskell', ''Queen's Park 1962'."We hit the Americans [and the British politicians] with every weapon at our disposal. We were on the side of anything that made them feel mad. The element of personal attack on the Kennedys was very popular in Scotland, but the US Folkways record label would not use 'Cheap-Jack the Millionaire' or 'The Rampant Lion' "because they made such consistent attacks on the Kennedys. And the Kennedys were untouchable." *Morris Blythman*

The theme of Eskimos arose when the West of Scotland Canoe Club and like-minded souls had turned up to escort the bad ship Proteus safely through the narrow entrance to the Holy Loch. "With a barrage of fire hoses, the United States Navy yesterday repulsed the sea-borne invasion of anti-Polaris demonstrators who tried to board the submarine depot ship Proteus in the Holy Loch." *The Scotsman 22/5/1961*

"The flotilla included kayaks, dinghies, launches, and a motorized house boat which bore a Red Cross symbol and the slogan Life Not

Death. The vessels were [confiscated] by the authorities, until three days later the canoeist in the last of the little fleet was tipped into the water by naval frogmen, but Sean Edwards had got within 20 yards of his target. At a press conference the ship's captain, Lanin, was asked by press persons what he thought of these insults to his vessel. He scoffed, 'They don't worry us. They're just a bunch of Eskimos'." *The Scotsman*

Blythman had developed a communal songmaking approach. The key creators were Blythman himself and Jim McLean. The Glasgow songsmiths grasped the wonderful metaphor delivered into their hands. First, a cherished surreal verse of a children's 'street song' that used the tune 'Let's All Go Down The Strand' celebrated the Eskimos.

Ma maw's a millionaire, blue eyes and curly hair,
Sittin among the Eskimos, playin the game of dominoes,
Ma maw's a millionaire.

Second, they were of the opinion that there were Eskimos in Alaska, Canada, Greenland and Russia, and that none of them had ever even participated in a war, let alone started one, so that to assert oneself as a Glesca Eskimo was to be peaceful, exotic and absurdly surreal all at once. Cue for a new lyric, 'The Glesca Eskimos'. The core demo singing group became known as 'The Eskimos'. In later years many who had been at one or other Holy Loch demo, had sung the songs or felt an association with the concept, claimed that they too were 'Eskimos', but Jim Maclean considers firmly that only the core singing group deserve that name. The 1961 'Glasgow Eskimos' lyric shows in trenchant and aggressive form the Eskimos' contempt for Captain Lanin and his supporters. The word 'spear' in the chorus employs a neat double sense, a fishing tool for the Eskimo but with a Scots sense of 'speir' meaning 'ask' when sung, and reminds us that many of the activists were in no simplistic way pacifists. Several were ex-soldiers, opposed to war but quite interested in discussing violent response.

A spear for Lanin, a 220 rifle to *"pick them aff the pier-o"* in 'Twa Twa Zero', and in 1967 "A second front at Holy Loch" and *" Victory for the Vietcong"* in 'L.B.J.' The 1980s SCND Buskers updated the 'Glesca Eskimos' chorus line from the outdated Captain Lanin reference to become *' We're no husky Ruskies, like Maggie might suppose'.*

Doon at Ardnadam, sitting at the pier,
When ah heard a polis shout: "Ye'll no sit here!"

Ay, but ah wull sit here!
Naw, but ye'll no sit here!
Ay, but ah wull! Naw but ye'll no!
Ay, but ah wull sit here.

'Twas Chief inspector Runcie, enhancing his career,
Prancin up an doon the road like Yogi Bear.

He caa'd for help tae Glesca, they nearly chowed his ear,
"We've got the 'Gers an Celtic demonstrators here."

He telephoned the sodgers, but didnae mak it clear,
The sodgers sent doon Andy Stewart tae volunteer.

He radioed the White Hoose, but aa that he could hear,
Wis...two...one...zero – an the set went queer.

For Jack had drappt an H-bomb an gied his-sel a shroud,
An he met wi Billy Graham on a wee white cloud.
Ye'll No Sit Here, tune Ye'll No S*** Here, words Thurso Berwick

In the 1965 'Rebel Ceilidh Song Book' the lyric is credited to T S Law, but Jim McLean created many of the lines. Other songmaker and singer members of the Glasgow Song Guild, based in Blythman's Balgrayhill Road home, included Bobby Campbell, Nigel Denver, Ray Fisher, Susan Haworth, Hamish Imlach, T S Law, John Mack, Gordon MacCulloch, Alastair MacDonald, Jackie O'Connor, Jimmy Ross, Ian Wade, and the key performer of the songs, Josh McRae, who "took a committed stand and gained great respect from all concerned". *Morris Blythman*

It was Blythman himself, described in 1994 by Gordon MacCulloch as 'The Magic Marxist and Eskimo Guru', who built and ran the 'collective mincer' that created these songs. "One of the most unusual features of this whole movement was the way in which many of the songs were born. Workshop techniques were employed, and as a result, many of the songs had a communal authorship. In at least one song as many as twenty people contributed to the final production." *Morris Blythman*

The songs were printed in the anti-Polaris chapbook style songbooks which were titled 'Ding Dong Dollar' and sold for sixpence. Eight 'editions' were published, though the '6th (New York) edition' was the LP of seventeen Holy Loch and independence songs issued on the American Folkways Records. The first was a duplicated production of seven songs in May 1961. By June 1962 seven printed editions had followed. For each edition the contents were slightly varied and at least one new song made. Edition Eight, published June 1962, hinted at the varied contents and contexts by listing the previous editions as: First (Duplicated), Second (Pirated), Third (Berserk), Fourth (Moscow), Fifth (Eskimo), Sixth (New York), Seventh (Comfort), Eighth (Boomerang).

"We found a publisher for them in Clydeside who brought out a new edition for almost every demonstration. There were maybe a couple of songs changed in each one. We must have sold thousands of them between us, me probably more than Morris, tens of thousands because they were only sixpence, and when people would say they'd bought it already, I would say 'Not this one!' and it would have a different picture on it." *Marion Blythman*

The core group of singers supported and encouraged the marchers not just at the Holy Loch, but at the annual Easter marches from Aldermaston to London. Veteran marchers have in conversation said that they sought out the Scots contingent because they always had the best songs.

In the USA, TV reportage of British marches caused jealousy in the breasts of songmakers developing their own approach to utilising song for political protest through the publications 'Sing Out!' and 'Broadside'.

"The people around 'Sing Out!' were envious of the British topical song movement. Alex Comfort, Ewan MacColl, and Matt McGinn were singing new and fresh songs that were both part of a tradition (Scot [sic] folk music) and of a mass movement (The Committee for Non-Violent Disarmament - CNVD). The films of the Aldermaston Marches drew long sighs as the folk singers and jazz bands made their way with tens of thousands along that country road to protest nuclear arming." *Josh Dunson*

They say that the atom-ships doon at Dunoon
Belang tae a big millionaire.
An I hope tae hell they'll be oot o there soon,
Afore we're aa up in the air.
The fella that sent them's an awfy nice chap,
He sent them owre here as a gift,
He heard the hotels in Dunoon were depressed
An he wantit tae gie them a lift.

Boomerang! Boomerang!
Juist send them back whaur they belang,
Along wi auld Adenauer, Kennedy's pal,
Signor Fanfani and Chairlie de Gaulle,
For we dinnae like gifts that go bang
Juist try wan an see if ah'm wrang,
The banners are wavin; Wha's next for the shavin?
So open the boom; boomerang!

Boomerang, tune Bless Em All, words Matt McGinn and Glasgow Song Guild

British folk magazine 'Sing' reported in May 1962 that "There's not much doubt about it, the stars of this year's Aldermaston march were the Glesca Eskimos." The report names Nigel Denver, Jackie O'Connor, Mrs Josh McRae and Morris Blythman, who at one point "sat side-saddle on a motor cycle swapping songs with Alex Comfort for over an hour... The group sang enthusiastically for several hours a day, fashioning new songs as they performed, not least a 'wee commercial' for the Holy Loch demonstration at Whitsun."

Morris wanted to get as many names of lyric writers shown as he could, so he would choose one key hand and ascribe the whole product to them. He told the author in conversation of how he wanted famed Glasgow songwriter Matt McGinn to be part of the process, but Matt was initially dubious. Morris had already worked out the basic idea and several lines for a song to the tune of the WW2 soldiers' favourite 'Bless 'Em All', with a central idea of sending the Yanks flying home like an Australian boomerang. He sang what he had to Matt, but suppressed the key word.

"Dud duh duh, duh duh duh, we'll send them back where they belang. I can't think what word to use there. Can you?" Matt hesitantly suggested 'Boomerang'. Morris was enthusiastically grateful and Matt was hooked and reeled in. He created so many of the lines that the whole lyric printed under his name, although Jim McLean made many of the lines for 'Boomerang' and other songs credited by Morris to other hands, including the 'Ding Dong Dollar' line about Mary of Argyll. McLean recalls, "When I wrote the line about spangled drawers, Jackie O'Connor nearly fell off the couch laughing."

"Morris had a gift for getting people involved in things. He was good at work-shopping. If you look at Matt's song, 'Boomerang', there are words that are just Morris – *'Adenauer...Signor Fanfani and Chairlie de Gaulle.'* 'Ding Dong Dollar' was credited by Morris to John Mack Smith. He was in the Labour Party and worked for the Licensed Trade Association, for the owners of the pubs, and he was a really smart guy, very astute and he wrote quite good songs. John Mack Smith started 'Ding Dong Dollar' and it was good but Morris work-shopped it to make it more singable. Morris changed it to "Ye canna spend a dollar when you're deid." *Marion Blythman*

But the Glesca Moderator disnae mind;
In fact he thinks the Yanks are awfy kind,
For if it's heaven that ye're goin it's a quicker way than rowin,
And there's sure tae be naebody left behind.

O ye canny spend a dollar when ye're deid,
Sae tell Kennedy he's got tae keep the heid,
Singin Ding ... Dong ... Dollar; everybody holler
Ye canny spend a dollar when ye're deid.
Ding Dong Dollar, tune Ye Canny Shove Yer Grannie, words Glasgow Song Guild

In 1968 Blythman wrote, "To take just one example of this communal origin: Glasgwegian John Smith ("Jak") heard George MacLeod of the Iona Community (now Lord MacLeod of Fuinary)

making a comment something like – 'And, of course, you cannot spend a dollar when you are dead." John then came up with 'Ye canna spend a silver dollar when ye're deid, In fact, it might as well be made o' lead.' The eventual version as sung became simpler, repetitive, so that the unassailable logic would stick with people. After all, to those making capital from the American presence, dollars would be poor consolation should the worst ever happen." *Morris Blythman*
This workshopped lyric was then credited in print to John Mack. It used humour, the vernacular, and sharp local references to sharpen its point. A small hesitation before the word 'jersey' allowed Scots listeners to recognize that it was a substitution for 'jaxie'
As well as the 'Glesca Eskimos' song, Morris created another that noted the absence of royalty in polar regions, 'The Eskimo Republic', which he described as "a sort of 'Big Rock Candy Mountain' visualisation of a Republic for Scotland".

O the Eskimo is a man o peace
He's never jyned the arms race
An ye'll find nae trace o a Polaris base
In the Eskimo Republic

When they mak a law, sure they all agree
For they aa sit on the com-mit-tee
An they've got nae Lords and nae M.P.s
In the Eskimo Republic

Now the Eskimo he is no like you
Every Eskimo has his ain i-ga-loo
An his mither-in-law has got an i-ga-loo too
In the Eskimo Republic

When an Eski wean he goes tae school
He sits up nice on an Eski stool

An he sings an he lauchs an learns the rules
O the Eskimo Republic
The Eskimo Republic, tune The Boys Of Garvagh, words Thurso Berwick

Marion Blythman explains Morris's aim. "The Eskimo Republic was a kind of ideation of what the best kind of society was going to be. It was to epitomise what was good in society and what we were aiming for, so that's why it started with '*There is nae class, there is nae boss, Nae king nor queen*'. At that time it had '*Willie Ross*' and that changed to '*damn the loss*' and *then 'You get boozed up for a six month doss In the Eskimo Republic*.' It was Morris's idea of a framework for a good society and that's what was important about it.
"Morris said he didn't know why the Labour Party wouldn't use [his concepts] because otherwise it was like fighting with one hand tied behind your back. Morris wanted the Communist Party to expel him, and he did everything he could to get them to do so but they wouldn't. I'd been kind of half Communist, I was always too independent minded. As soon as somebody said to me 'Everybody says' – I'd say 'Oh really?' I joined when I was a student but then I came out of it quite early, '47 or '48, at the time of Czechoslovakia, and then there was Hungary. Somewhere in the interim, Morris finally left, stopped paying his dues, but that wasn't what he wanted, he wanted to be expelled. He thought they had become bureaucratic and anti-Scottish, they weren't interested in that side of it.
"There was a definite ideological split at that time [re what kind of language to use in new political song]. Morris thought the purpose of the songs was not literary, the purpose was polemic. Morris wouldn't have stopped writing, absolutely not. He would have been writing anti-Iraq-war songs. Everything that came up that was important to Scotland, he would have written songs about it. Morris put his money where his mouth was. If he set out to do something, he would do it."
Marion Blythman
Jim McLean was Blythman's key lieutenant in the Glasgow Song Guild. He went on to write many more songs of Scotland and to create

themed records. In about 1959 he created Radio Free Scotland, a hotly pursued pirate radio station which broadcast in the Greater Glasgow on the BBC television frequency from various locations, including the homes of Hamish Imlach and the McGillverays.

"In 1957 I served 6 months in Barlinnie for registering as a Conscientious Objector to my National Service. I went abroad for a couple of years when I was released and came back from working in Germany in 1959 as a translator. I was a TV engineer, and got a job in Glasgow. I built a radio, put it in back of my work van. We broadcast Republican Scottish material which the SNP knew of, I was not a member, too many fascist elements at that time. They sent us a message, to wait till the Queen's has been played, don't upset people. About this time I wrote and co-wrote a number of songs for the 'Ding, Dong, Dollar LP'.

"It started when I met Morris. In 1960 I went to the Glasgow Folk Club, Geordie McIntyre took me there, I was just back from Germany. I heard these songs, fantastic. I went away home and wrote 'Maggie's Weddin' and 'NAB For Royalty'. I'm a musician, not a singer. Dominic Behan said I sing like a duck. Other people sing them, I tell them what the melody is. I wanted others to sing them. Some are solo songs most are group chorus songs, to get people singing on the marches, on the ferry [to Dunoon], like 'The USA are Giein Subs Away'. Morris wanted no 'cult of personality'. Everybody knew Morris and Hamish Henderson, the rest were 'unknown'. The Eskimos were Morris, me, Jackie

Rebel Ceilidh Song Book No 2 lyrics
Sing a song o tax an woe
Empty pooches in a row
The Chancellor's collectin dough
Aa for Maggie's Waddin
Tune Mhairi's Wedding, words Jim McLean

There lives a family in oor land
The famous Royal crew, man,
They willna work they willna want
They're living on the Broo, man

It's NAB for Royalty
Free milk for wee Prince Andy,
Tae pey the cook an claith the Duke
The Welfare State's gey handy!
NAB For Royalty, tune The Deil's Awa, words Jim McLean

O'Connor, Josh McRae and Nigel Denver. Not Hamish Imlach, I was surprised to see his head in the photograph of the 'Ding Dong Dollar' album, that was taken on the Dunoon ferry. I don't really remember him there.

"Our message was 'Here we are, and we don't like you'. The US sailors didn't know what the songs were about, they enjoyed them. We were not talking to them, but being a morale booster for the marchers, and entertaining ourselves. That's why we'd use one line two or three times. Give the passersby a chant, a line out, trying to bring people in."

The songs used humour, as well as positive energy. The comparable English songs emphasised doom, gloom and terror. "Alex Comfort in his little book of his own songs said the Glasgow songs and the 'Ding Dong Dollar' movement were a breath of fresh air. Why use humour? One of my first songs, 'Maggie's Weddin', was the only way to treat the subject, we tend to laugh at people, for example some of the bothy ballads, their pawky humour, the human spirit won't lie down." *Jim Maclean*

Rebel Ceilidh Song Book No 2 lyrics

Oh dear, Yuri Gagarin
He flew tae the moon when it looked like a farthing
He said tae the boys at the moment of parting
Ah'm juist gaun awa for the Fair

Yuri Gagarin, tune Johnny's So Long at the Fair, words Roddy McMillan

☙

Far frae ma hame ah've wandered
An ah never will return
Frae ma ain hame in the Gorbals
Juist alang frae Jenny's Burn
For they're pullin doon the buildin
An ah doot ah canny bide
For they're gonnae mak the Gorbals
Like New York or Kelvinside

An it's oh, but ah'm longin for ma ain close
It wis nane of yer wally, juist a plain close
An ah'm nearly roon the bend, for ma ain wee single-end
Fareweel tae dear old Gorbals an ma ain close

Ma Ain Close, tune Ma Ain Folk, words Duncan Macrae

Henderson's great anthem 'The Freedom-Come-All-Ye' was also on the 'Ding Dong Dollar' album. His dedication of the song says it was created 'for the Glasgow Peace Marchers, May 1960', but it is usually sung as a slow march, and its progress in entering the singing repertoire was initially slow. It eventually became a favourite song of the Revival and is repeatedly urged as a new Scottish National Anthem, although Henderson himself opposed this idea.

Blythman added the first crop of agit-prop peace songs to the 1965 second 'Rebels Ceilidh Song Book', with another wonderful cover by Jimmy Dewar that includes references to at least twelve of the songs in the booklet.By the time the song book appeared the songs it contained were widely known, had appeared on record, and were sung with gusto in folk clubs and concerts throughout the land. In the 1965 Preface Blythman acknowledges that, through the developing Folk Revival, popular involvement with Scots song had changed since the pioneering efforts in Bo'ness.

"With our first issue we were well ahead of the market. Today, after several editions of the Rebel and Patriot Song Books – and in the face of the tremendous job done by Hamish Henderson and the School of Scottish Studies, and the growth of Folksong Groups everywhere – the Bo'ness Rebels Literary Society find themselves well ahint. The present publication is an attempt to get up to date, and as such, mainly records songs that have been already sung at hundreds of Ceilidhs and at Folk Clubs and Festivals throughout Scotland. Many of the present songs have already been published elsewhere, many recorded. Most are by well-known authors. Mainly they are rebel songs.

"While only one or two of the most popular items are retained from the 1951 [sic] publication this collection repeats our endeavour to group together the different types of rebel song being sung in Scotland today. Naturally many are anti-authority. Scotland suffers in some measure, no matter what power group rules from London and this feeling is reflected in the songs. Let it not be said that these songs are anti-English, or anti-American, or anti-German. As Dominic Behan says: '*The love of one's country is a terrible thing*'. These songs are pro-Scottish. None of them has the death wish.

"Where MPs fail, and that is often, these songs provide a VOICE for Voiceless Scotland. They bind Scottish Labour inevitably to the Scottish Nation.

"Yet curiously, as in 'Ma Ain Close', they show a communal conservatism worthy of the best of our traditions opposing a modern sterile bureaucracy. If anyone feels aggrieved he may reflect wisely with one of our Scottish Kings that perhaps his only ultimate claim to fame or immortality may lie in the fact that 'they pit me in a Ballad'."

Morris Blythman

Rebel songs and ballads, literary debates, ceilidhs with speeches as well as dancing and music and song, political action, celebration of Scotland's culture, and the joy of fellowship. The Bo'ness Rebels Literary Society helped put the voiceless people of Scotland into songs, then the old and new songs gave those people back their voices to sing and to write their own

Rebel Ceilidh Song Book No 2 lyrics

Hey hey ho, the Yankees bluff and blow
Here's the dough dough dough, if Castro shoots the crow
But Fidel says "No, we'll have another go
By the Bay of Pigs in the morning"

Fidel Says No, tune Banks o the Boyne, words T S Law

ꟹ

Have ye heard o Lady Chatterly
Sick and starved o love wis she
Hey hey, pair wee Lady Chat

Good Sir Clifford wis her man
He got shot in the war an he couldnae stand

But Lady Chat wis fou o pluck
She went doon tae the gairden tae try her luck

Lady Chat, tune Honey Have a Whiff on Me, words Jim McLean

ꟹ

O, Billy Wolfe'll win, hullo! hullo!
O, Billy Wolfe'll win, hullo! hullo!
O, Billy Wolfe'll win. Yes, he'll walk right in,
An it's ta-ta Tammy, oot ye go.

Now the wey that Tammy's built,
Hullo! Hullo!
Now the wey that Tammy's built,
Hullo! Hullo!
Now the wey that Tammy's built,
Och, he shouldnae weir the kilt,
An it's ta-ta Tammy, oot ye go.

Election Ballad, tune I Married a Wife, words Thurso Berwick songs. There are 39 songs, of which only six are also in the first Song Book. There are nine 'Ding Dong Dollar' Holy Loch songs. The rest are all political and social comment songs. They include four anti–royal songs by Jim McLean, three by Blythman, and two by Dominic Behan, an Irishman hen domiciled in Scotland, who also contributes 'The Patriot Game'. There is a comment on book censorship, praise for cosmonaut 'Yuri Gagarin', and songs about enforced rehousing from Adam McNaughtan and Duncan Macrae. No Gaelic songs are included this time.

There is also the first of what would be a flood of SNP campaigning songs, Blythman's pro SNP and anti-Tam Dalyell ' Billy Wolfe'll Win'. A few ruder verses were excluded, for example, "*Tammy is a ....., Oh, you've got the word quite right*". Wolfe later said, "We adopted all the anti-Polaris songs. We were very much outnumbered in those days by the Labour Party on those peace marches, they and the Communists were the speakers, and dominated in meetings. Keith Bovey, chairman of SCND, and I were the only nationalists. The logic was that the only way you can get rid of the Holy Loch is by being independent. But they could not see that."

Criticising voices were raised. In Autumn 1962 'Folk Notes' magazine, Vol.1 No. 1, carried an advertisement for Edition 8 of the Ding Dong Dollar song book, songs and an article, 'We Can Write - & Must', by Matt McGinn, and an article by Josh McRae on his trip to Moscow, the welcome the Eskimos' songs got, and the experience of hearing his recording of actor Roddy McMillan's 'Yuri Gagarin' played on loudspeakers strung on the city's lampposts as he walked along the streets.

But the issue also had an article, 'Political Pops?', by an Ian Campbell (there have been several Ian Campbells active in the Folk Revival) that began, "The increasing inclusion of political songs in singers' repertoires is a dangerous sign for the future of folk clubs. The adoption by singers of such songs is an indication of the influence the audience is having on the choice of songs. It cannot be disputed that the jingoistic political song proves to be more appealing to sections of club audiences than many, in fact the majority, of the better and grander examples of folk song." He continued, "It must be understood that I am deploring particularly the ultra-simple parodies fitted to tunes which are obvious vehicles for the makers of parody." Campbell makes various other points on the problems a folk club faced. A club could become "The wearer of a political tag, and its music suffers". Campbell calls for singers to in effect re-educate their audience.

Campbell was not alone in condemnation. In the next issue of 'Folk Notes' Gordon MacCulloch in a general survey of the Folk Revival's 'The Past and the Future" responded to the "critics of the folk song movement" who " claim that it has purely political motives". McCulloch refutes this, but comments, "It is true that the folk revival is in general anti-establishment. A very short experience of folksong clubs serves to show that the revival draws its very life's blood from its rebel leanings".

"While the American song movement began to grow in strength, in Scotland "public demonstration reached its peak and lost its impetus after a time, but the songs did not die out. We could have gone on and on publishing new editions of *Ding Dong Dollar* had we not made the decision to call a halt. We got many, many requests from bookshops and from individuals up to two years after we ceased publication. We stopped at the time the missiles went to Cuba and were turned back by the Americans. The numbers at demonstrations had fallen off and we had written the songs to back up these demonstrations. [...] Every campaign encounters its peaks of feverish activity - and its troughs of apparent inactivity - as breath is drawn for the next stage in development." *Morris Blythman*

For Blythman and some of his collaborators the next stage was to be support for the SNP Independence campaign, although he was never an SNP member, seeing their political victory as a necessary step towards his unwavering goal of a Scottish Workers Republic.

It fell aboot the time o valentines
When the G.P.O.'s gey busy-o
Wi pillar boxes full o billets doux

That a high explosive wan wis sent tae Lizzie-o

Wha's the chiel that sent it? Naebody can say
Polis, press nir postie-o
But there's none that can deny that his principles wis high
An that Lizzie's smile is weiran kinda frosty-o

Gelignite or dynamite
T.N.T. or the pouther-o
Maks a valentine incisive til a queen that's ill-advised
An it maks the face o Scotland aa the smoother-o
Billet Doux, tune Corn Rigs, words Thurso Berwick

Cooncillors Cooried In Conclave – Songs Of Local Politics

In the days when we were Radicals a short time ago
We spouted much of Labour's wrongs and of the people's woe
We held that Whigs and Tories both had always tyrants been
And bawled the people's rights were lost those robbers vile between

And when we find that we shall need the people's aid again
We'll soon forget that Whigs we've turn'd although 'tis now so plain
Our voices shall be raised once more as loud as e'er they've been
To spout and sing our treason songs and laugh at Prince and Queen
And thus again we'll gull the crowd with pleasant wordy show
As we did when we were radicals a short time ago
In the Days When We Were Radicals, tune In the Days When We Went Gypsying, words Edward Polin, from 'Radical Renfrew'.

Alongside Chapter Eight's account of songs on national issues, there are the local political songs about local political issues, in which councillors and landlords get kickings, alcohol is condemned, and local volunteer soldiers are praised.

1830s Paisley weaver Polin hammered ex-Radical town councillors with 'In The Days When We Were Radicals'. The songs of national politics are an exception to the general rule that Scottish political songs make frequent use of humour, and are almost invariably serious going on deadly in tone. Songs about local politics employ the weapon of humour mercilessly. Attacks on town councillors featured much. Warfare references were mixed into such songs. In 1842 Queen Victoria visited Edinburgh, but when she landed at Leith the Edinburgh councillors were still abed. Two broadsheets fired broadsides at them.

Hey Jemmie Forrest, are ye waukin yet, or are your Bailies snoring yet
If ye were waukin I would wait, ye'd hae a merry merry morning

The frigate guns they loud did roar, but louder did the Bailies snore
And thought it was an unco bore to rise up in the morning

The Queen she's come to Granton Pier, nae Provost and nae Bailies here?
They're in their beds, I muckle fear, sae early in the morning
Jemmie Forrest, tune Johnnie Cope

Up in the mornin's no for me, up in the morning early
The Bailies and I could never agree to rise in the morning early

Bright shines the sun frae east to west, the breeze is blawing rarely
The royal squadron's at the Pier, the Queen is landed fairly

It's braw to tend on Majesty, and princes deck'd sae rarely
But what's thae pleasures to a nap? It beats them hollow fairly

The Provost sabb'd and sigh'd and moan'd, "O, had I just been near her
I'll greet and grunt and groan and die, neglect shall ne'er pay dearer"
The Provost's Nap, tune Up in the Mornin Early

In Glasgow a broadsheet lyric assailed the Reformed Town Council, "Ye idiots of the rabble hail, Wha now in power so smoothly sail." Another demanded 'Who diddled the paupers?' A Dundee broadsheet 'New Comic Song' made gentle fun of the Duke of Argyll at a civic event.

The Art Gallery had been opened don't you see
By the Duke in style so fairly
So he dressed himself in style wi the Lass O Ballochmyle
And cam doon tae the Carse O Gowrie Dairy

When socialists eventually gained political power and proceeded to enjoy in comfort the fruits of office they in turn came in for a bashing, of course. To the tune of 'The White Cockade' Iain Nicolson speaks in about 1950 of The Labour Provost of Glasgow.

Wi ma ermine coat and my office seal
For Socialism I am fu o zeal
The principles of socialism are aa very well
Bit ye mustnae forget tae look after yersel

So when the Queen cam's tae see us aa
Republican sentiments we'll banish awa
On bended knees, or if it suits
On hunkers doon we'll lick her boots

Verses of the Bo'ness 'Lea-Rig' song commented on various councillors, and said,

The Labour Councillors were there
Aa cooried in conclave
Keir Hardie's Ghost wis pitten oot
Fur turnin in its grave

Local events could inspire satiric comment. 'The Battle of Balfron', warfare again, was a bloodless broadsheet tale of 1859 when the navvies of the Glasgow Water Works came to the town and threatened to riot. The citizenry sent to Stirling Castle for help from the 42nd Regiment, and the navvies retreated to their camp. The air is 'Guy Fawkes'.

High glory to the old Black Watch, and dauntless Seventy-One
And glory to the Ninety-Two, who have such laurels won
And honour to the illustrious few who bravely led them on
To the deathless and the bloodless field of the battle of Balfron

'Twas the morning of the eighth of March, and seven by the chime
When rushed down from the Water Works some hundreds in their prime
Two hundred Irish labourers and Highland navvies ran
Like a torrent from the Water Works to the battle of Balfron

I have already quoted William Campbell's lauding of Glasgow and Paisley Volunteers, and Burns' celebration of the Dumfries Volunteers in 'Does Haughty Gaul Invasion Threat?' The slim poetry volumes in Stirling Library, unlike those in Paisley Library, offer few political comments other than songs that praise extravagantly the Volunteers of Stirling, Grangemouth and Leven.
'Radical Renfrew' offers us a song published in 1850 that seems at first to laud Volunteers in Paisley but proceeds to satirise them.

When I wi the laird did enlist, a volunteer loyal and clever
I swore fair or foul to resist the claims of the people forever
And with my sword, pistol and horse, I'm still ready, willing and able
To scatter by physical force the low lousy radical rabble

O, hing up the speech making loons, an riddle them through with your bullets
Infesting like rattons the towns and ready to pounce on our wallets
And try if the cat-and-nine-tails can keep them content wi their drummock
Wha basely the corn-law assails for pinching their back and their stomach

What were the land-owners to do wha now in their carriages caper
An live aa so het and so fu, were victual and land to be cheaper?
Nae doubt it would better the poor, and mak them more happy and healthy

But wha such a change would endure when made at the cost of the wealthy?
When I Wi The Laird Did Enlist, tune Tak it Man, Tak It, words Alex McGilvray

Volunteer songs in Stirling Library's collection are more straighforward, though the assertions of high military prowess of local forces is suspect. David Taylor's praise of Stirling heroes and their ability to repel French invaders was published after France and Britain had been allies in the Crimea. Garibaldi had just won his great 1859 and 1860 successes in Italy.

Foul fa the louns wha jeer an gibe the scions o the hero tribe
Let's rather honour still ascribe to our leal Volunteer boys
Hey the winsome, ho the handsome, gallant Volunteer boys
Blessins on them ane an aa, our valiant Volunteer boys

The British lion's a towsie tyke, an let the French come when they like
They'll settle them wi ball and pike, our bold brave Volunteer boys
Great Garibaldi, true an brave, wha gars the flag o freedom wave
Wad be richt proud, I ween, to have sic noble Volunteer boys
From 'Poems and Songs', David Taylor, published Stirling 1862, tune not named

Robert Buchanan of Falkirk goes further over the top. His mighty heroes, like Campbell's Renfrew Volunteers, were ready to take on and thrash Napoleon before any other Volunteers got there. 'Nap Hectoring' refers to Napoleon loudly seeking to act like brave ancient Greek hero Hector.

Come sing the glorious victories won of yore, by land and sea
The gallant deeds of valour done by Scotia's sons, the free
But here's a nobler roundelay, which all delighted hears
Tis the name, and the fame, and the dauntless game of the Grangemouth Volunteers

Once on a time, mid war's alarms, Nap Hectoring, o'er the way
For Waterloo resolved to make Old England reckoning pay
But ere his precious schemes were formed, a glorious host appears
And firm in the van of the mighty clan were the Grangemouth Volunteers

From 'Falkirk', by Robert Buchanan, sung at an 1865 supper in Grangemouth, tune The Breist Knots

Katherine Drain's more sober admiration is for what were later called Territorial soldiers, intended to fight close to home, but here being honoured for active service, presumably in South Africa.

Last week I went to Stirling to see the grand review
Our gallant active service men, our brave red white and blue
Called out by Sergeant Lindsay, they marched up bold and free
And foremost stood our Leven lads of D. R. V.

King Edward's representative, who everybody knows
Buchanan Castle's noble lord, his Grace Duke of Montrose
He gave the badge of honour then, a glorious sight to see
What joy it gave our sturdy men of D. R. V.

From 'Loch Lomond Rhymes', Katherine Drain, published Glasgow 1902, tune not named

Temperance movements fought to rid cities and towns of the scourge of the bottle. In the 1951 People's Festival Ceilidh the temperance song 'The Ale House' was sung. Another such, 'Nancy Whisky', became a Revival favourite and was localised from Dublin to the Calton in Glasgow though the anti-drink message was not noticed by singers, and other hymns to sobriety faded from sight. The radical weavers of Paisley, and Sandy Rodger of Glasgow, balanced verse and song on the evils of drink against other effusions praising the festive bowl.

Local campaigns against perceived injustice were supported in song. Sandy Rodger wrote three songs supporting the 1823 action for "securing the liberty of the banks of Clyde, when the public were likely to be deprived of that privilege by the rapacity of Tam Harvey", who had barred a public footpath.
In 1920 a rent strike began in Clydebank against unreasonable rent increases by the factors. The strike lasted till 1927, and was organised and led by Clydebank women. Inventive tactics of mass action and non-violent resistance, and legal arguments were used. When an eviction took place, as the furniture was being carried out of the house it would be put back in through the windows, and the 'theme song' of the strike was said to be the children's song, "*Go in and out the windows, Go in and out the windows, Go in and out the windows, As you have done before*".
In the 1980s broadcaster and writer Billy Kay made a series of programmes for the BBC, 'Odyssey, Voices From Scotland's Recent Past'. The programmes mixed interviews with old songs and new ones specially written. One programme was on the 'Clydebank Rent War', for which the author wrote a number of incidental lyrics, some based on children's songs, from which the following verses are drawn.

Two versions of 'Nancy Whisky', various tunes used
This seven long years I've been a weaver
Until my wages they were pulled down
And to buy myself a new suit of clothes
I took my way up to Dublin town

As I was walking up Dublin city
Nancy Whisky I chanced to smell
I thought it proper to call in and see her
For seven years I had loved her well
Published by the Poet's Box, Dundee

Ah'm a weaver, a Calton weaver
Ah'm a rash and a rovin blade
Ah've got siller in ma pooches
Ah'll go follow the rovin trade

As ah gaed in by Glesga city
Nancy Whisky ah chanced tae smell
I gaed in, sat doon beside her
Seven years I lo'ed her well
Glasgow version, as sung by Hughie Martin of Shettleston

Hard up, kick the can, Clydebank factors have a plan
They'll be sorry they began when they see the Rent Strike
Hard up, pockets out, tell them what it's all about
Wave yer banner, raise the shout, we support the Rent Strike

What's the factor greetin for? Tripped himsel, skint his jaw
Noo he's greetin for his maw, canny get his rent increase
Tell yer boss, no more snash, tell yer boss, no more cash
Tell his nibs he's no on, we live here and we're no gaun

Special handbells were cast in the shipyards and rung to summon help when someone was threatened with eviction.

If ye see the factor comin, ring the bell
Be an educated wumman, ring the bell
And he'll never pit ye out, for we know what it's about
And we'll aa be there tae shout "Go tae hell"

In January 2001 the Southside Baths campaign began in Glasgow, and was strongly supported through song. Key songmaker Alistair Hulett explains.

"I got involved in that campaign because I was living right in Govanhill where the baths are located. Glasgow City Council decided, against the will of the majority of residents in the area, to shut the facility down. A decision was taken by local activists to occupy the building and we maintained that occupation for over 150 days. It was a huge operation, self-organised by the local community. So long as we had people inside the building we needed a 24 hour picket outside. People who had never taken part in any political campaign in their lives were signing up to sit outside a darkened pool building throughout the night and we kept that going right through winter into spring and summer.

"One of the ways to keep ourselves solid and strong was to sing, and I began making up funny wee parodies about the pool campaign. People in the campaign got well into it and songwriting became a big craze on the picket line. 'It's A Lang Way Tae Bellahouston' and 'This Pool is My Pool' were two of the most popular early ones. We were doing a kind of 'flying picket' thing as well, visiting other council facilities around Glasgow and occupying them too, to publicise our campaign. The songs were a good way of defusing any tension and keeping these actions light hearted and non threatening to the council workers at these other facilities.

"Every Wednesday night we all used to gather outside the pool to show solidarity with the ones inside and sing our songs. Soon we had enough for a songbook that we produced locally and sold to get money for the ongoing occupation. Later we made a CD and sold that in the local chippie. Other folk singers in the area got involved in that too, Mick and Irene West, Gavin Livingstone and Claire Quinn and some others. It was totally a grass roots thing, and once the local campaigners got the songwriting bug, they were all at it.

"At Xmas time we went out carolling with a songbook of 'Pool Carols'. 'Storm The Halls Of City Chambers' was my personal favourite, that and 'God Help Ye Hairtless Cooncillors'. The upshot has been that the reopening of the pool is moving forward steadily, although after 150 days the police were sent in to smash the occupation. That was a huge stooshie but several hundred people fought bravely to save our control of the building.

"The cops and sheriff's officers wrecked the place though, so the occupation was no longer feasible. Anyway, there's a date set now for the reopening, thanks to the stalwarts who have fought on through other means to save the pool, so that's an example of political song, albeit pretty light-hearted stuff, helping keep a campaign going that eventually won." *Alistair Hulett*

Two CDs of parodies were recorded. The campaign's Christmas song book uses and misuses several carols.

God help ye hairtless cooncillors that stole oor pool away
Tae pay ye back we'll kick ye oot come next election day
We'll gie ye aa yer jotters, ye'll be signin on the broo
An ye'll no be toddlin doon tae the front o the queue

ꟹ

On the first day of Closure the Cooncil gied tae us
A pool ye cannae reach wi'oot a bus

On the twelfth day of Closure the Cooncil gied tae us
Twelve mair campaigners, Eleven points of grievance
Ten horses chargin, Nine weans a-greetin
Eight polis lyin, Seven metal shutters
Six Sheriff's men, Five hundred cops
Four white vans, Three hired hacks
Two useless stooges and a pool ye cannae reach wi'oot a bus

Other carols included 'The First No Well' when local councillors called in sick and missed the crucial voting, and 'Deck the Halls' turned into 'Storm the doors of City Chambers'.

Storm the doors of City Chambers
Fan the flames and waft the embers
Let them know when we assemble
We're the wans who'll mak them tremble

Kick the Cooncil up the backside
Celebrate the new Red Clydeside
John Maclean is here in spirit
His tradition we inherit

ꟹ

When it's all been done and dusted
Power tae those who can be trusted
Down with all who push and shove us
Drunk and bloated on force and guile
Down with all who stand above us
Power tae the rank and file

Here Come the Folk Clubs

It wis at a Rangers-Celtic match I'm sure ye'll a' hae mind
O' the fighting and the cursing in the days o Aul' Lang Syne
Noo Jamie was the boy ye ken wha stopped the hulla-baloo
Intae the Pavilion he did slip afore the game wis due

Says Big McGrory: "I protest, that ba' has an awfu sheen!
For one hauf it wis pented blue an the ither hauf wis green
"God's truth" he said, "for boldness, that lad ye canna beat."
For the mighty deed wis done by our hero, James McPhate
Baron James McPhate, tune Big Kilmarnock Bunnet, words Andrew Hunter

ꕥ

Ma wee laud's a sojer
He works in Maryhill
He gets his pey on a Friday night
An buys a hauf-a-gill
Goes tae church on Sunday
Hauf-an-oor too late
He pu's the buttons aff his shirt
An pits them in the plate
Ma Wee Laud's A Sodger, traditional

ꕥ

There was a lady in the north
I ne'er could find her marrow
She was courted by nine gentlemen
And a plooboy lad frae Yarrow
The Dowie Dens O Yarrow, traditional ballad

ꕥ

'Twas poor Tom Brown from Glasgow, Jack Williams and poor Joe,

We were three daring poachers, the country well did know
At night we were trepanned by the keepers in the sand
And for fourteen years transported unto Van Dieman's Land
The Poachers, traditional transportation ballad

☙

My love he stands in yon chaumer door
Combing doon his yellow hair,
His curly locks I like to see,
I wonder if my love minds on me

Will ye gang love, an leave me noo?
Will ye gang love, an leave me noo?
Will ye forsake your ain love true
An gang wi a lass that ye never knew?
Will ye gang love?, traditional

The above range of lyrics, all drawn from Norman Buchan's '101 Scottish Songs' - social comment, children's fun, new national song, old ballad, broadside ditty, love song – show some of the song mix that became popular as folk clubs began to open and prosper around Scotland, and performers of professional standard began to develop. As did confidence and ability in songmaking, with political song lyrics taking a prominent place in the 1960s.

From 1959 through the 1960s the Scottish Folk Revival gathered strength. A new key source of songs appeared. Norman Buchan began a weekly 'Bothy Ballads' song column in the 'Weekend Scotsman' newspaper. In 1962 he gathered these and other songs into '101 Scottish Songs', a small format book with a red cover that was dubbed 'The Wee Red Songbook'. The range of songs is wide and well selected, most of them going quickly into the repertoire of young singers. Only a few of them had already appeared in the Bo'ness chapbooks.

In his Introduction Buchan says first, "The task of editing a small book of this kind is immense, for one is faced with the mass of Scottish song, perhaps the richest treasury of all Europe." He explains that "firstly we had to reject 'kailyardery'." He seeks to change "the popular repertoire in a direction more suited to the needs of the present time". He abandons piano accompaniments, instead indicating suitable guitar chords. Buchan thanks "all the members of the Rutherglen Academy Ballads Club who showed me that a love of the best in Scottish song can go hand in hand with a liking for guitar strumming, banjo-picking and American hoe-downs."

Buchan had begun the Ballads Club in the Academy, the second folk club started in Scotland, in 1957, where he was a teacher. (The third club was the Edinburgh University Folk Society.) In concerts organised by him and Janey Buchan in Rutherglen, in Ballads And Blues nights in the Iona Community's Clydeside premises on Glasgow's Broomielaw, in concerts and ceilidhs the enthusiasm for song and singing was spread. Young singers were performing wherever they could corral an audience – social clubs, talent competitions, bingo halls, and especially clubs for the elderly.

In 1959 Janey and Norman Buchan asked a group of young singers to their home, and proposed the formation of a folk club open to the public. A committee was formed, but little progress made till Janey Buchan found a possible location, a large lunchtime eatery in the Trongate. The committee had by now dwindled to Drew Moyes and the author. On the first night enthusiasts came in herds, and the Glasgow Folk Club became the fourth folk club in Scotland and the first to operate as a weekly self-funding club. There were drawbacks. Singers had to stop in mid-verse when trams rattled past on the Trongate, until after a few weeks two young men brought in a mysterious setup of microphone, wires and boxes, and singers could conquer the trams. After a few weeks the club had its first guest, Jimmy MacBeath, who was paid a fee of £8, more than he'd ever before got from singing.

The singing backbone of the Glasgow Club was a ramshackle assembly of singers who shared a repertoire of political and other chorus songs through their participation in an ongoing 19 month long party that was held at Hamish Imlach's house in Broomhill. Imlach, Josh and Sheila McRae, Jim McLean, Archie and Ray Fisher, Bobby Campbell, Jackie O'Connor and the author were known collectively as the 'Broomhill Bums'. Another, more organised, ceilidh venue was the Blythman's house on Balgrayhill where frequent ceilidhs had run since the mid-1950s.

Jimmie Macgregor wrote in his appreciation of Blythman and the Balgrayhill ceilidhs in the 'Scotsman', "Some of the young people involved have gone on to become well-known and successful in the world of folk music – Matt McGinn, Archie Fisher, Robin Hall, Josh McRae, etc, but more significantly, many more gained a lifelong interest in their own traditions."

Songs of Glasgow

As I was walking one summer's evening
A-walking doon by the Broomielaw
It was there I met with a fair young maiden
She'd cherry cheeks and a skin like snaw

The Bleacher Lassie O Kelvinhaugh

☙

I love the lassies, Ah'm gaun tae wed them aa
When the broom blooms brawly on the bonnie Broomielaw
But in the meantime we'll hae tae sail awa
Till the broom blooms brawly on the bonnie Broomielaw

I have a bonnie lassie, Brigton's her address
And Jimmy Maxton's written tae wish us baith success
He's gaun tae get his hair cut just tae gie's a new mattress
And I love my lassie, oh she's fine

The Broom Blooms Brawly, Music Hall song

☙

As I went out by Cardowan bings I heard a young man say
Once I was a miner but they've ta'en my job away.
I used tae work the coalface of that mine ower the field
We always made our quota, we always got good yield.
But a man came from America, I curse him to this day
McGregor rationalised me and he's ta'en my job away.

Ta'en My Job Away, tunes and words John McCreadie

Within two years of the opening of the Glasgow Folk Club the author went to work in Africa, and Drew Moyes moved the Folk Club to its own premises, to become the Glasgow Folk Centre in Montrose Street, where it ran several nights with visiting guest performers every week. There were instrument lessons during the day. Drew proceeded to open a network of other folk clubs in the Greater Glasgow area.

Ronnie Clark was drawn in. "I first heard a traditional song on the early evening UK country wide TV programme, 'Tonight'. Rory and Alex McEwan, or Robin and Jimmie. There was little else available to choose from then, only Guy Mitchell. I then went round Glasgow record shops, seeking, learning more, finding people like Blind Lemon Jefferson.

Glasgow Songs, the second written in response to the first

Oh where is the Glasgow where I used tae stey?
The white wally closes done up wi pipe cley,
Where ye knew every neighbour frae first floor tae third
And to keep your door locked was considered absurd.
Do you know the folk steyin next door to you?

The Glasgow That I Used To Know, tune traditional, words Adam MacNaughtan

Oh where is the Glasgow I used to know?
The tenement buildings that let in the snow
Through the cracks in the plaster the cold wind did blow
And the water we washed in was fifty below

We read by the gaslight, we had nae TV,
Hot porridge for breakfast, cold porridge for tea
Some weans had rickets and some had TB,
Aye, that's what the Glasgow of old means tae me

Farewell To Glasgow, tune and words Jim McLean

"Two years later, in about 1962, I was chatting with a girl at work, she told me she went to a folk club, I went along to Drew Moyes' Folk Centre in Montrose Street. That was it. I had found a set of rails to put myself on and learn a lot more. Hamish Imlach and Nigel Denver were the first singers I heard. My first interest was antiquarian, as for many, but this was something native to me as well, and I could identify with the history, and I could speak to the people delivering it.

"In 1963 or 4 we started the Grand Hotel Folk Song and Ballad Club at Glasgow's Charing Cross. The idea was pushed by Geordie McIntyre, Carl MacDougall was brought in, he in turn brought in Ian Philip from Aberdeen. We had a policy, our view of what a traditional singer was. We brought the best guests, A L Lloyd, Ewan MacColl, Jeannie Robertson.

"We had political song nights, structured the night around that idea – Irish, French, Spanish, it didn't matter. Lloyd and MacColl would make a point about singing political songs when they came. The local younger guys, like Peter Ross, Jimmy Ross, would give you a few of their songs. And older political songs – Harlaw, World War One, Jacobite songs. What songs are sung depends who is there. In a club, people pay hard cash, and have a set of expectations. You have to not change songs, but maybe introduce others to humour the house.

"Matt McGinn would come and sing at the club, not as a paid guest, but always welcome to sing a few songs. I had great respect for him as a cobbler of songs. Nothing that will last forever, but songs on a general political theme that people could sing and were happy to sing with. Ironically I think Matt did not like folk song, but as a vehicle for him to cobble his own stuff. He never sang any folk songs himself, and he'd sometimes be very dismissive of the singing of people like Joe Heaney and MacColl. Matt McGinn and Danny Kyle have become legends. How does that happen? It is in part tied to an individual's ability to promote themself. Which is their right, but don't expect me to swallow it.

"Arthur Argo came to the club with Peter Hall. Arthur had a genuine interest in the music, not just in promoting himself. He was very important to the Revival at the time, he was a collector for a start, he was of the family of Gavin Greig, through his job in Aberdeen radio he got some good work out on radio. He created some good records, he was happy to tour and to sing songs without looking for anything in exchange. He was a nice human being. Arthur created 'Chapbook', Carl and Ian provided the West of Scotland aspect of the magazine.

"Geordie McIntyre was also important. He discovered singers - Duncan Williamson and Arthur Lochhead, who gave us a brand new version of 'Lamkin'. The club waxed and waned. It was hard to keep up the enthusiasm, and by the 70s I had a family to bring up, a career to build, I faded from the scene." *Ronnie Clark*

Jim Brown lyrics

I felt so sad just standing there in a place I'd once loved well
Now used without permission asked to store the very teeth of Hell
But all these folk who strive for peace
My heart went out to all of them
The struggle's on, it mustn't cease
I tell you now, as I told myself, that day upon the road

As I Walked On The Road

☙

Come tae your dad, don't stand in the cauld
A chill wind is blawin through Cumbernauld
Well, you're feelin young but yur dad's feelin auld
We'll make a great team together
Bein on the dole is no much fun
Times seem awfu bad
But no for you to worry, son
Why, you're just only a lad

Come To Your Dad

☙

My old man in his day, to my brothers and me he used to say
Never let them grind you down,
Build yer union strong and sound and the boss won't get his way.

My Old Man

Later in the 1960s an informal venue became the centre of the Glasgow folk scene. Ye Olde Scotia Inn at the foot of Stockwell Street was next door to the closed Scotia Music Hall where Harry Lauder had had his first paid gig. Singing in the public bar of pubs was now legally allowed, and the left half of the long curving bar was a centre for 100 voice chorus singing. The right half of the bar was reserved for the local chapter of the motorcycle Hells Angels, who entered by a separate door from the folkies, and tolerated the noise to their left. At the far left of the bar was the Wee Back Room, where twenty early comers jammed themselves in and sang together. The Scotia had its own newspaper, co-edited by poet Freddie Anderson who would enter the pub and distribute cyclostyled copies of his latest political lyric.

Linked to the Glasgow scene were other clubs. Danny Kyle started one in Paisley. Members of the Cumbernauld Little Theatre started a club and ran concerts and classes.

One key member was Jim Brown, a shipyard worker who had moved to Cumbernauld. In 'Song And Democratic Culture In Britain' Ian Watson says Brown developed a distinctive melodic guitar accompaniment style, and made songs that "exploit fully the medium of song through both text and melody, a commitment to democratic culture in songwriting, performance and practical organisation, a stubborn realism and an ambition to capture and activate a working-class public". Watson devotes a whole chapter to Brown's work, hoping to help "gain recognition for a songwriter who, by virtue of his social and artistic circumstances, remains unknown to a national public".

The Folk Song Revival, the Lallans poetry movement and other outpourings of creative writing before and since in Scotland and other countries, produced other makers the equal of Jim Brown whose work deserved much better recognition and valuation than it got. Fortune does not always favour the talented over those assiduous in self-promotion. See what Pete Heywood has to say on page 302 about John Watt's positive influence on the Scottish folk scene.

In its early days, the Glasgow Folk Club exchanged fraternal visits with the Edinburgh University Folk Society. One trip by the Glasgow club was on the flatback of an unladen coal lorry, and in Edinburgh they were entertained by a group that included Dolina MacLennan and Jean Redpath. A previous temporary venue in Edinburgh had been The Howff, organised during the Festival by visiting English singer Roy Guest. Other Festival time venues featuring folk song followed.

Dolina MacLennan became heavily involved in the ongoing Edinburgh folk scene.

"I came to Edinburgh in 1957. The 18th of April 1958 was the date the University Folk Society opened, and I met Hamish Henderson that night. My friend Christine was going to a party, after the first night of Folk Soc. It was incredible. I didn't understand it. It was the beginning – of the end! Without it I would have been very boring." Dolina eventually took over as Folk Soc president. "I recently found a notebook from those days, with the entry, 'New girl, Jean Redpath, sounds promising'.

"I was the only Gaelic folkie around when I came down to Edinburgh. There had been Kitty and Marietta MacLeod and Flora MacNeil. I sang everywhere, every political party thought I was one of theirs. In 1959 I started singing in the Waverley Bar on St Mary St, upstairs in the lounge. There was no singing allowed in pub bars in those days, no music allowed in Sandy Bell's till later. We got other people started. I gave the Corries their first gig, at the Waverley, and showed them how to use the mike.

"We were singing the songs, but I didn't quite understand what they meant. The folk scene was very left wing and very political in the beginning.

"Every night I had to sing the 'Coronation Coronach' and the 'Wee Magic Stane'. That went totally out in the late 60s, early seventies. It got competitive. Before that, if you got a gig you brought other singers in, shared the performance and the fee." *Dolina MacLennan*

Folk clubs in pubs began to spread. Nancy Nicolson came from Caithness to study, and was brought in by a friend.

Songs from Edinburgh

Ye ladies wha smell o wild rose,
Think ye for your perfume to whaur a man goes,
Think ye o the wives and the bairnies wha yearn
For a man ne'er returned from huntin the sperm.

My Donald, Owen Hand

ঔ

But no content wi howkin deid – a ploy that aye gets harder –
They cast their een on livin folk an start committin murder.
But Reekie toon can sleep at last, the twa sall hunt nae mair –
It's the gallows tree for William Burke and a pauper's grave for Hare.

Burke and Hare, Broadside Ballad

ঔ

Dalry, Kilbirnie, Johnstone, Kilmarnock and Ayr,
Glasgow, Coatbridge, Airdrie and the whole of Lanarkshire,
Falkirk, Fife and Gallowa and the Lothian men aw say
That colliers should, like other men, but work eight hours a day.

Colliers' Eight Hour Day

"My friend Dot said 'Nancy, we are all gaun to the folk club'. 'What's a folk club?' 'Just come and you'll see.' It was the Crown Folk Club in Lothian Street, run by Archie Fisher, Owen Hand and Wattie Wright. I found it was what my own folk had been doin at home. I just sang the choruses. And to find people like Owen Hand who wrote his own songs, I thought, 'That's something!'"

Hand's best known song was 'My Donald', about the whaling industry. Is it political? Nancy Nicolson thinks so. "It was not protest, but of course it was political, they had to go oot because they'd no ither job, the situation was far more dangerous than people should have been bein put into. But because the companies needed oil for the perfume for the ladies in the Strand, of course these boys had to die. Oh yeah?" *Nancy Nicolson*

John Greig came from Inverness to study in Edinburgh, and he found folk clubs. "The whole place was really awash with music. There was the Crown, the folk club of the University, which had different names and moved through lots of lifetimes. There was the Triangle, there was one in George Square. I met a friend of mine who had been 2 years in front of me in Inverness and had sung in a group, and we were going for a pint – and it all really came from that. He said 'We'll go to Sandy Bell's' and we met in Forrest Road and he says 'This is Sandy Bell's' and I thought, 'No it's not, it's the Forresthill Bar.' The chances of getting in were not high, but once you did get in, there was very little you didn't come across. Whether it was the people playing at the time or 'Wow, Archie Fisher drinks in here!' You suddenly realise you're in a different world entirely.

"From there it really went through the University Folk Club. There was a guy called Abby Sale, an American. He was a Jewish guy who'd lived on the West Coast, lived in New York, had been all over and knew everybody, Jean Ritchie, all those people. He really got a hold of the Club and hammered it into shape, so it was a very good club. He also introduced the idea of getting a guest and making it pay, and he had very good taste in guests, so it did pay. It wasn't the kind of club where they'd bring on a guy who could sing three songs, people would actually go and pay to see these guests." *John Greig*

"We had money in hand, we decided we should pay singers. Dick Gaughan, Dolly MacLennan, Rod Paterson who used to sing Hamish Henderson songs wonderfully. We paid them £5, at that time they were semi-pro working artistes. Why not support them? We did a few more concerts than previously. We hired a location, and started a Fringe Festival Club. A wonderful endeavour. We were very sad when after three years it was time to leave. I now own a Folk Soc 50th anniversary T shirt." *Abby Sale*

John Greig recalls, "I used to go with my tape-recorder and I think probably the first time I saw most people was in that club - they all came and played. I remember Jimmy Ross coming across with a big crowd of Glasgwegians, who were all singing. Glasgow was overtly political at that particular point, very much so. There was a lot to do with the SNP as well. In Edinburgh, I was getting up and singing, but it was all the stuff I'd learned in Inverness – I was the guy who introduced them to bothy ballads. But then you'd come across people like Hamish (Henderson) who was busy out there singing 'We Are The D Day Dodgers' and 'Banks Of Sicily', all that sort of stuff. " *John Greig*

John Barrow, later an agent for Dick Gaughan and many others, had come to Edinburgh from Tyneside. "I bought a guitar in Edinburgh, I was in digs in the 60s with two students with lots of songs. At the Agricultural Society on a Wednesday night there would be a big circle of guys just singing. I was learning songs, and began to

Songs sung in Aberdeen

We shall overcome, we shall overcome
We shall overcome some day
Deep in my heart I do believe
We shall overcome some day
American freedom song

ɞ

Achanachie Gordon he is but a man
Although he be pretty, whaur lies his free land?
Saltoun's houms they lie bonnie, his tours they stand hie
Ye maun mairry Lord Saltoun, forget Achanachie
Achanachie Gordon, as sung by Joe Rae

ɞ

I aince hid a lass, I likit her weel
I hate aa the people that spak o her ill
But whit have I gotten for aa ma great love?
She's awa tae be wed tae anither
I Aince Hid A Lass, as sung by Elizabeth Stewart

acquire political points of view, and Scottish songs, learning the history of something I'd never heard of before. I was busy studying to get a degree, bypassing student protests. Then I felt I should vote, and I voted on the left because I was conditioned by what was around me.

"During the 60s I ran the University Charities appeals concerts. Matt McGinn, politics seemed to seep out of him, he was the one guy at the time I'd call a political songwriter and singer. Dick Gaughan was not really a political singer then, not till Allende and Chile. There was a club at the Royal Terrace in 1967/8. Pub singers didn't go there, they were singing the jolly songs that would get across to an audience.

"Then the Vietnam War and 'We Shall Overcome' songs came in, but even then where I was, not much. Thank God I didn't get to Sandy Bells at that time or I might never have graduated. I looked for it two or three times, but I wasn't looking for the Forresthill Bar. I would have bumped into

Songs sung in Aberdeen

Twa recruitin sergeants cam frae the Black Watch
Tae merkits and fairs some recruits for tae catch
But aa that enlisted wis forty and twa
Enlist ma bonnie laddie, and come awa
For it's over the mountains and over the main
Through Giberaltar tae France and Spain
Pit a feather tae yer bunnet and a kilt abune yer knee
Enlist, bonnie laddie, an come awa wi me

Twa Recruitin Sergeants, old ballad

☙

This is nae a sang o love, na, nor yet a sang o money
Faith, it's naethin verra peetifu, it's naethin verra funny
But there's Hielan Scotch, Lowlan Scotch, butterscotch an honey
If there's nane o them for aa there's a mixture o the three

McGinty's Meal An Ale, G S Thomson, bothy ballad

☙

Tae get ma rooster hame I got onto a bus
I sat doon in a corner seat awa fae aa the fuss
The folk come crowdin on, I squeezed up tae the top
"Excuse me, madam," I shouted,"ye've sat doon on ma
Cock-a-doodle-doo, it's nothing to do wi you
It's a jolly fine bird and it's aa I've got
It's ma cock-a-doodle-doo"

Cock-a-doodle-doo, music hall song

Hamish Henderson earlier." *John Barrow*
In the Central Belt folk song was being revived, but in Aberdeenshire the picture was of continuing life and vitality in the songs. Danny Couper explains. "Aiberdeen is different tae the rest o Scotland. Robbie Shepherd said there was no such thing as Revival singers. He was correct as far as Aiberdeen is concerned. Aiberdeen is made up of fishing and farming. Fishing has a living tradition of singing and choirs. There was a lively scene about the farming Bothy Ballads in Aiberdeen, there was 'Bothy Nichts' on TV, radio had 'Down at the Mains', a live thing was going on in Aberdeenshire. And where the travellers settled doon in agricultural communities, they were accepted there, the farmers were dependent on them for labour. In Fetterangus there are four or five traveller families, including the Stewarts.
"Another lively thread was there was a lot o instrumental dance bands playing. Jean Stewart of Fettercairn had her own dance band, with Elizabeth playing piano - Lucy Stewart the great ballad singer bade wi Jean in Fetterangus. Curly MacKay had a band, he was a traveller, he played in all the halls in Aiberdeen. I played in a band. When I was 19 I was playing wi a traditional jazz band and playin a bit of skiffle, the band was Bill Bruce an the Gaybirds. Before that I'd played wi another band, nae a jazz band. Bill Bruce was a seed merchant, we played in halls, with me singin 'MacPherson's Rant' and Irish rebel sangs, learned frae mother and frae uncles, nae Revival songs frae books. Intertwined wi that wis the skiffle and the jazz. Ye'd Jimmy MacBeath, Davie Stewart, these people who in the 40s and 30s sang in the feein markets.
"What little influence I had, there was a pub in Aiberdeen, 'P Peep's Bar' in Commerce Street. It's proper name was the Commerce Bar, the sign over the door said 'Commerce in, or ony wye ye like'. I'd a friend, at university, he also played with Bill Bruce, we started a singin evening in the pub. When we started it Arthur Argo cam doon. The place was packed. Arthur said 'Why don't we form a folk club?' At the same time I was a member of the Young Communist League, a few of them were interested. One of them was a member of the Arnold Wesker Society, and wanted the club to be part of that [group

of allied cultural local organisations throughout Britain]. Arthur was not keen. There was not real Communist Party influence, but CP people were part of the folk scene naturally. It was politically driven in Glasgow, but it didn't need to be driven up here.

"When Hamish Henderson and Alan Lomax came here and they found Jeannie Robertson they styed wi the Lennoxes, the singer Annie Lennox, that's her family. The Lennoxes understood the political significance of folk song, what it was about, that ye canna separate songs frae politics. They understood this. The Aberdeen Folk Club was supported by people in the CP, by fellow travellers, by left wingers. Peter Hall came here, and he and Marion got involved. Peter was involved in CND.

"So Aiberdeen was and is different, there's a continuity and a mixture of influences. Ewan MacColl's approach uses a dead tradition you can control. In Aiberdeen the tradition is live all the time. The travellers didn't think of the old songs as folk songs, they sang them but they also sang country and Jimmy Rodgers songs."I sing songs, I'm an Aiberdeen supporter, travel wi the team, they're nae party supporters, nae CP, but I've had Arthur Johnstone up, and they love his songs. You wouldnae get that wi upper class or the middle fringe of Tories, English people, but ye get it in Scotland, Young Tories joining in."
Danny Couper

In Fife the best known clubs were St Andrews, The Elbow Room in Kirkcaldy, and the Dunfermline club. Dolina MacLennan says that she and Robin were the first guests, at the opening of the Dunfermline club. "At a party near Dunfermline we had met John Watt, he said 'This is new'. He and Robin got together, John started writing songs, and started the club." Watt went on to be a major songmaker in the Revival.

Fife punched above its weight in the Revival. Was it a generational thing, or the impetus of activity? In Aberdeen they were so occupied with the cornucopia of living tradition on their doorstep that they had little need to spread the word or to develop a strong songmaking movement. Fife had more clubs, and singers and songmakers who became active outside their home area.

Fife songwriter Rab Noakes says, "I was first aware of folk song through its commercial aspect – Robin and Jimmie, the White Heather Club. I went to St Andrews Folk Club, the people there were really interested in a wide range of things.

"Young Davey Stewart, Rod Sinclair singing Scottish songs, Ewan MacColl songs from the Radio Ballads. Pete Shepheard was more interested in the older material, Jimmy Hutchison was singing songs learned from Jeannie Robertson. Other people coming in - Davie Craig, Artie Trezise – were welcomed.

"I got more deeply into Scottish tradition from hearing older singers, I was getting contact with the tradition. Now in the club I had a vehicle where I could write my songs in a different way. The Great Fife Road Show was about tradition and identity and new songs.

Young Davey Stewart heard about an English

Lyrics from Fife songmakers

Espana ye bled from Bilboa to Seville
While the ghosts of your dead, oh they walk the beaches still
So while you're busy getting laid and you're raising merry hell
Think on what the price was paid for yer dirt cheap San Miguel
Owt For Nowt, John Watt

☙

She's just a Kelty clippie, she'll no tak nae advice
It's "Ach, drap deid, awa boil yer heid or ah'll punch yer ticket twice"
Her faither's just a waster, her mither's on the game
She's just a Kelty clippie but ah love her just the same
The Kelty Clippie, tune Maggie Cockabendy, words John Watt

☙

I heard some men out talking on a street corner
And some of them were saying their lives were getting bad
I head one of them saying, "Friend, I can't make any money"
And the friend replied, "Well, I think we're being had"
Don't Keep Passing Me By, Rab Noakes

☙

I see you take your orders from above
The iron fist held in a velvet glove
And you always hurt the one you love
Would you break your sweetest vow
How can I believe you now
How Can I Believe You Now, Rab Noakes

travelling show, we decided to do that. Our first outing was to Belfast in 1969. They wanted old Davie Stewart, and we built a show around him. Then we did a tour of East Anglia. 1970 was our first Scottish tour. It was all to do with song. John Watt's songs were important in the show, all Fife related, very layered and deep." *Rab Noakes*

John Greig tells about Inverness. "Inverness was really the source of a lot of it for me. There was a guy called Duncan MacLennan ran the folk club in Inverness until quite recently. Duncan had been to Aberdeen University, he'd known Jeannie Robertson well, he knew lots of people, and so I grew up with a proper folk club, with people who had the required attitudes of the time. One or two people were a bit older than me. Hamish Grant had sung with the Dubliners in the Aberdeen Concert Hall as their second act and he had a tremendous voice for bothy ballads and for big ballads. I didn't think there was anything particularly strange about doing these things because from the age of 14 or 15 that's all I was really interested in. Once I'd heard it, that's what I wanted to do. That included the blues, I'd heard that, and Dylan coming along. It wasn't just the Scottish music, it was everything, it was astonishing. I remember Dylan's first LP coming out about 1963. I was in school, I'd wander round the town as you do, looking at the record stores and wander back to school again. Nothing else to do, no money, but I remember these things happening. So I had plenty of

Sheila Douglas lyrics

In the wee sma oors of mornin there was sudden blazin death
Three hundred desperate miners ran and fought for a breath
Fire at Michael Colliery. Black smoke underground
Six men dead in a pit of hell, and three who were not found

Michael Colliery

As I cam in by Peterheid
I saw it changing sairly o
For the tankers grey stand in the bay
And the oil is flowin rarely o

The men o the north are aa gane gyte
Aa gane gyte thegither o
As the derricks rise tae the northern skies
The past is gane forever o

The Men O The North

songs when I left Inverness, it wasn't as if I had to come down [to Edinburgh] to learn songs." *John Greig*

The Perth area benefited from the presence of teacher, singer, author, organiser, songmaker, collector, storyteller, promoter of the use of the Scots language and all-round powerhouse Sheila Douglas.

There was perhaps less folk song activity in Dundee, though the songs of poetess Mary Brooksbank became staple fare in the Revival. The key 'acoustic' songmaker to emerge from Dundee was Michael Marra, whose wonderful songmaking has some affinities with folk song, but ranges far wider. Re political protest, Dundonian Stuart McHardy says, "I was excited about CND, thousands of people demonstrated in Glasgow, a few dozen of us in Dundee. Similarly, in the 90s there was a massive Glasgow march against the Iraq war."

Oh dear me, the warld's ill divided
Them that work the hardest are aye wi least provided
But I maun bide contented,dark days or fine
There's no much pleasure living affen ten and nine
Oh Dear Me, Mary Brooksbank

London-based Ewan MacColl's work was very influential in Scotland, through recordings and broadcasts, through his touring along with Peggy Seeger, through his flow of fine new-made songs, and through his work developing the skills and knowledge of younger singers in the Critics Group. Scots who at various times 'studied' with MacColl include Enoch Kent, Bobby Campbell, Bob Blair and Gordon MacCulloch. Others like Ray Fisher and Gordeanna McCulloch were involved in recording projects with MacColl.

Through the 1960s many folk clubs opened and folk song concerts became more frequent. Particularly popular Glasgow based singers included Josh McRae, Hamish Imlach, Alastair MacDonald who sang with the BBC TV orchestra at times, but always held Republican and 'Stane' songs in his repertoire, and Archie Fisher. Soon Matt McGinn came back from studying in the south. Other young Scots were developing their performance and songwriting skills, among them Glasgwegians John Martyn, Billy Connolly, and Fifer Barbara Dickson. Fewer singers emerged from Edinburgh at that time, but Owen Hand,

Bert Jansch, and soon Dick Gaughan and the McCalmans became professional singers. Three of these very popular professional Revival singers, McRae, Imlach and McGinn, were particularly known for politically committed songs.

Glasgwegian Ronnie Clark says of the Grand Hotel Club, "The Holy Loch or Republican songs were very popular. There were factions within the audience and the singers – SNP, Communist, Scottish separatist – they showed it in how they structured their repertoire, how they introduced their songs. People sang the Clancy Brothers chorus songs, and people were always very happy to join in and raise their voices to make a noise with the Holy Loch songs. MacColl was very dismissive of the Holy Loch songs because they did not have the qualities that the English had managed to create in their peace songs. I thought this a stupid thing to say, he had a different perspective and he was a different being anyway.

"He considered we should write thought pieces as political songs. I think there is a purpose in the English perspective, but the Scottish songs were made to work on the street, to say 'Don't do that'." We need a broader context to put political song into."

Ronnie Clark

Josh McRae's intense involvement in and identification with

Songs sung by Hamish Imlach

Cheap-Jack's a millionaire
(a very nice feller)
He wants tae send us up-the-stair
(or doon tae the cellar)
But up the stairs we arnae gaun
For Wall Street and the Pentagon
Or Cheap-Jack the Millionaire

Cheap-Jack The Millionaire, tune Ma Maw's AMillionaire, words Glasgow Song Guild

❧

I didn't raise my son to be a soldier, and go off fighting heathens round the Horn
If God required to show that men were bolder, they'd wear uniforms and swords when they were born
Why should we have wars about religion, when Jesus came to teach us not to kill?
Do Zulus and Hindoos not have the right to choose?
I didn't raise my son to be a soldier

New verse by Ewan McVicar for 'I Didn't Raise My Boy To Be A Soldier', 1914 American popular song the 'Eskimos' was reflected in his performance of peace and republican songs along with old ballads and American material. He and Hamish Imlach shared many stages, singing for whoever invited and paid them. Hamish Imlach said, "The political lines weren't so tightly drawn then. I remember Archie, Josh and I singing for the Young Communists and the Young Conservatives on the same night. Or the Communist Party gigs that Aly Bain's older brother used to organise in Glasgow."

Jim McLean does not remember Hamish going on Eskimo demos at the Holy Loch. Hamish said that he sang at a lot of the demos, and in the book 'Cod Liver Oil and the Orange Juice' tells various tales, including one about the singers being bussed a mile ahead of the march at Sandbank Pier, finding themselves surrounded by "three or four hundred Yank sailors who were thinking 'Not much of a mass demonstration, this! We were singing away, and selling them copies of Morris's 'Ding Dong Dollar' songbooks at sixpence a time. They were buying six or ten copies each, as cheap souvenirs of Scotland. Eventually the mini bus came back and took us to the right place."

Hamish said he sang on the 'Ding Dong Dollar' album, which was issued in the USA. "And in Russia, "where they translated all the songs and used them on the front page of 'Izvestia'. No British company would issue the record, and when the American Folkways company eventually agreed to do it they insisted that the specifically anti-John F Kennedy songs be removed. Unfortunately they

Matt McGinn lyrics

I have heard men complain o the job that they're daein
While they're howkin the coal or they're diggin the drain
But whatever they are, there is none can compar'
Wi the man that stauns shovelling manura man-ya

Noo I'm feelin gey sour, for my job's been ta'en ower,
And everything noo is mechanical power:
And the roses that grow have nae odour oh no! –
Nae manura, manura, manura man-ya

Manyura Man-ya, tune The Kerry Recruit

☙

I'm looking for a job with a sky high pay
A four-day week and a two-hour day
Maybe it's because I'm inclined that way
But I never could stand being idle

I'm Lookin For A Job

were the songs I sang. After the recordings had been made Kennedy had been assassinated and become a saint, so my songs were out."
Imlach says he was apolitical till he met Josh McRae and Morris Blythman. "I was if anything Conservative as my parents had been." His singing and recording of political songs led eventually to him being blacklisted. "In 1989 the 'World in Action' TV programme reported I was on a political blacklist I had never heard of – The Economic League. They had me down as a communist sympathiser when I'm one of the very few professional folk singers who has *never* been a communist."
In his autobiography Imlach says that Glasgow songwriter Matt McGinn "didn't spend enough time polishing his songs. He'd lose interest in a song in a week, and instead of polishing a brilliant idea that was nearly there, he'd go on to a new brilliant idea. He'd have a sudden burst and write six songs in a day, and one or two would have the kernel of a great idea, if only he'd spent a bit more time rubbing the rough edges off. Later I realised this was part of his strength, and made his work unique as a songwriter." *Hamish Imlach*
McGinn was the first political songmaker of the Revival who also became when opportunity offered a professional performer. An eloquent and openly politically dogmatic singer-songwriter, he continued throughout his career to create a welter of songs on a wide variety of lyric topics, his political values firmly expressed in the mix.
"Matt was a clever operator, I never saw him perform live, but my wife did, in Blantyre Miners' Welfare. Several times he was the Sunday lunchtime spot and he would do funny songs, two or three fairly risqué jokes, and then he would slip in a political song – and the audience was with him all the way – pretty clever." *John Powles*
McGinn had an engagingly rough voice and rather pugnacious but winning singing style. Most beginning folk song makers begin by manipulating parody elements – sometimes working off key parts of the original lyric, sometimes appropriating and reworking a song in a way that refers back tangentially to the original or older known song. This is different from the folk tradition's way of making use of a tune

held in common but without referring in the new lyric to any older one.

The more tangential approach is shown in McGinn's song 'Manura Man-ya', which was made widely known by Pete Seeger. McGinn took a traditional comic Irish song of a Kerry Irish lad enlisting in the army, with a chorus beginning "*With my toora nanya, my toora nanya*". McGinn made it into an hilarious tale of a street collector of horse dung, the chorus beginning '*Wi manyura man-ya, manyura man-ya*". He includes enough references in his lyric to the hardships of the job, and being put out of work by 'mechanical power', to make it possible to squeeze the song into my widest definition of political song.

A much simpler example is the way he took the Israeli dance song 'Havana Gila', and made it into "*Have a banana, have a banana, have a banana, eight pence a bunch*". In performance he could coax out thunderous audience participation in such slight material.

Matt McGinn lyrics

Our faithers fought this fight before, and thought that they had won
You should have seen the boss turn green and how that man could run
But when our faithers turned their backs, the boss came again to dodge his tax
But the next time we'll no be so lax, and we'll have a May Day then

We'll Have A May Day

Too-ra-loo-ra-loo-ra-loo
There's twenty four hours in the day it's true
And we'd ha worked the twenty two
If it wisnae for the Union

Men and women listen tae me
It's time tae rise up aff yer knee
So raise the flag of Unity
And forward with the Union

If It Wisnae For The Union, tune Join The British Army

A McGinn political parody that works off an original song is in a cyclostyled collection of his first lyrics that was dedicated 'To my grannie'. This includes, to the tune of 'Tipperary', an attack on unwaged wealthy people who wintered in the south of France.

It's a long way to the Riviera, it's a long way to go (without your bankbook)
It's a long way to the Riviera and to dear old Monaco
Goodbye to dear old England, her praises we shall sing
And to prove that we are patriotic, we'll be back next spring.

His choice of tunes is eclectic at this time. As he developed he drew more on traditional song tunes, though nearly always making new tunes out of old ones. This first batch uses a music hall tune, a religious tune, Sir Arthur Sullivan's 'Tit Willow', 'Poor Old Joe', 'Harry Was A Bolshie', and some tunes of his own devising. His other lyric topics there are criticism of the powerful, of racial prejudice, of unemployment, of taxation and financial hardship, of Joseph Stalin, of trade union leader Arthur Deakin, of 'My Foreman'. None of the broad comedy, children's songs and romantic ditties he would later intermingle with such politically explicit songs as 'Three Nights and a Sunday', 'If It Wasny for the Union', and 'We'll have a Mayday'.
His 1964 collection, 'Scottish Songs of Today' has 26 songs. A few are about relationships, nature, or alcohol, the majority mingle elements of the problems of employment, humour and political comment. The 1987 posthumous collection of his writings and 61 of his songs, 'McGinn of the Calton', has the same mixture of elements, though the proportions differ. The 1987 book has in proportion more reflective or romantic songs. 'Mambo was a Dusky Man' and 'My Faither was Born a Hebrew', both songs about prejudice, are the only two included in all three collections.
McGinn's songs did not fade from sight with his early death in 1977. Memorial shows featuring a mixture of his output continued to be produced and toured in 2009. Other political songs of his that remain popular include 'The Ballad of John Maclean', 'Can o Tea', 'Coorie Doon', his first song 'The Foreman O'Rourke', 'I'm Looking for a Job', `The Little Carpenter', 'Lots of Little Soldiers', and 'With Fire and with Sword'.
'Scottish Songs of Today' is dedicated to 'the greatest guy I know, Pete Seeger'. His widow Janette's Introduction to 'McGinn of the

Calton', and McGinn's own 'Excerpts from Autobiography' in the book, share many anecdotes about his performance skills, social influences and amusing incidents told from his partisan viewpoint, but little about creation of his political songs. Janette tells us, "First of all he would have an idea, then words and music would come together. Never, ever, was anything ever noted on paper. He relied on memory and sang everything aloud line after line, again and again."Matt inaccurately credits Josh McRae with being the leader of the anti-Polaris movement and of the 'Eskimos', and says he himself was "very much on the fringe" of the emerging songmaking at the start of the '60s. He quite quickly found himself taken up by American Pete Seeger and whisked over to perform as a headliner in a concert at New York's Carnegie Hall. Further down the bill was a polite and rather nervous young singer songwriter, Bob Dylan. McGinn wrote, "I started at the top. From then on it had to be down all the way."

In fact from then on he, with McRae, Imlach and Fisher, was in the first rank of best known and best loved performers of the '60s folk scene. Vol 4 no 4 of 'Chapbook' magazine in 1967 devotes most of the issue to McGinn, with seven songs and a 'very tall tale' by him, and two articles about 'Matt McGinn: Minstrel'.

In their 1968 second last issue, vol 5 no 1, the editors of 'Chapbook' wrote, "Three and a half years ago, in defiance of all the prophets of doom, a rather slim magazine was launched in Scotland to cater for the interests of Scottish folk song enthusiasts. That was Chapbook, that was. In the intervening years, our magazine has grown in both size and in stature – to such an extent that copies are sent to over 30 countries of the world and sales have more than doubled."

The publication 'Chapbook' was a co-operative venture. Ronnie Clark says that Aberdonian organiser and activist Arthur Argo created the magazine, with Aberdonian relocated to Glasgow Ian Philip, and Glasgwegian writer Carl MacDougall providing the West of Scotland aspect. It carried month to month news about folk clubs, singers and personalities, record reviews, old and new songs, photographs, and extended articles on song topics and song makers – I quote elsewhere in this book from several of these articles.

It was at first published by Aberdeen Folk Song Club, and vol 2 no 3 carried the first three prizewinning entries in the Club's contemporary song competition. Two of the three take the topic of war. Zetta Macdonald's 'Dunkirk, a Scot Remembers', was based on the first hand account of one of her brothers. In Lindy Cheyne's 'Sing a Song of Buttercups' his love laments Johnnie who went to fight in the war, and 'lies in a lonesome grave'. When Arthur Argo eventually moved to work for the BBC in Edinburgh the magazine went with him.
'Chapbook' continued to feature songs with an implicit or explicit political element.
Vol 4 no 2 was an issue largely devoted to new songs, nearly all from weel-kent songmakers. The songs included a trenchant attack on Charles De Gaulle's refusal to join the Common Market, eloquent accounts of the hardships of working to build the Shira Hydro-Electric Dam and of the tragic coaltip accident at Aberfan.

Verses from Chapbook Vol 2 No 3, "prize-winning entries in a contest run by the Aberdeen Club", 1965

Mony miles between hame o mine, beloved scene
And that bombed and bloody beach o Dunkirk
Oh ma hert was sair – wid I see hame ivirmair
Bit I micht – Bit I micht – Bit I micht
Dunkirk (A Scot Remembers), Mrs Zetta Macdonald

Sing a song of buttercups
Sing a song of rain
Johnnie's gone to fight in the war
And he'll never come home again
No he'll never come home again

Withered yellow buttercups
Cryin' drops of rain
The men will go and fight in the wars
And the women will cry in vain again
The women will cry in vain
Sing A Song Of Buttercups, Mrs Lindy Cheyne

An anti-militarist song of Scots soldiery, one expressing contempt for the self-seeking rise into parliament of a trade union official, a comment on Glasgow gang religious bigotry, and "a page of political lampoons, tending very much towards the street song style, gathered from various sources".
From 1964 to 1968 Chapbook was the guidebook and diary of the Scottish Folk Revival. It folded at a time when the number of folk

clubs was high, but the community energy was waning, commercialism was gaining strength, the distance between active audience and performer growing and the nature of their relationship changing.

Lay down the borrowed guitar, lay down the fiddle and bow
You'd like one more drink at the bar, but the manager says you must go

All the tunes in the world are dancing around in your head
The clock on the gantry says 'Playtime is done', you'll just have to sing them instead

Everyone here feels the same, yes, you deserve one more tune
But you know the rules of the game, it's time to go howl at the moon
All The Tunes In The World, tune The South Wind, words Ewan McVicar

Far Ower The Faem – International Connections

Hie sits oor king in Dunfermline
Sits birlin at the wine
Says "Whaur eill I get a bonnie boy
That will sail the saut seas fine
That will hie owre to Norraway
To bring my dear dochter hame?
Sir Patrick Spens, traditional, as sung by Amelia and Jane Harris, 1859

Political folk song in Scotland was never isolated. First there were the accounts and complaints about violent interaction with our English neighbour, then borrowings back and forth in song with Ireland. Scottish ballads had travelled with emigrants to northern America, then Scots learned about and borrowed from the increasing popularity of folk song in the USA. By the time of the Folk Revival the interaction with English songs and singers had become peaceful, and the process of political songmaking was interactive if at times competitive. Scotland's singers and makers also drew on the events and songs of other countries for topics and tunes.

The political folk songs of Scotland drew and draw on the songs, history and approaches to political song of other countries, and have in turn made an impact on the political song cultures of other countries. Songs and singers came to Scotland, Scots singers performed and toured and their recordings were sent outwith their own borders. Formerly song lyrics were exchanged with people in foreign parts through manuscript or printed versions, with or without music notation, then by disc or tape recordings. Now through the

Internet song lyrics and performances of them can be accessed freely and fairly easily.

IRELAND

Scottish song has interacted with Irish song far more than with English song. Pro and anti IRA or Orange chants are staples of Scots football match singing. The Orange songs, 'The Sash', 'Dolly's Braes', 'The Old Orange Flute' and others are mostly sung within enclaves. But stirring tunes played by Orange marching bands were appropriated for 'The Coronation Coronach' and 'The Eskimo Republic'. Pro Irish republican songs abounded in the 50s ceilidhs and 60s folk clubs, sung by Dominic Behan or the Clancys, or by five hundred imitators. 'Kelly From Killane', 'Kevin Barry', 'The Foggy Dew', 'The Row in the Town', 'The Bold Fenian Men', 'Follow Me Up to Carlow', 'The Patriot

Irish rebel songs sung in Scotland

What's the news, what's the news, oh my bold shemalier
With your long barrel guns from the sea
Say what wind from the south brings your messenger here
With a hymn of the dawn for the free?
Goodly news, goodly news do I bring youth of Forth
Goodly news shall you hear Bargy man
For the boys march at dawn from the south to the north
Led by Kelly the boy from Killane

Kelly The Boy From Killane

ꟹ

I'll sing you a song of the row in the town
When the green flag went up and the crown rag came down
'Twas the neatest and sweetest thing ever you saw
And they played the best game played in Erin Go Bragh

The Row In The Town

ꟹ

The midnight hags were sweeping round the castle of Drumboe
While patriot blood was running red in the sodden soil below
Their crime that they had left their homes, a tyrant to o'erthrow
And by Irish hands they were murdered in the castle of Drumboe

The Castle Of Drumboe

Game', 'Johnson's Motor Car', 'Boolavogue', 'The Smashing of the Van'. Many more.

In reaction to the Republican and Orange bigotry, songs aiming at reconciliation and tolerance like Adam McNaughtan's 'Derry and Cumberland Boys' and Jim McLean's 'Forget the Old Orange and the Green' came from the Revival.

Winnie Ewing tells how she heard an Irish priest sing 'The West's Awake'. "The words seemed so entirely appropriate, then and now for Scotland as well as Ireland – *Alas and long may Erin weep when Connaught lies in slumber deep. The good creator never planned for slumbering slaves a home so grand.*"

She and a Labour activist sang 'The West's Awake' together at a reception after the opening of the Scottish Carfin monument to Irish famine victims, "greatly to the shock of all the others".

As well as songs from Ireland, Irish issues feature in some Scots songs – 'The Battle of Balfron', about a non-fight between Irish navvies and Scots villagers, another Irish worker accused of being 'a traitor' in the industrial song 'Hot Asphalt', 'Erin Go Bragh' about a rebellious Scot accused of being a Paddie.

Some of the songs were filtered through another continent. The Irish Clancy Brothers had made their name in the USA, their

A Scottish-Irish song

The other night a copper comes and says to me,"McGuire
Will you kindly let me light me pipe down at yer boiler fire?"
He planks himself right straight in front, with hobnails up so nate
"Oh", says I, "me dacent man you'd better go and mind yer bate"

He turns and yells, "I'm down on you, and up to all yer pranks
Sure I know you for a traitor in the Tipperary ranks"
Boys, I hit him from the shoulder and I gave him such a welt
That he landed in the boiler full of hot asphalt

With the rubbin and the scrubbin sure I caught me death of cold
And for scientific purposes me body it was sold
In the Kelvingrove museum, boys, I'm hangin by the belt
As a monument to the Irish stirrin hot asphalt

Hot Asphalt

recordings had come to Scotland, then they came to tour Britain. The new politicisation of American song was added in.
Donald Smith says, "I spent a lot of time in Northern Ireland as a youngster and it wasn't until the Civil Rights thing began to be taken up and happen in Northern Ireland, that I began to make the connection with what was happening round me and this media, record culture, where all the action seemed to be really in the States. Maybe that was typical in many ways of Scotland – all sorts of aspects of our popular culture were really coming from America.
"Ireland and America – for me, those would be the two influences. But then there was what I can only describe as a kind of conversion experience – and Northern Ireland was quite instrumental in that, because of the strength of local culture – as I began to sense that these cultural energies were flowing in our own society and community.
"There's another aspect of political song. I was in Wexford for their Storytelling Festival and for the opening night, they trail round all the pubs in Wexford, trying to tell stories in various impossible situations. And I'm there kind of as the token Scot – and I'm in the George Moore pub – he had some connection with great Irish poetry and song – and I thought "What am I going to do here?" And I got up and sang 'Scots Wha Hae', and silenced the whole place. It was not just about the Scottish-Irish connection but about Burns – so celebrated in Ireland, on all sides. Burns was a great supporter of the democratic cause in Ireland. If he'd still been on the go in 1798, he's have supported the Rising, as many Presbyterians did. But it's a universal language. Burns shows that in political songs there's an immediate struggle. 'Scots Wha Hae' is really about the democracy movement and the sentencing of Thomas Muir to transportation. There's an immediate occasion but he has to use an historic metaphor because otherwise he'd be put in prison and be transported himself for saying it."
At the time Smith talks of, the increasing violence and atrocities of the Northern Ireland struggles of the 1960s and 70s led to the gradual abandonment of rowdy Irish rebel songs in the Scots repertoire. To sing them was to associate the singer not with the fights of 1916 and

the 20s, but with the current horrors. There was a real discomfort with violent terrorism. People reacted against the inappropriateness of singing these songs at that time. 'Johnson's Motor Car' and other humorous ones lingered on. But the hard-hitting ones, the Black and Tans, dropped out. At the time of those 1920s events these were not retroactive songs, but if you sing them later they are retroactive, and you are associating yourself with current violent action because the songs have been claimed as the identifiers of those currently involved in or supporting violence. When sung before they were telling of what seemed justified action.
Geordie McIntyre says, "If 'The Freedom Come-All-Ye' became associated with bombing English people, we would stop singing it. There is a sense of ownership of certain songs by singers with whom they are strongly associated. But, unlike a poem, once a song is out there it takes on a life of its own. There are innumerable examples of how powerful political songs can be. Not long ago you could not sing at all in Glasgow pubs. It was assumed the songs sung would be inciteful of violence."

USA

The links between American and Scots songs, political and otherwise, are many and varied, old and new. There were remembered in Appalachia many American versions of the ancient 'Big Ballads' that were and are also sung in Scotland – 'Barbara Allen', 'Lord Thomas and Fair Ellen', 'The Cruel Mother', 'Lord Randal', 'The Twa Sisters'. Few of the intensive political songs of 16th Century cross-border theft and strife, the Border Ballads, were sung outwith the Scottish Borders, but one, 'Jock o the Side', furnished lines and couplets for 'The Escape of Old John Webb', a 1730 broadside from Salem, Mass. The North-East ballad 'The Bonny Lass o Fyvie' moves to become 'Pretty Peggie', a traditional version of which was recorded by Bob Dylan. On occasion he is credited with writing it, but it came to him from husband and wife duo George and Gerry Armstrong (a Borders surname).

American tunes used for Scots kids songs were in turn appropriated for Holy Loch and SNP campaign songs. 'She'll Be Coming round the Mountains' becomes "Ye Canny Shove Yer Grannie Aff a Bus' became 'Ding Dong Dollar', 'Twa Twa Zero' and 'Ye Cannae Push Auld Scotland Aff the Map'. In the 1980s the same tune was still in vogue, for 'If You've Nuclear Weapons Ready', 'They're Building Fallout Shelters For The Queen' and 'No Nuclear Weapons Wanted Here'. 'Marching Through Georgia' became 'The Glesca Eskimos'.

A Scottish-American connection
Full fifteen stane o Spanish iron
They hae laid aa right sair on me
Wi locks and keys I am fast bound
Into this dungeon dark and dreirie

The first strong door that they cam at
They loosened it without a key
The next chain'd door that they came at
They garr'd it aa to flinders flee
Jock O The Side, 16th C Borders

There was eighty weight of good Spanish iron
Between his neckbone and his knee
But Billy took Johnny up under his arm
And lugged him away right artfully

And Billy broke locks, and Billy broke bolts
And Billy broke all that he came nigh
Until he came to the dungeon door
And that he broke right manful-leye
The Escape Of Old John Webb, 1730 American

Gospel songs 'I Shall Not be Moved', 'Michael Row The Boat Ashore' and 'I'm Gonna Rock My Soul' were employed for 'We Dinnae Want Polaris, 'Shout To The Man In Number Ten – Independence', and 'I'm Going to Change My Vote'. 'John Brown's Body' became 'Ban Polaris – Hallelujah'. 'Yankee Doodle' was used for 'Gie The Man A Transfer' and later for Ian Davison's 'Star Wars For Reagan'. There were more.

American strike songs were employed on British picket lines – 'Hold The Fort', and 'Solidarity Forever' – and songs from the International Workers of the World Little Red Song Books in concerts – 'You Will Eat By And By', 'Hallelujah I'm A Bum', 'The Banks Are Made Of Marble', 'Roll The Union On', 'The Union Maid', 'Which side Are You On?'. Two US country music coal mining songs with a political tinge – 'Down In The Mines' and '16 Tons' - were adopted into the Scottish political song repertoire, and Ewan MacColl even recorded '16 Tons' commercially in the 1950s, though later the London Ballads and Blues Club passed an edict against such intercultural performances.

Among US influences were the parodies of the Wobblies (I.W.W.) particularly Joe Hill, the songs of white songsmith Woody Guthrie and black singer Leadbelly, songs shared by animateur and collector Alan Lomax. The group the Weavers, who featured banjoist Pete Seeger, were influential as just about the only folk group available on record, and Seeger went on to create anthemic politically committed songs. His songs and his performing inspired many young Scots. He and other US singers introduced Scottish folk club audiences to songs of the Civil Rights movement, and records by Phil Ochs and his New York contemporaries showed how songs could be 'singing newspapers'.

American Union lyrics

Hold the fort for we are coming
Union men be strong
Side by side go marching onward
Victory will come

Hold The Fort

Oh, why don't you work
Like other men do?
Tell me how can I work
When there's no work to do?

Hallelujah I'm A Bum

Come all of you good workers
Good news to you I'll tell
Of how the good old Union
Has come in here to dwell

Don't scab for the bosses
Don't listen to their lies
Us poor folks haven't got a chance
Unless we organise

Which Side Are You On, tune Lay The Lily Low, words Florence Reese

Come all of you good people
You women and you men
Once more our backs are to the wall
We're being attacked again

It's time for a decision
And you really have to choose
Support the miners' struggle
Or the next in line is you

Which Side Are You On, new words Dick Gaughan

Most of all, songmaker Bob Dylan carved his mark on 1960s Scottish political, folk, and popular song. John Powles comments, "Janette McGinn says that when Matt appeared with Dylan in Carnegie Hall in

1962, Matt reported that Dylan was a very nice young man, very polite, and had asked Matt if he could borrow a pair of nail clippers."Dylan [as a political songwriter] started off with 'This is wrong' songs. He didn't dwell quite so much maybe on 'What can we do about it?' From the beginning I think he was posing difficult questions. In 'A Pawn In Their Game' the perpetrator was seen to be as much of a victim as the actual victim was. He was already saying, 'This is difficult.' But of course he moved the whole thing to a totally different level when he started to move away from that kind of anthem, or preachy or straightforwardly political songs. Why he did that again is complex, like everything is to do with Dylan. I think that as he said himself, he was getting worried about how big a figurehead he was becoming. In 1962 he became particularly worried that people were being bumped off all around him, and he could be the next one. And he pulled back and he produced complex songs like 'My Back Pages' which to me is the absolutely seminal Dylan song, in realising that things were much more complex – "I was so much older then, I'm younger than that now." He's seen through the glib questions. Glib questions actually have very complex answers." *John Powles*

Donald Smith says, "For me the 60s is the Dylan decade – the American decade. I was only a lad then, born in '56, and we didn't even have a telly until the mid 60s, but one's sense of politics in the 60s as a Scottish middle class child, was that it happened somewhere else. We didn't have politics in Scotland. Now that may sound crazy, but that was the kind of impression that was given. It was Vietnam, all that, and there's no question that your Dylan man caught the mood and tone of all that and expressed it, and that was the beginning of energising huge waves of popular, political protest. Alongside that, the other big thing was the Civil Rights movement, again largely centred on the States and the struggle for Afro-American rights." *Donald Smith*

Ian McCalman says, "Woody Guthrie's songs were poetically smooth, but Dylan writes real intellectual poetry, using imagery to get his songs over in a different way. Then you suddenly get to know about Holy

Loch, the LPs, you meet your Hamish Imlachs and realise there is so much more to it in Scotland."

In the opposite direction, Dylan and others were affected by Scottish political and traditional songs. Dylan made use of various traditional Scots songs and tunes. His 'Times They Are A-Changing' uses the tune of 'Farewell To Sicily', and his 'Lonesome Death of Hattie Carroll' draws on 'The Queen's Four Maries'.

Pete Seeger got the 'Ding Dong Dollar' songs printed in New York's 'Broadside' song magazine, and lobbied to get the 'Ding Dong Dollar' album released on the US Folkways label. I have noted earlier how the 'Broadside' community were envious of the incorporation of song into British peace marches. In her book 'Bob Dylan, Intimate Insights', Kathleen Mackay tells of a conversation Liam Clancy had with Pete Seeger. Clancy says Seeger "was bound to the cause [of social justice]. I felt he was talking through me to humanity. He was sending me a message. One time he told me to learn a Scottish song called 'Freedom Come-All-Ye', and it was a Communist anthem. Yes, Pete was preaching."

ENGLAND

While in Scotland the 1950s impetus and examples that spurred on the 60s Scottish Folk Revival were developing, a parallel push and example-setting was happening in England, spurred on by singer, collector and author A L Lloyd and singer, playwriter and songmaker Ewan MacColl. MacColl was born in Salford of Scots parents who both held fine repertoires of traditional song. In London Lloyd, MacColl and his partner, American singer, musician and songmaker Peggy Seeger, developed the concept of a Ballad and Blues folk club. This became regularised in Britain as a weekly event run by an organiser or organisers, usually themselves singers, with some support from a committee of volunteers, usually in a pub 'back room', where a central performance by a professional or semi-professional singer was supported by 'floor spot' songs from club regulars and perhaps a resident group of performers.

There was much cross-fertilisation of songs and performances between Scotland and England, and many young Scots singers developed their performance skills at home then went down to seek employment and fame in London, where there were more performance opportunities, and access to national broadcast media and record companies.

The 'Ewan MacColl and Peggy Seeger Songbook', their own compositions, has section headings that show their writing priorities.

Various Trades
Contemporary Broadsides
The Iron Road
Road Builders
The Bold Fishermen
Coalminers
Lovers
Songs For Survival
Just Songs

Some of the titles show a little of the strength of their political commitment and creativity.

Go Down, You Murderers
That Bomb Has Got To Go
Brother, Won't You Join In The Line?
March With Us Today
No Agents Need Apply

Some Scots singers succeeded in 'The Smoke'. More found part time employment touring the developing network of folk clubs in England.

Many of the first wave of these young people had been moved to take up a guitar and try out their singing voices by the recordings of Glasgow born London based Cockney accented 'Skiffle King' Lonnie Donegan. Later waves got their inspiration from established Scottish performers, or from recordings and performers coming from the USA.

Those who began to make a living from touring in England left at home the polemically critical Independence songs. English performers and audiences had little or no knowledge of the Scots political songs that protested about English and Royal Family power and actions.

MacColl and Seeger and the Singers Club they ran continued to dominate the English folk scene, they incorporated Scots singers into their Radio Ballads, and Scots songmakers' work was included in their political song chapbook series the 'New City Songster'. Their recordings and song books of traditional songs, and of their own songwriting, and their frequent touring of Scots clubs, fuelled and fired many Scots singers and some songmakers, though other Scots songwriters drew more on native models and approaches, and on local topics. In his autobiography 'Journeyman' Ewan MacColl wrote that in the early days of the Folk Revival "only Scotland differed from the general pattern." He identified three distinct categories of song in the folk clubs. The traditional songs "popularised by Hamish Henderson's ceilidhs", a category "made up almost entirely of the songs of Woodie Guthrie" and the skiffle repertoire, and songs about the Stane. MacColl makes no reference to the key influence of the Bo'ness Ceilidh Song Books. The Singers Club decision that folk singers should only perform songs from their own birth area was less adopted in Scotland than in England. Scots singers were and are always more eclectic in their selection of their repertoire.

A few English songmakers other than MacColl and Seeger were also admired and influential in Scotland, but the traffic was more from north to south. Young Scots went to study with MacColl and Seeger in London, and political songs by Scots, especially Matt McGinn, featured in issues from small commercial London based recording companies and songbooks.

WALES

I am a London Welshman, I am a Cymro da
Like Gwyn and Iori Thomas and Dai Llewelyn are
I'm much more Welsh in London than I have ever been
I stand up for my country and for God Save the Queen
The Exile's Song, tune God Bless The Prince Of Wales, words Meic Stephens

For two nations with such similar political issues there is remarkably little social, cultural or song interaction between Wales and Scotland. Morris Blythman was very pleased to be able to include in the 'Second Ceilidh Songbook' two songs from Meic Stephens. 'The Boys From Gwent' exploded a bomb at the site of the new Bala Dam being built to supply water to the

English Midlands. 'The Exile's Song' criticised the 'London Welshman' who sentimentalised from afar. But these songs are lone exceptions.

AUSTRALIA

Australia was one of the major destinations for emigrating Scots, some not in accordance with their desire, as in broadside ballads about 'Hardie, Baird and Wilson' and 'Jamie Raeburn'.

One voluntary emigrant, Eric Bogle of Peebles who went in 1969, had run a folk club in his home town, and had sung and begun songwriting, but his talent bloomed in his new home. In 1971 he wrote a now famous song about the Anzac troops' attack on Gallipoli in 1916, 'The Band Played Waltzing Matilda'. In 1975 he wrote another tremendous anti-war song 'No Man's Land', now better known under the title used when it also became a hit record in Ireland sung by the Furies, 'The Green Fields of France'. This song tells of a World War One Scots soldier killed in Flanders.

Did they beat the drum slowly, did they play the fife lowly?
Did the rifles fire o'er you as they lowered you down?
Did the bugles play the Last Post and Chorus
Did the pipes play 'The Floors o the Forest'?
No Man's Land, Eric Bogle

Is Bogle a Scots political folk song writer? He is Scots, and a wonderful songmaker who shows his fierce political commitment in many of his lyrics, and performs to acoustic guitar accompaniment. A few of his lyrics relate to memories of Scottish issues, and strong identification with his anti-war songs is voiced not just by the left but also the right in Scotland. On the other hand, his melodies draw more on soft US country music than on Scots airs, and he is territorially claimed by Australia as an adopted native son – and also by Ireland because of the chart success there of his songs. Like Ewan MacColl, Bogle's work is not driven by the mainspring of Scots political song, but is considered by singers to be part of the Scots heritage.

In 1996 Scots singer-songwriter Alistair Hulitt returned from 25 years residence in Australia where he was active on behalf of Aboriginal rights, to express in his own songs and repertoire his commitment to political issues, including the Glasgow South Side Baths struggle.

France

Scotland has always been more aware of the ancient Auld Alliance with France than the French have been. I mentioned elsewhere links between the two nations through the tune 'Hey Tutti Taiti', and Robert Burns's initial support in songs for the French. Revolution. I also wrote earlier about Scottish right wing revulsion at the French Revolution, expressed in songs condemning the horrid concept of 'democracy', and supporting gallant local Volunteer soldiers.

ITALY

Avanto o popolo, alla riscossa
Bandiera rossa, bandiera rossa
Avanto o popolo, alla riscossa
Bandiera rossa trionfera.

Bandiera Rossa la trionfera
Eviva il socialismo a la liberta
Bandiera Rossa

The Scots folk song movement acquired a small Italian connection through Hamish Henderson's enthusiasm for the Italian partisan songs he had gathered on active service. There is still in Rome a successful Hamish Henderson Folk Club. A connection better known in Scotland arose through the adoption by singers of the Italian songs 'Bella Ciao'and 'Bandiera Rossa' (Advance, people, to the barricade, the scarlet banner will triumph). It is still a Scots favourite. In the late 1980s the SCND buskers were singing in Clydebank to welcome the marchers arriving in the annual commemoration of the 1941 Clydebank Blitz. The march was led in to the shopping complex by the Barrhead and Neilston Pipe Band playing 'Bandiera Rossa'. The pipers, who had never heard anything musically louder than themselves when playing, were visibly startled to hear the Buskers joining in, singing the lyric over the PA.

SPAIN

In the 1930s many Scots communists and socialists went to fight supporting the national government of Spain against General Franco's invading fascist armies. The author's mother's father, ex-soldier Hugh Reynolds of Plean, sought to go and fight with the International Brigades but was rejected as too old at 40.

The songbook 'Canciones de las Brigadas Internacionales', published in Barcelona in June 1938, holds some 120 songs (the multiplicity of translated versions makes it difficult to give an exact tally) in 16 languages. They include James Connolly's 'Rebelsong', 'Bandiera Rossa', and another that is still held in British singing repertoires, 'The Peat Bog Soldiers', a song from the German concentration camps. The songbook does not give 'Los Cuatro Generales', a sweet-tuned Spanish account of the four generals who "tried to betray us", which was sung in Glasgow folk club settings in the early 1960s, nor 'Viva la 15 Brigata', an Italian song of the Spanish fight from which Hamish Henderson took the tune and refrain line for his 'Rivonia'. The volume has many German and Italian songs and lyric translations, reminding us that Italians and Germans fought on both sides in Spain.

Songs of the Spanish Civil War

There's a valley in Spain called Jarama
That's a place that we all know so well
For 'tis there that we wasted our manhood
And most of our old age as well

Jarama, tune Red River Valley, words Alex McDade

☙

He's gane frae the shipyard that stands on the Clyde
His hammer is silent ,his tools laid aside
To the wide Ebro River young Foyers has gane
To fecht by the side o the people of Spain

In the fecht for Belchite he was aye to the fore
He focht at Gandesa till he couldna fecht more
He lay owre his machine-gun wi a bullet in his brain
And young Jamie Foyers in battle was slain

Jamie Foyers, tune traditional, words Ewan MacColl

It does not hold the best known Scottish song of the Spanish Civil War, "*There's a valley in Spain called Jarama*", made by Glasgow Brigader Alex McDade to the tune of a then current cowboy ballad. The other song of that War very popular in Scotland is about a Glasgow ship worker killed fighting in Spain, written in the 1930s by Ewan MacColl, using the tune and first verse of the Peninsular War Scots song 'Jamie Foyers'.

RUSSIA

Earlier I gave Josh McRae's account of 'Ding Dong Dollar' songs, in Samuel Marshak's translations, being published in Russia.
The influence of the Communist Party in the 1950s development of the Revival was strong, but only one Russian political song, in praise of the Russian Air Force and included in 'Canciones de las Brigadas Internacionales', was sung in Scottish folk settings in the 1960s.

Higher and higher and higher
Our emblem the Soviet star
And every propeller is roaring
Defending the U S S R
Red Air Fleet

AFRICA

In Scotland the opposition to the African-American Slave Trade involved both 'left and right wing' songmakers. There were in effect still slaves in Scotland till 1799, coal miners and salters, and there were various court cases seeking to free black slaves brought to Scotland as servants.
Robert Burns' 'The Slave's Lament' is currently much sung and recorded, and adduced as evidence of Burns' compassion on the issue. Dr Gerard Carruthers, a lecturer in Scottish literature at the University of Glasgow, questions this, considering that the class-conscious bard was

It was in sweet Senegal
That my foes did me enthral
For the lands of Virginia, -ginia, O!
Torn from that lovely shore,
And must never see it more,
And alas! I am weary, weary, O!
The Slave's Lament, Robert Burns

strangely silent on slavery at a time when abolition was a big issue. Carruthers claims this points to a lack of concern.

Carruthers writes, "Even supposedly right-wing contemporary Scottish poets wrote more against slavery. For instance, the Glasgow poet William Campbell, who was against the French Revolution, published poems in Glasgow newspapers passionately protesting against the crimes against humanity that Britons were committing on a daily basis both in their own country and overseas against black people. Burns only writes one mediocre song, 'The Slave's Lament', which has very little to say about the plight of the slaves."

But white man's joys are not like mine
Dho' he look smart and gay
He great, he proud, he haughty, fine
While I my bonja play
He sleep all day, he wake all night
He full of care, his heart no light
He great deal want, he little get
He sorry, so he fret
Bonja Song, Robert Dallas

Scots Anti Jacobins also wrote ambivalent slavery songs. In the 1820 'Union Song Book' is Anti Jacobin novelist Robert Dallas's 'Bonja Song', in which the happy Jamaican slave has none of the white man's cares, but can sing all day and sleep all night, and play his bonja [banjo].

When the South African freedom movement began to gather strength, Scottish songs in support appeared, most notably Hamish Henderson's 1964 'Rivonia', calling for the release of African National Congress officials sentenced at the Rivonia Trial, with its refrain 'Free Mandela'. A recording of the song sung by the Corrie Folk Trio was sent to Mandela in his Robben Island Prison, and was later translated into and performed in at least one African language.

Geordie McIntyre sings Hamish's version of the song. "Mandela was a statesman, his political stance re forgiveness. Singing it in USA, it goes down extremely well with general audiences. So does 'Peat

They have sentenced the men of Rivonia
Rumbala rumbala rumba la
The comrades of Mandela
Rumbala rumbala rumba la
He is buried alive on an island
Free Mandela, free Mandela
He is buried alive on an island
Free Mandela, free Mandela
Rivonia, Tune Viva la 15 Brigata, words Hamish Henderson

Bog Soldiers', it's about hope against adversity. And look at all the people on the planet today who have hopeless lives. There are exceptional songs that transcend their period."

It has been suggested that the line "*And a black boy frae yont Nyanga dings the fell gallows o the burghers doon*" in Henderson's 1960 'Freedom Come-All-Ye' is about Mandela. Certainly there were political riots in Cape Town's Nyanga in 1960 at the same time as the more famous Sharpeville riots, but Mandela's home area is hundreds of miles away on the other side of South Africa from Cape Town, where maps record no place named Nyanga, he worked in Johannesburg, and in 1960 he was not permitted to travel in his own country.

The Nyanga student could just as well have come to Scotland from Nyanga in Zimbabawe. At a time when Henderson was unwell I visited him, and I asked about the Nyanga reference. He could not recall any specific person or event that had occasioned it. Morris Blythman had years before told me an eloquent story of a Glasgow demonstration where the protesters were stood beside a piece of the old gallows of the city, commenting on the injustices associated with it but still respecting its age. One of the group, a black African university student, challenged this attitude, and leapt up and tore the wood down. A good story but I've been unable to substantiate it or even find a reference to such a structure remaining in Glasgow.

Later when in internal South African violence people were killed by burning tyres around their necks in 'necklace killings' several songs were penned by outraged Scots. In 1983 Glasgow was the first city to make Nelson Mandela a freeman.

Glasgow's Royal Exchange Square, home of the Glasgow Stock market, had been renamed by the city fathers Nelson Mandela Square. On the night in 1990 that Mandela was released from prison, the bus services had to be rerouted - Mandela Square was full of people celebrating in song and dance in the darkness. Glasgow women's Eurydice Choir sang 'Nkosi Sikelele Africa' then, and again on the George Square platform in October 1993 when Mandela came to a public meeting in Glasgow's George Square to thank the city, and in heavy rain, during the music that followed his speech, he danced on the stage.

Ian Davison's song 'Mandela Danced in the Square' speaks of this moment and the crowd's response. I asked Davison if the song, telling of a moment of community pleasure, could be called political in nature? "Absolutely. So many political songs are dire - sad, or banal. My Mandela song became very important. There are many people who think [wrongly] that they were arrested at the Holy Loch, and there are many people who think they were at George Square. It's an imaginative trap for people. Mandela dancing on a British public stage happened there for the first time, he later did it elsewhere also. He knew what he was doing, he was hitting the off beat. My memory was that it was spontaneous, he was pulled into it, grabbed in by the South African pop singer there, she was married to a Scots engineer and sang to a backing tape."

We'd sung about him for years, and there were speeches every where
But I'll never forget the cheers when Mandela danced in the square

When Nelson came to Glasgow after all his pain
Ten thousand people met him and listened in the rain
The big umbrellas folded, many heads were bare
But every face was shining when Mandela danced in the Square

When Nelson talked of duty you could feel us hold our breath
We were just a bit uneasy when Mandela talked of death
And when he talked of trouble there was tension in the air
But we faced the future smiling when Mandela danced in the Square
Mandela Danced, Ian Davison

Swing to the SNP

All together - swing to the SNP
All together - swing to the SNP
Make up your minds and make up for those wasted years
Swing to the SNP

The times they are changing - swing to the SNP

Watch your sons and daughters - swing to the SNP

Labour is out-dated - swing to the SNP
The Tories antiquated - swing to the SNP
Make up your minds and make up for those wasted years
Swing to the SNP

Swing To The SNP, tune I Shall Not Be Moved, words Glasgow Song Guild

In the late 1960s political songmaker skills were harnessed by Morris Blythman in support of the developing success of the Scottish National Party, and for issues of republicanism, employment and land reform. The role of Hamish Henderson as exemplar, encourager and superlative songmaker came to the fore.

We'll cut a trench along the border
We'll cut a trench along the border
We'll cut a channel from the Solway to the Tweed
And sail away from England wi the SNP.

We'll keek in every corner, roon the North Sea tae the Clyde,
For naebody will stowaway when we sail wi the tide,
We'll make sure the Duke O Edinburgh's on the other side!
When Scotland sails away!

The Scottish Naval Patrol, tune John Brown's Body, words Jim McLean

In 'The Nationalist Movement in Scotland' Jack Brand considers that "the rise of the folk song movement" was much more important in the growth of nationalism than the teaching of history. Although the way the songs "provided a set of Scottish symbols which could be manipulated by Nationalists in order to attract the young voters" was not the major reason for "the support which the SNP has had from young people ...the folk song movement gave them a direction in which to press their efforts". Brand argues that the singing of folk songs helped develop "a general belief about the condition of Scotland, and, after this, that folk songs were used as a weapon" to organise support. "Many of the young people who went to folk clubs also supported CND. The songs sung at the Holy Loch therefore gained a wide currency and with them the more specifically nationalist ones... It is not surprising then, that when the Nationalist wave started to roll they should use folk song, ceilidhs and singalongs as a method of attracting young people."

O Swing now, O Swing now,
Swing to the SNP,
Time now to change your vote –
Swing to the SNP

There's changes here in Hamilton, Swing to the SNP

We've got the big boys on the run, Swing to the SNP

O Swing Now, tune Pay Me My Money Down, words Glasgow Song Guild

Brand goes on to detail a couple of the campaign songs developed by Morris Blythman and his crew. In his notes he acknowledges that his whole chapter is "based on the article 'Rebel Songs of Scotland' in Chapbook, vol 4 no 6." In that article, which I quote from liberally earlier and later in this book, Blythman writes, "Our obvious decision was to back [the SNP] up as the movement most likely to bring Scottish independence. They had become the popular movement in the same way as the CND had been the popular movement some years before.

"So we started writing, and we decided the thing to do, to fit in with the ideas of the Scottish people, was to press home the concept of electoral victory. We felt they would go for this." One 'deplorable' handicap for the songmakers was that the SNP held no demos, and only one march a year, to Bannockburn.

"Then came the [1967] Pollok by-election. Alastair McDonald, Susan Haworth, Ian Wade, Jimmy Ross and myself started work on a pattern of material aimed purely at election campaigning. The interesting thing about these songs is that they were not fully fashioned songs in the main. They were really slogan songs which we had developed from previous campaigns – ramming across points and playing to crowds over loud-speakers." *Morris Blythman*

I'm fed up wi votin Labour
And so is big Jock ma neighbour
"Jesus freeze us, Jimmy," Jock he says tae me
"What the Hell dae they think they're daein' wi' ma economy?"
I canna hae a Friday on the skite, noo,
Or nip in for a hauf afore ma tea,
So I think I'll gie ma vote tae Geordie Leslie
An shift tae the SNP."
(Shift wi' Jock now)
I'm Fed Up Wi Votin Labour, tune The Means Test Man, words Glasgow Song Guild

ɞ

I'm going to change my vote and swing to the Nationalists
Change my vote - swing to the Nationalists
Change my vote - swing to the Nationalists
Swing to the SNP

I'm feeling sore, I'm going to change my vote
Like the man next door, I'm going to change my vote
Like thousands more, I'm going to change my vote
I'm Going To Change My Vote, tune Rock My Soul, words Glasgow Song Guild

Blythman had for the 1964 West Lothian General Election written a forerunner of the approach, his 'Billy Wolfe'll Win' song.

Blythman wrote, "We tried these songs at Pollok and they proved a central point in the campaign. We tried them again at Hamilton – and they made a major contribution to the victory. They were morale-boosters for the workers. They got over certain ideas where straight political propaganda would have failed. And we found that when there were radio and television interviews people were actually quoting the words of the songs." *Morris Blythman*

The Hamilton by-election came later in 1967, contested by Winnie Ewing, who noted "Our tapes played in cars stationed all over the constituency." Billy Wolfe recalled, "I think we were first to broadcast music from cars. In the West Perth and Kinross by-election [1963, Alec D Hume was the Tory candidate] we had a huge megaphone on top of the Land Rover. You could hear it a mile away. We had a wind-up gramophone that played 78s, we just played Jimmie Shand and similar things. There is a long straight bit of road going up from Gleneagles, and we blasted this at the countryside. There was two men diggin in the ditch at the side of the road, and they louped oot o the ditch and did a dance, birled each other in front of us in the middle of the road. I became convinced you just need to play Jimmie Shand. It doesn't appeal to everybody, but to the majority of Scots. We went into songs after that." *Billy Wolfe*

On the 'Tartan Express' train chartered to take Ewing to London on the night of 16/11/1967, were "fiddlers, pipers, accordionists, tin-whistlers and of course singers." At Euston she was "lifted shoulder high by Angus McGillveray and Hugh MacDonald." Both men were central in the SNP song movement.

Blythman acknowledged that "we don't use Scottish tunes as often as we would like. For slogan songs you need swing tunes and most of the best swing tunes for our purposes are American. We are not exploiting the tunes. We admire many of them and would never use them callously." His comments apply equally to the 1960s and 1980s Scottish CND songs. The lyrics at times attack the actions of powerful Americans, but the tunes and musical idioms used show the deep knowledge and love of American traditional music that permeates the Scottish Folk Revival.

Marion Blythman says, "He started writing songs for Winnie, and then for Billy Wolfe and Margo MacDonald (Govan 1973). These songs were made for the elections. And Morris used to say that you had to ball these songs into slogans, so that when you sang them, it was like a missile."

Blythman himself wrote, "A friend of mine worked it out when he was talking about the various forms of folk-song. He described these songs as 'contrived banality'. No-one was given the chance to miss what we were saying. We hammered it over, clearly and carefully chosen, and kept emphasising it until they began to repeat it. It got through - operating below the threshold of consciousness. Subliminal, if you like, but it was openly subliminal. We thought along the lines of the Marxist term agit-prop - agit being agitation and prop being propaganda. Agitation is the immediate action and propaganda the long-term." Blythman explained the 'Swing' songs quoted above were all 'agit', while 'Shout!' and 'The Map' quoted below were 'prop'.

Marion Blythman recalls, "Winnie Ewing was a lawyer whose husband was an accountant. She stood for Hamilton, but they had this big flat at Queen's Park. She had a think tank on a Sunday night, and Morris used to spend a good bit of Sunday afternoon having a sleep, because he knew he was going to be up all night."

Winnie Ewing's nationalism is steeped in Scots song. She wrote in her autobiography that she became a nationalist at the age of nine, on a trip 'doon the watter' to Kilchattan Bay in Bute, when she heard a band play 'The Road to the Isles'. "In school, during our music lessons, we heard and sang many Scottish songs which told the story of our past in a way which stays with you for the rest of your life."

When she was a lawyer, dinners in the Inns of Court were followed by ceilidhs. "I of course could not resist the singing

Shout to the man in Number 10 – Independence!
Scotland will be free again – Independence!

River Tweed is a great divide – Independence!
Take your stand on the Scottish side - Independence!
Shout!, tune Michael Row The Boat Ashore, words Glasgow Song Guild

ᏣᏰ

O ye cannae push aul' Scotland aff the map,
Naw ye cannae push aul' Scotland aff the map'
Though ye freeze us and ye squeeze us, in the end ye'll hae tae leave us
Cause ye cannae push aul' Scotland aff the map

Noo the Labour party are the boys in power
An' they're peyin' the M.P.'s ninety bob an hour
Oor share o' their enjoyment is double unemployment
So ye see they're just anither Tory shower
The Map, tune Ye Cannae Shove Yer Grannie, words Glasgow Song Guild

and soon became much in demand, particularly when introducing the English to the pleasures of Jacobite songs!"
At the Glasgow Bar Association dinner dance after Ewing's 1967 victory, "Jim Murphy (an SNP candidate in the same chambers) wrote songs which were sung in close harmony. They included one called 'In Good Queen Winnie's Golden Days' and another to the tune of an IRA song, 'Off to Dublin in the Green',"

My name is Winnie Ewing
And I live in slavery
But I know what needs doing
So I joined the SNP
So I'm off to London in the morn in the morn
For I'm Scotland's new MP
And I'm off to heckle Willie Ross
Till he joins the SNP

Brand says that by 1970 and 1974 the workshopped songs had "become part of every SNP campaign at national or local level." The singing of traditional Scots songs and newly made ones that fitted into the traditional mould became part of the SNP identity. In 2008 Glasgow SNP councillor Alison Thewliss said "political song is a way of bringing people together. It's quite strange, I imagine it happens in other political organisations. In the SNP, at the end of the night everyone comes together and spontaneously bursts into song. Nobody has a control over it, it sort of happens. That's a good thing. There are songs that belong to a movement, belong to an organisation. It's part of each party or organisation's politics. It brings people together." In 2009 former SNP leader Billy Wolfe said, "We sang the songs, they were our songs. There was a marvellous period in the party, in the 1970s, for about three years, you could go several places and be sure to have a ceilidh. Hugh MacDonald lived in Busby, a Gaelic speaking Highlander from Maryhill, there was a ceilidh in his house all the time. He could sing for twenty four hours and no repeat himself. His favourite song is 'Stirling Brig', which I think should be our national anthem.

"One of Winnie Ewing's favourite songs was an Irish one, 'The Three Flowers', about Wolfe Tone and two others. Winnie Ewing had a competition in Europe with an Irishman who considered himself to be a real expert in Scottish and Irish songs - and Winnie won. Her father was a singer, she learned all her songs from him." *Billy Wolfe*

When Ewing herself had lost Hamilton and was back working in the courts, another new song about her was sung at the Glasgow Bar Association cabaret.

Yesterday, life was like a television play
Now I'm cooking spuds and mince all day
Why they voted so I don't know, they wouldn't say
I did nothing wrong but my salary's gone away

At the end of his 1968 article Blythman lays out his principles of political songmaking for campaigns. Song-writers should pay attention to people's conditions and immediate needs, read the political situation closely, know when to push a topic and when to ease up on it. However, artistic and traditional considerations are paramount.

"Never let the political aspects take precedence over artistic considerations. Most of all they need an understanding of the tradition. The Scottish literary tradition is quite clear. You speak out for the people all the time. It is a people's tradition, a radical tradition. Whoever or whatever happens to coincide with the people's tradition, be it CND, Sky-High Joe, the people who took the Stone of Destiny; you back them up and you don't split hairs." He emphasises that his aim is always a Scottish Workers Republic. The first thing is to establish Scottish independence and you can argue afterwards". *Morris Blythman.*

As well as party political songmaking and remaking, political songs on social issues were appearing. Chapbook vol 5 no 1 featured 20 'Songs for '68'. As with vol 4 no 2, nearly all the makers were active writers or Revival singers. The politically committed songs include a soldier's account of the 'bloody affair' of Aden, one blaming the ''perfervidum ingenium' of the English and one castigating Harold Wilson personally, another on Goverment finance mismanagement, a lyric about a 'born overtimer' who is '*fechtin for the shorter week to get mair overtime*', a song on racial prejudice, songs on war and injustice from Ewan MacColl and from Peggy Seeger, and an anti-Lizzie complaint on the naming of the liner Queen Elizabeth. Also included was a page of three hard-hitting song lyrics written to support the campaign for revolutionary Daniel Cohn-Bendit to be Rector of Glasgow University. The songs are given as 'Anonymous', but Morris Blythman told me that Jimmy Ross and he were main contributors, and that one chorus was self-censored as too explicitly challenging.

Upper Clyde Shipbuilders Songs

I've heard it's been said, there's trouble for Ted
If ever he steers oot o' the channel,
If he tries the Clyde, we'll boot his backside
And make Edward sign on the Panel.
Noo Nero was fiddlin' when Rome went on fire,
But Edward's been fiddlin wi rowlocks and wires.
Let's finish his trick wi' two well placed kicks
And stop all his fun up the channel.

Head Teeth, tune Messing About On The River, words Jim McLean

Monday morning early by the clock
The Clydeside men were working on the dock
When the gaffer comes round, he says "Bad news,
"The Upper Clyde is bound to close"

So pack your tools and go. Pack your tools and go
For the word's been said, the yards are dead,
The big old gates are closing,
So pack your tools and go

Pack Your Tools, tune Drill Ye Tarriers, words Jimmie MacGregor

Chase the Senate and the Court, chase them down to Dover
Chase the Senate and the Court, wee Dannie's takin over

had been

Chase the Senate and the Court, chase them holus-bolus
Chase the Senate and the Court, and chase the Glasgow polis

The following 'Chapbook' was the final one, Vol 5 No 2. In that final edition Andy Hunter made criticism of some other songmakers. "Patriotism need not be an inhibiting factor in your life, especially if you succeed in eradicating racial (anti—English) prejudice from your outloook. This is the great tragedy of many of the recent Nationalist folk-songs which frankly drag a long way behind the new and praiseworthy objective of the S.N.P." He mentioned no names. Who did he have in mind?

In the same year of 1968 Jim McLean showed rebel outright bloody-minded defiance. He gathered 25 of his trenchant and uncompromising songs into 'Scottish Rebel Songs'. His introduction note says, "He is a dedicated Republican and fighter for Scottish Independence," details international experiences, and ends, "To dismiss him therefore as a 'narrow nationalist' is witless". His songs are fiercely and inventively anti-Royalist, anti-Polaris, anti-privilege, anti-Unionist politician, pro-republican and pro-Scottish. His humour is trenchant verging on

Jim Mclean song lyrics

Remember what Marx said to you and me,
'No one who rules another can be free!'
So while the English crown
Keeps another nation down,
Every Englishman's denied democracy.
Workers of the World

Ꞵ

We stood with heads bowed in prayer
While factors laid our cottages bare,
The flames fired the clear mountain air
And many were dead in the morning.

Where was our proud Highland mettle?
Our men once so famed in battle
Now stand cowed, huddled like cattle,
And soon to be shipped o'er the ocean.
Smile In Your Sleep

Ꞵ

While Scotland is bound to Elizabeth's crown
We're held down by the blue-shirts and green,
Let's put all our hate on the Sasunnach State
And forget the old Orange and Green.

Forget the old Orange and Green
Forget the old Orange and Green
The Queen's Union Jack's been too long on our backs
Let's forget the old Orange and Green.
Forget the Old Orange and the Green

black. McLean wrote and organised the recording and release of several themed albums of his own and traditional Scots songs, first with singer Alastair McDonald, then later Nigel Denver. McLean in his own song book and themed recordings does not make use of the simple 'agit-prop' songs he had had a hand in.

"In 1972 I wrote 'Head Teeth' for an LP called 'Unity Creates Strength', an Upper Clyde Shipbuilders album. Danny Kyle approached me and asked if we could make an LP celebrating the shipyard work-in at the Clyde yards. I had a meeting with Jimmie Airlie and Jimmie Reid in Glasgow. Danny and I gathered a few singers including Dominic Behan, Alex Campbell, Iain Campbell (from Glasgow), the Laggan, and I produced the LP in London. We all gave our services free and I delivered 1,000 LPs to the yards at a total cost of £500, which paid for studio time, sleeves and the cost of pressing the LPs. They were sold by the workers at a higher rate and helped to fund the work-in." *Jim McLean*

Into the 1970s there were twin developments of the emergence of more singer songwriters under the influence of Bob Dylan, and a performance style that emphasised comic material and monologue over song, so that the fare in folk clubs and concerts moved from communal singing towards solo performance and a more passive audience. The 1960s wave of political songs suddenly faded from the repertoires of professional singers, though political songs were still sung on protest platforms, on marches and on recordings.

Political songs in one theatrical show had powerful strength. Billy Wolfe recalls that in 1972 the 7.84 play 'The Cheviot the Stag and the Black Black Oil' was performed in Edinburgh. "It had a tremendous effect on the audience. I said to author John MacGrath, 'That was my total political message.' We asked him to put it on at the SNP Conference. The Corran Hall was packed, the players became involved in an emotional way. John MacGrath spoke to the audience and said, 'I think I should tell you that none of us are nationalists.' He was wrong. Within a year half of the players had joined the SNP."

Dolina MacLennan was one of the cast. "At the SNP Conference Liz MacLennan came out of character, angry because there was a standing ovation, and both she and her husband John MacGrath were totally against nationalism. We all made the songs in the 'Cheviot and Stag' together. I was the only singer there, so I introduced the tunes, e.g. I Will Go, for coming back from the war and no land left for the soldiers. Marie Mhor's song '*Remember you're a people and fight for your rights'* – nobody had ever heard of it till I introduced it. Only one song did not use a tune suggested by me, but a Gilbert and Sullivan tune."

Rob Gibson recalls, "I saw the first performances, it was inspiring. In Oban the SNP 'petit bourgeois' lapped it up, which was educational for 7.84. In Alness the play got a hostile raw reception, people there were working for the oil industry. If there had been no 'Cheviot', then there would have been no 'Black Watch'. The ceilidh play changed the form of theatre in Scotland." *Rob Gibson*

Also in 1972 came Morris Blythman's next work, co-edited with T S Law, the booklet 'Homage to John Maclean'. Blythman had been instrumental in the 1967 forming of the John Maclean Society, and became Convenor of the Research and Publications Committee, then Society Chairman. Most of the works in the booklet are poems, a few are songs. Ronnie Clark instances one of them, 'Dominie, Dominie' by Matt McGinn, to illustrate how we could scale songs "on a 'folk idiom' spectrum, a spectrum that needs to be quite broad, if not re-defined, when it comes to political works as opposed to the everyday songs in the 'folk idiom'. [Hamish Henderson's] 'The John Maclean March' ticks all the boxes. In Matt's 'Dominie' the language is OK, the veracity of the events is not, the tune is like something from a '50s cowboy series." *Ronnie Clark*

Jim McLean develops a related point. "Political song is not just a matter of expressing what *you* feel. When I was writing, I did it trying to convince other people, whatever the politics I had in mind and I thought were important. I wrote these songs basically as propaganda, you can call it that. That's what political song means to me, basically it's propaganda."You can write about someone, maybe John Maclean, but to me that was very obliquely political. A lot of people just wrote about what he did, his life story. You could do that about anyone. My point would be, "This is what this man's done, and you should emulate Maclean". In my song 'The Man in Peterhead' I said, "He's there for you", so emulate him, not just write a wee life story, pastiching about him, follow that man's life." *Jim Maclean*

Comrade John Maclean's the man we want to top the poll!
A fighter born and bred, he's in the fight with heart and soul.
So if you meet a man who seems to hesitate or doubt,
And don't know who to vote for, just go up to him and shout:

John Maclean – he's come out of Jail again –
John Maclean – the Tyrant's enemy!
If you want to end the Workers' grief and pain,
Make him Mr John Maclean, M.P.
Mr John Maclean M.P., tune Private Michael Cassidy V.C., "author unknown, an election ballad of 1918, originally published as a broadsheet."

In 1973 another collection of '118 modern and traditional folksongs', 'The Scottish Folksinger', was edited by Norman Buchan and Peter Hall.
It was intended as 'a handbook for singers' in the Revival.
The sections on 'The Warld's Ill-Divided' and 'Come, Lay Your Disputes' contain several songs quoted in this book.
For author, playwright and cultural projects organiser Donald Smith, "It wasn't until the 70s that that really began to connect for me, and it was a heads-up scene – the language, the culture and the politics all working together, and these things actually happening, here and now. And that was, of course, the beginning of political activism. You know, we were fighting, then moving towards the devolution debate and campaigns, moving into the '79 referendum.
"So you were activated from then on in, it was battle, either political or cultural, after the '79 defeat. It was almost like that shoved more emphasis on to the cultural side. In a sense, the song, the theatre, the story, were all feeding off each other.The song would be part of the public utterance. This is Hamish again, and this is the extraordinary thing, that somebody like Hamish Henderson, he's a senior academic, he stands up to give a speech or a pronouncement about something –

cultural, political – and he's quite a declaimer, you know, and – he'll sing. In the middle of it he'll sing and that was "not culturally appropriate."

"At the same period, you've got James Hunter and 'The Making Of The Crofting Community' and looking at the whole history of land use in the Highlands. When you go back to the land struggles, the 19th Century Napier Commission and the various campaigns for land rights in the Highlands, that directly picks up on the Gaelic tradition of using song made for a specific purpose, to announce, to lament, to denounce, whatever. It seems to me that that was an important bit of the jigsaw as well, but maybe we'd rather lost touch with that as the 20th century went on.

"In the Gaelic tradition, the song was part of the

Hamish Henderson song lyrics

Ye can talk aboot your Moray loons,
Sae handsome and sae braw;
The Royal Scottish Fusiliers,
A scruffy lot and a'
The Cameronians frae the South,
They sure are mighty fine,
But in the Battle of Anzio
'Twas the Banffies held the line.

Ballad Of The Banffies

☙

O horo the Gillie More
Whit's the ploy ye're on sae early?
Braw news, sae tell it rarely
O horo the Gillie More
News o' him, yon muckle callant
Whistlin' at the smiddy door.
Tak yer bow, for here's your ballant
O horo the Gillie More

Song of the Gillie More

☙

Quo life, the warld is mine.
The floo'ers and trees, they're a' my ain.
I am the day, and the sunshine
Quo life, the warld is mine.

Quo daith, the warld is mine.
Your lugs are deef, your een are blin
Your floo'ers maun dwine in my bitter win'
Quo daith, the warld is mine.

Quo daith, the warld is mine.
I hae dug a grave, I hae dug it deep,
For war an' the pest will gar ye sleep.
Quo daith, the warld is mine.

Quo life, the warld is mine.
An open grave is a furrow syne.
Ye'll no keep my seed frae fa'in' in.
Quo life, the warld is mine.

The Flyting o' Life and Daith

public utterance, it wasn't a private "I'm moodily reflecting on my state of being, in this lyric". It was a powerful public utterance that sat alongside speech, story, ritual, event. So that was maybe an underlying energy in Scottish culture, never lost, that speech and song would go together in whatever public thing was happening." *Donald Smith*

In Edinburgh Hamish Henderson was continuing to collect and write songs and to influence performers from his base at the bar in Sandy Bell's pub, Foresthill Road.

Singer John Greig says, "If you were interested in folk music you would at some time find Sandy Bell's, and you would run into Hamish Henderson. Hamish would just be sitting at the corner of the bar delivering lectures to anyone who was prepared either to drink or to listen. He was an academic and he talked like an academic, that's the way he worked. From the things he said to me, especially round about the late 60s, when I spoke to him most, he wasn't very keen on the folk scene at all – at least if he over-drank, he wasn't.

"He was obviously very enthusiastic about anyone doing anything – that's part of his persona, his nature, he wasn't putting people down, in that sense, but I don't think he thought [the folk Revival] was going the right direction. I don't think he was overwhelmed by what was going on. He had one or two people he particularly disliked, but I don't think he particularly liked a lot of things that were going on. I don't think he saw it going quite where he had envisaged it. And that was the attitude he took to a lot of things – he was an intellectual whose interests took in poetry, literature, politics and who knows what else. He used to feed me songs that he thought I should sing – "You've got the right sort of voice for this" – that sort of attitude. And up to a point I thought that was OK, but I didn't like that attitude either – he was always trying to not bully, but corral people into where he wanted them to be! " *John Greig*

John Barrow gives an example of Henderson's approach. "The Edinburgh Folk Club Songwriting competition arose from a conversation with Hamish. He said if you get a lyric, set a tune to it. It is not written anywhere that 'this is where the tradition ended', so use tunes. Or if you found a tune, write a lyric. Or like MacColl, take a tune and bend it. I went away and said to the guys, we should have a folk song writing competition. Hamish was a great proselytiser, wanted to expand. Lesser mortals felt there were songs, and we sang them that way."

Nancy Nicolson found in the Edinburgh Folk Club in George Square the impetus to begin to sing solo and to write songs. "There was brotherliness, friendliness, mutual support in the Folk Club for everybody. The feeling of togetherness, and also the fact that a large number of the songs were what we would call protest songs. We didna feel we were just there to look at how clever or how pretty our voices were, we had a bit of purpose in it. Then John Barrow started the Club's Songwriting Competition, and told us all to go home and write a song. I wrote a little song, and was utterly delighted to come second to Sheila Douglas. A whole squad of us then started to write towards the song competition. I remember in particular Andy Mitchell from Ullapool, and Dennis Alexander from Fife. We greeted each other as a threesome of sisters and brothers at each annual get-together." *Nancy Nicolson*

Nancy Nicolson song lyrics

Cuddle, cuddle, cuddle against the war
Use your arms for cuddling, that's what arms are for
Escalation could be bliss
Start off with a cuddle, end up with a kiss

Cuddle a Russian, peasant or Czar
And he may show you his samovar
They say the Russians answer "Niet!"
I've never had that answer yet
Cuddle

ᴓ

Listen tae the teacher, dinna say dinna
Listen tae the teacher, dinna say hoose
Listen tae the teacher, ye canna say munna
Listen tae the teacher, ye munna say moose

He's five year auld, he's aff tae school
Fairmer's bairn wi a pencil an a rule
His teacher scoffs when he says "hoose"
"The word is 'house' you silly little goose"
Listen Tae The Teacher

Nancy Nicolson's song 'Cuddle Against The War' makes a positive statement about what the individual can do. She took the central idea from a badge she was given at a peace gathering. The tiny badge had two stick people reaching out to each other. The legend said "Arms are for cuddling with". Her 'Once There Was A Lion, Once There Was A Bear' makes a wry statement about being 'piggy in the middle' between two fierce warring animals, and her 'Ah'm I Man At MUFed It' jams a tickling stick into the ribs of the embarrassed staff at Dounreay Nuclear Power Station in her native Caithness, and in her native dialect suggests what may have happened to the nuclear MUF [material unaccounted for], and how local people were turning it to useful purposes.

John Greig tells in detail about the Edinburgh folk pub, Sandy Bell's. "You start to socialise with all these people because you're in Sandy Bell's, and the list is endless of people you meet. Some were people coming up from England, not so overtly political, more historical with their politics. They were singing about the blackleg miners when they'd never met a miner. But that gave you an impetus, it was all happening and somehow in Edinburgh you seemed to catch everybody. I've seen concerts with Tom Paxton and Matt McGinn. What was that like? Pretty strange, but good.

"You couldn't avoid it unless you were in the mind to avoid it, which you weren't – you got the whole thing. There's nothing like that whole movement today. I don't mean that people today aren't good at what they do, but they make records which in some ways is the death of politics in the folk club. I'm very ambiguous about the whole notion of writing it down or setting it down – I realise it has to be done – but it's a double-edged sword in many ways. It kills a lot of things off or it kills people's willingness to act, to be part of it.

"Hamish Henderson didn't exactly steer clear of it, but for him all this was probably old hat, he'd been through a lot of that stuff and he didn't seem to have a lot to do with it. He spent a lot of time having minor battles with people in the literati

We used to be a nation but we're not right now
We seem to be short of a lot right now
We used to have a parliament, we used to have a government
Take a look at what we've got right now
We Used To Be A Nation, tune I Used To Be A Hippy, words Ewan McVicar

scene that turned up at these things. I thought, just keep out of corners, otherwise somebody's going to get stabbed and I hope it's not me! But quite often it was me in a weird way. Hamish would say to sing a particular song and I'd stupidly do it and realise he was only wanting to really annoy someone else. You got to know what Hamish was up to – if not you'd soon find out because this person would be coming towards you with a sword in their hand more or less, ready to stab you and you're going "It wisnae me, it wis the Big Guy over there!" That never worked. I was astonished by what would cause fights." *John Greig*

Nicolson and Greig sang and occasionally were paid for performing, but got their primary income elsewhere. So did the songwriters who made and contributed new songs for a fundraising cassette of 'Songs for a Scottish Parliament' in 1979 – John McCreadie, Sheila Douglas, Jim Brown and the author.

A small group of Scottish folk singers had the performance and presentation skills and commitment to become professional touring musicians. They sometimes collaborated with others, or engaged in theatrical or musical productions. Those who featured political and social comment songs prominently were Matt McGinn, Hamish Imlach, Iain Mackintosh and most prominently Dick Gaughan.

Gaughan became identified as a political singer. One key song he wrote is 'Do you Think that the Russians Want War?' 'Both Sides the Tweed' is a James Hogg lyric to which Gaughan made a few crucial lyric alterations, turning it from an anti-Jacobite song to an aspirational appeal for peace and harmony, and then creating a beautiful new tune to carry the words. The above singers, and the McCalmans group and others, increasingly found their work touring the Continent.

Other singers who had learned their trade in the Scottish folk scene left to become well-known in other music and drama genres – Barbara Dickson and Rab Noakes of Fife, Billy Connolly and John Martyn of Glasgow. Although neither Connolly nor Martyn were tagged with political songmaking, both made over the years a few songs with marked political content, for example each made a poignant anti-war song. Connolly wrote 'Sergeant Where's Mine?', and Martyn made

'Don't You Go My Son'. Archie Fisher has remained one of the best-known Scottish Folk Revival singers, and has written several songs of social comment.

Watch your daughter's children play, thirty years ago today
Echoes of your last young summer never seemed so far away
Smiling at the gathering storm, in your khaki uniform
As you marched along the High Street, did you listen to your heart beat?

Did you find what you were looking for
In the somewhere over there?
Was the answer found on the battleground?
Was the question really fair?
First Of The Few, tune and words Archie Fisher

Work And No Work Songs

They'll tip you on the shoulder, an speir gin ye're to fee
They'll tell ye a fine story that's every word a lee
They'll tell ye a fine story, an get ye to perform
But lads, when ye are under them, ye'll stand the raging storm

He promised me the ae best pair I ever set my e'en upon
When I gaed hame to Barnyards there was naething there but skin and bone

The fairmer o yon muckle toon he is baith hard and sair
And the cauldest day that ever blaws, his servants get their share

Like many o my calling, I soon began to find
That Benton's study ever was his servants for to grind
Cuttin being over, and leading weel begun
The Banton thocht he would get me awa frae him to run

But Martinmas it has won on, my fee's into my pouch
And sae merrily merrily I will sing, 'I'm oot o' the tyrant's clutch'

Ah'll maybe see old Adam there, a suppin at his brose
Ah'll gie him a len o ma handkerchief tae dicht his snottery nose

Verses from various Bothy Ballads

Most songs about aspects of work are descriptive or anecdotal, but some address and comment on conditions and issues in ways that involve or touch on protest or social comment. When the oldest settled activities of farming and weaving change from being self-employment to employment and at times exploitation of others, song lyrics report and reflect. As industry develops the mills and mines songs develop, strikes and industrial action are supported by song, and unemployment and poverty are condemned in verse.

Elsewhere in this book you will find assertions that all songs are in some sense political. Some singers go less far, but feel that songs to do with the 'the common man's' working conditions are all political in essence. This chapter takes a narrower view, that political songs of work and no work are those that do not just describe or complain about work and workers, but that protest about working conditions, criticise employers, or urge change.

FARMING

Many of the bothy ballads that tell of life on 19th Century farms in the North-East complain about work conditions or the character of the farmer, but the planned solution is not in joint action but in the release at term time to seek work on another farm. Or if a new place of employment proved unsatisfactory, the worker could 'run away' and seek work at a Rascal Fair held a few weeks after the term time. Are these protesting ballads political? Singers like Jimmy Hutcheson and Geordie Murison say yes.

"Bothy ballads had quite a political slant to them, because they were quite anti, they were protesting in their own way about the conditions on the farms at the time. The hard conditions then." *Jimmy Hutcheson*

"Ah consciously learned aa these bothy ballads, which ye ken on reflection is just full a political statement - and of course aa the songs, they aa look intae this cry oot for help, or there was some statement bein made aboot the conditions an 'at." *Geordie Murison*

Ian A Olson disagrees. "The idea that the bothy ballads are a significant form of socio-economic protest ... is a fairly modern one, unsupported by contemporary evidence." Olsen says the idea is "arrived at by a combination of simple assertion and a highly selective quotation of verses", as shown above.

However, since modern singers consider the relevant bothy ballads to be political, and introduce and sing them as such, then if they were not political in their original setting, they become political when sung

in some modern settings – as with the songs of warfare referred to in Chapter 4.
In the Lowlands two broadsheet ballads were also general in their criticism and praise.

Our farmers now they are aa growing braw
And getting quite fat on the Corn Law
Among them a tradesman can scarce make his bread
I am told it is so by the Laird o Loanhead

You bonny lasses brisk and gay, that comes to Falkirk on the feeing day
I hope you'll join with me this day to sing the praise of ploughmen
The very Queen that wears the crown, and brethren of the sacred gown
And dukes and lords of high renown, all live by the gallant ploughmen
We have in Scotland Lords and Thanes, with powdered heads and glancing canes
That think themselves nae sheep shank banes, yet they all live by the ploughman

'Twa Recruitin Sergeants' is a Scots bothy version of a song about a recruiting party seeking to entice a farm worker off to war. It is discussed by Rab Noakes later in this book. Later bothy ballads were made to be sung in the emerging music halls, and moved towards broad humour rather than complaint.

WEAVERS AND WEAVING

The hand-loom weavers and the early spinners worked at home and were self-employed. They were at times exploited by the middlemen who bought their finished work, and in Paisley by the 'corks' who sold the weavers machine-made thread then bought back the completed cloth, and their livelihood was at times threatened by foreign imports, but songs about these issues are few. Instead we get a broadside that sings 'In Praise of the Gallant Weavers', and another that praises the weavers who behaved riotously at a wedding in Elgin. In Tom Leonard's 'Radical Renfrew' he helpfully categorises the works of weaver poets he has selected. Though most of the pieces he classifies as 'Employment', 'Unemployment' and 'Trade Unions and Co-operation' are strongly political, each one was made as poetic verse, not as song.

We're a' met thegither here tae sit an' tae crack
Wi' oor glesses in oor hands, an' oor wark upon oor back
For there's no a trade amang them a' can either mend or mak
Gin it wasna for the wark o' the weavers.

If it wasna for the weavers, what wad they do?
They wadna hae claith made oot o' oor woo',
They wadna hae a coat neither black nor blue
Gin it wasna for the wark o' the weavers

There's smiths an' there's wrights an there's mason chiels an a'
There's doctors an' there's meenisters an' them that live by law
An' oor freens that bide oot ower the sea in Sooth America
An' they a' need the wark o' the weavers
The Wark O The Weavers, David Shaw

Ɑ

Oh all you Trades and Callings
To offend you I am loath
But if the Weavers be not fine
From whence comes the fine Cloath?
Wat is't that makes us gallant?
Comes not from that Ingine
Who works the Silks and Satins
Strips, Stuffs and Cloath so fine
Proper New Ballad In Praise Of The Gallant Weavers, broadside

Glasgow weaver poet Sandy Rodger's songs are challenging enough to explain why he was locked up in Glasgow in the Government panic of 1820 that followed the Radical War, and how his bellowing out his verses tormented his jailers. He wrote widely and richly on political topics, but not on weaving.

In Chapter 19 I tell of the modern use and mining of Forfar weaver David Shaw's early 19th Century song 'The Wark o the Weavers'. The song begins *"We're aa met thegither here, tae sit an tae crack"*. Shaw's humorous song is in praise of his fellow handloom weavers. Shaw also talks of other trades, including 'hireman chiels', and drops in an internationalism reference to *"our friends in Sooth America"*, who were at the time with Bolivar freeing themselves from the yoke of Spain. Shaw also points out how our own soldiers and sailors *"couldna fecht for cauld"* without cloth, and begins and ends with a celebration of the joys of social consumption of alcohol.

We do not find complaints in song either about the often horrific factory conditions in the cotton mills after the hand-loom was smashed by machinery, though songs from cotton spinners' strikes resulting from complaints about work conditions and payment are given below.

Dundee jute mill worker and "leader of a left-wing militant group" Mary Brooksbank was also a fine song and poem maker of the first half of the 20th Century, and her songs of mill life survived to become popular in the Revival. Her best known song, 'Oh Dear Me', was a development of a verse that she first heard in 1912, "They used tae sing it in the street and up and down the Passes between the frames in the mills".

Oh dear me, the mill's gaen fast
The puir wee shifters canna get a rest
Shiftin bobbins coorse and fine
Wha the hell wad work for ten and nine?

In the Revival, noted singer Sheena Wellington made a new song lauding the work and determination of the 'Wimmin o Dundee'.

COAL MINING

Coal mining is rich in songs. Up until 1799 the colliers, and the salters, were in effect slaves. Not only the workers, but their families, were thirled to their place. So in the love song 'Collier Laddie' the girl

who prefers a collier lad over a noble suitor is choosing not just 'the wee cot hoose', but slavery for her children.
Later, in a broadside 'The Truck Masters' of Gartsherrie and Summerlee in Lanarkshire are castigated for their system of truck shops, where colliers had no option but to buy goods on credit from the master at such a cost and rate of interest that they were in effect still tied by unpayable debt to the pit.

As for some of our masters they are great men
And one of them a ruler of our native land
I wonder what's the reason he does not stop
The infamous system of a truck shop

The reason is obvious and plain to be seen
The profits are great altho' they are mean
They rob the poor man in every stage
And they very soon make him a small enough wage

In another broadside, 'The Pitman's Union', a miner steps up apologetically to a pretty maid a-milking.

Your pardon is granted, young collier, she replies
But do you belong to the brave union boys?

He equivocates, but he is a pitman "*as black as any sloe*" as her father was, so she "*put her arms around him like violets round the vine*".
As with the bothy ballads, old mining songs that have no political content are in Revival performance labelled as political. Pit disaster songs tell of loss, but not of blame. 'The Blantyre Explosion' is a lament for the dead. In 'The Donibristle Moss Moran Disaster' of 1901 some error was made, "*someone put in a stopping*", but who?
Humour is deployed as a weapon in miner poet and dramatist Joe Corrie's song 'It's Fine to Keep in Wi the Gaffer', in his play 'Hogmanay'.

For mony a year I hae wrocht doon alow
But never in bits that are wet or are low
For I mak it my business wherever I go
Aye tae keep in wi the gaffer

When the singer has a foreman who is a Mason, he 'beards the goat in its den', when he works under a musician he learns to play cornet, for a Salvationer he carries the lamp, but when his gaffer bets on the horses, the singer ends with 'my shirt in the pawn'.

As the Revival was beginning, in 1959 at Auchengeich Colliery near Glasgow 47 miners were killed in an underground fire. Norman Buchan wrote 'The Auchengeich Disaster', to the tune of the song that had so pleased him in 1951, 'Skippin Barfit Throu the Heather', and was delighted when within a few years the new song appeared on a recording labelled 'trad', given the accolade of acceptance into tradition.

The author's mother was from the mining village Plean near Stirling, and my maternal grandfather, Hugh Reynolds, told me first-hand about a 1921 disaster in one of Thorniecroft's Plean pits. I researched more information in the local newspaper, learned whom an investigation had found to blame for the deaths, and took my information to the primary school where my mother and her siblings had studied, and had been attended by the dead miners. I worked with a Primary 6 class in Plean Primary school, and together we wrote a song, 'My Collier Sweetheart', using the first verse of one old song and the tune of another old ballad.

My mother said I could not have a collier, if I did it would break her heart
I didn't care what my mother told me, I had a collier for my sweetheart

But one day up Cadger's Loan, the siren screamed at Pit Four head
All of Plean ran to find out, "How many living, how many dead?"

Down in the dark of the Carbrook Dook the young shot-firer fired his shot
Dynamite blew up the section, twelve lads dead, seventy caught

Their holiday bags were lying waiting, the men were lying down below
The wee canaries they died too, salty tears in the sad Red Rows

The young shot-firer had no certificate, my young collier lost his life
Fate was cruel to my sweetheart and I will never be a wife

STRIKING AND UNION ACTION

Strike songs are preeminently used for direct action, and often are more chant or roughly worked couplet than song. Their use is to taunt or chastise bosses or strike-breakers, to assert solidarity and sometimes to explain themselves to passersby or the reporting media. Other than in media reports the lyrics seldom survive. A rare exception was discovered by Professor Christopher Whatley in court papers relating to an 1824 strike of Glasgow cotton spinners where violence had included a strike-breaker being shot. Strike-breakers were called Nobs, and the girl workers on strike gathered around the works gate where they "shouted and hurrad and sang what they called the 'Nobs Song'". Whatley gives us lyrics for only two of the five or six Nobs Songs the strikers are reported to have known. One begins

We are the braw chiels that belongs to the wheel
That earns their bread by the spinning o't

And continues in criticism of the mill owners

I think they would tak both the quick & the dead
And howk up a Corpse for the Skinning o't
Their houses are Shinny their children are braw
Their tables are costly, their privies warst of a

But when they go on they will soon get a fa
And wha will they be the beginning o't

The other song refers to the shooting, saying "*Wasn't he a fool to come out and be shot?*" Both songs are set to old Scots tunes. Roy Palmer reports that in 1837 there was another strike of Glasgow cotton spinners, and passes on the remark of historian Dorothy Thompson that the very influential Cotton Spinners case "really led straight into Chartism." A blackleg was shot, union officials were arrested and sentenced to transportation for seven years, their crime was "being leaders of an association engaged in illegal activities (mainly picketing)". Palmer prints a broadside ballad about them, 'The Cotton Spinners' Farewell', which says that

Our trial they postponed for time after time
Indictment on indictment, and crime upon crime
Which turned out all a humbug, for this was their claw
To prevent combination in Caledonia

The accused were sent by ship from Glasgow's Broomielaw to the hulks at Woolwich, and pardoned in 1840. In 1903 Robert Ford wrote that prior to the 1850s Crimean War the children of Glasgow sang in the streets, to the Jacobite tune 'Wha Wouldna Fecht For Chairlie',

Wha saw the Cotton-spinners?
Wha saw them gaun awa?
Wha saw the Cotton-spinners
Sailing frae the Broomielaw

A 19th Century Dundee broadside song, 'It's No' the Clean Tattie Ava', has two verses about a railway strike, then moves on to criticise young laddies who marry before they've enough income, to praise the "*wee chapper laddies*" who work for only "*three hanies a week*", and then cheers the success of the local football team, who won "*the Coonty Cup*" last year and should "*scope it this year*".

Noo the great railway strike that did happen, I'm sure it upset ane an aa
An ye may think it's fun what the blacklegs have done, they're no the clean tattie ava

Noo, bad luck tae aa head men o' railways, an may they sune get a doon fa
For to work day and night, it's far far frae right, it's no the clean tattie ava

Unusually, the composer of this song is shown. "Written composed and sung with success by William Gordon, Dundee." This suggests he was a music hall artiste performing between 1880 and1900.
The Dundee mill lassies knew how to keep their emotional energy high on the picket line. A newspaper photograph from 100 years ago shows shawled Dundee jute strikers playing 'Jingo-ring' as they dance 'The Merry Matanzie'. That same spirit, and the combination of bouncy old tunes and simple determined lyrics, also typified the mass Holy Loch peace protests of the 1960s.
Mary Brooksbank, poetess of the Dundee mills, in the early 20th Century created her own version of an older strike song, to a tune by George F Root that began life as an American Civil War marching song, 'Tramp, Tramp, Tramp'. It was applied to the US hymn 'Jesus loves the little children' but also used in many political campaigns to advocate that hearers 'Vote vote vote for [insert candidate's name here]'.

We are out for higher wages
As we have a right to do
And we'll never be content till we get our ten per cent
For we have a right tae live as well as you

Nigel Gatherer (1985) comments, "It is easy to imagine Mary Brooksbank leading the singing of this song during a strike", and suggests she must have based her rhyme on an older song, since a song about a Dock strike in London in the 1880s has the chorus:

Strike boys, strike for better wages
Strike boys, strike for better pay
Go on fighting at the docks, stick it out like fighting cocks
Go on fighting 'til the bosses they give way

Another strike song, from the 1926 Miners' Strike, tells of the arrest of the author's grandfather and other Union officials for peaceful picketing in the village of Plean where he was Union Branch Secretary. He was sentenced to six months hard labour, and blacklisted from the mines. The tune is 'The Wearing of the Green'.

Oh the model village Plean, oh the model village Plean
They're going to build a prison wall round the model village Plean

You go into the court, and you stand before the Dean
And the Prosecuting Council says, "It's Reynolds frae the Plean"

Fife Playwright Joe Corrie's 'In Time O' Strife' play of 1926 begins with a song borrowed from America, with the tune 'John Brown's Body'.

We'll hang every blackleg to the sour apple tree
As we go marching on

Glasgow shipyard union official Josh Shaw wrote songs and sang them in meetings and on the picket line in the 1950s and 60s. His 'The Lockout Song' says

The shipbuilding bosses are hon'rable men
They sign their agreements wi' gold-plated pen

But for all that they're worth sure, it's only a farce
You might as well use them for lighting the gas

To the tune 'Caroline' he wrote, "*Nothing could be finer than to form a picket lina in the morning.*"

The 1971 Upper Clyde Shipbuilders sit-in was strongly supported by West of Scotland singers and songmakers at concerts and demos. Matt McGinn wrote two songs, so did Jim McLean, who then recorded and issued an album of UCS songs [see p177-8].

In the Political Song Archive at Glasgow Caledonian University is a typed song lyric headed "Dedicated to the Lee Jeans Girls, to be sung to the tune of 'Joe Hill'". The 1981 Lee Jeans factory women workers occupied their factory to save their jobs. There are no clues on the song's provenance. Here are verses one and five. In the latter the writer says there will be support from other trade unionists.

I dreamt I saw a girl last night, astanding by my bed
She said 'I want to keep the right to earn my daily bread'

You'll have workers from the pit, the workers from the yards
They're on the side of girls of grit, who will not take their cards

In 1985 Edinburgh school teacher Nancy Nicolson wrote one of the rare anti-agents-of-the-law songs, a sombre protest about the use of police horses to charge coal miners on strike, 'Maggie's Pit Ponies'.

Here come the cavalry, here come the troops
Here come Maggie's Pit Ponies
Watch for the batons and watch for the boots
And watch your back, Miner Johnnie

Nicolson's bus to work passed the road-end where there were pickets for Bilston Glen [coalmine].

"It was just heartrending seeing these guys standing there. Then, at a teachers' meeting in Edinburgh we were watching a piece of newsreel, of horses running into and through a picket line. My friend said, 'Those bloody horses'. I said 'The horses are just doing what they were trained to do.' And I looked at the boys on their backs, doing what they were trained to do. I told my husband Denness, and he said, 'Aye, some bloody pit ponies'. The song just grew itself.

"I sang it at a concert, an this fine lookin man in a suit came marchin towards me, I thought 'I've done it, this is the day I'm gonnae get bopped in the face'. He says, 'That song', I says 'What song?' 'The miners song, where'd ye get it?' I put my chin up ready to be hit and said, 'I wrote it'. He took me by the lapels to be even closer, and he says, 'On the button, hen! On the button!' He was Jackie Aitchison, one of the miners' leaders." *Nancy Nicolson*

Nancy sang her song at an 1985 'Writers For Miners' fund-raising event organized by Jim Kelman in Glasgow's Third Eye Centre. The list of performers is a roll call of politically committed artists. Poets reading their work included Liz Lochhead, Edwin Morgan, Freddie Anderson, Aonghas MacNeacail, Hamish Henderson and Tom Leonard. Peter Nardini sang his furious 'Now That Hitler's Back In Style', Danny Kyle sang a protest blues called 'If You're Black Get Back', other singers and musicians were Dave Anderson of Wildcat Theatre, Alan Tall, Jim Daily and the writer of this book, Gerda Stephenson. And Rab Noakes, who sang the World War One song 'When This Bloody War Is Over'.

Small squibs made to be sung in trade union settings only accidentally get into print. There have surely been many such songs, undocumented, over the years. Nancy Nicolson sang the author "a very political song that you won't have heard, because I just used to sing it among teachers in E.I.S. thingies [Educational Institute of Scotland union meetings] about the heidie [head teacher]. "There's lots of splendid heidies now, but there's still a few of this ilk."

Ah'll butter ma breid on baith sides, eat ma cake and have it
Ah'm the heidie, Ah'm the boss, Ah run the E.I.S.
Ye needna work, ye needna strike, buy a Rover no a bike
Transfer the staff ye dinnae like, join the Heidie Tong

UNEMPLOYMENT

Why have you no songs, Poets,
For the men who march through the towns?
Demanding bread for their children,
And rags for their naked bones.
Why have you no songs, Poets,
For the right against the wrong?
For the slave against the tyrant,
To make him proud and strong?
The gift you have, oh, Poets,
Is the greatest given to man,
But while the poor march songless,
You spend your lives in vain.

Joe Corrie's poem of the 1930s 'Hunger Marchers' pointed out the need for song to support the marchers as they trudged along, and to explain who they were and why they marched. Though Corrie says they had no songs, when in 1933 a national march came to Edinburgh, and camped in Parliament Square, "from parts of the encampment came snatches of song." Probably popular and national song, but equally probably small squibs of topical parody. The march was reported in 'The March: the story of the historic Scottish hunger march', written by Comrade Harry McShane and published in 1933 by The National Unemployed Workers Movement.

The police kept the surprised Edinburgh citizens from 'loitering' to talk with the marchers, and Princes Street Gardens were kept closed from them when on the second night they camped along Princes Street.But the marchers had won a tactical morale victory on the first day that sustained spirits, with a spontaneous act of song-led mass trespass on Royal ground that was reported only in the Communist Party's 'Daily Worker', although the other aspects of the marchers' activity in Edinburgh were reported in the Press.

The marchers' road to a mass meeting at the Edinburgh Meadows lay down the Royal Mile, "leading to the historic Royal palace of Holyrood. Down go the swinging columns, down right to the gates of Holyrood. 'Turn to the right', says a police official. The March leaders turn a deaf ear. 'Straight on!' 'Straight on!' it is, right through the Palace grounds itself. The pompous official in charge at the Palace almost took an apoplectic fit! His eyes literally bulged out with mixed astonishment and horror.
"In go the columns, a mile of flaming, flaunting scarlet banners, headed by the Maryhill [Flute] Band playing Connolly's 'Rebel Song' as if their lungs would burst. What a sight! The proletariat, the indomitable proletariat in their ragged clothes, have stepped into the most sacred precincts in all Scotland!" Co-leader of the 1916 Dublin Easter Rising, Edinburgh born James Connolly's 'Rebelsong' was followed by "the thunderous battle cry of the world's workers, 'The Internationale'." The age of the two songs played and sung makes the point that the march had no key song of its own to sing.
Wry selfmocking parodies like the following clever Dundee song of unemployment and 'signing on' at the Bureau, to the flighty tune of 'Bye Bye Blackbird', would have worked well when sung on a march or picket line, but its detailed lyric and lack of chorus make it a soloist's song, not one the marchers could have joined in with.

We're the boys fae the tap o the hill, we never worked, we never will
We're on the Bureau
Just like the lads fae Peddie Street, mention work – we tak tae oor feet
We're on the Bureau
We went doon ae Thursday for oor money
The cash clerk said, "Noo lads, youse think you're funny
You're oot o here ye see, for noo ye're on the UAB"
Bureau, bye bye

Many noble aspirational ballads or sarcastic squib songs were surely sung from platforms at demos, or annually on Mayday on Glasgow

Green or at the Miners' Gala on the Edinburgh Meadows. Before the Folk Revival was there a lack of songs that all could join the chorus of on the marches and at demos to encapsulate whatever point they were making? If there were such songs other than 'The Red Flag' and 'The Internationale', I have not located them.

POVERTY AND HARD TIMES

And still must he labour mid hardship and care
At delving, at ploughing, or spinning o't
Wi belly aft pinched, and wi back nearly bare
For comfort, there's now a sad thinning o't
His substance is seized on for taxes or rent
The priest comes and tythes him, then preaches content
Wi sickness and sorrow his frame's sairly bent
Pale want on his face shows the grinning o't
The Spinning O't, tune The Rock And The Wee Pickle Tow, words Sandy Rodger

Speak no ae word about reform, nor petition Parliament
A wiser scheme I'll now propose, I'm sure ye'll gie consent
Send up a chiel or twa like me as sample o the flock
Whase hallow cheeks will be sure proof o a hinging toom meal pock
And sing, Oh waes me

Tell them ye're wearied o the chain that hauds the state thegither
For Scotland wishes just to tak gude nicht wi ane anither
We canna thole, we canna bide, this hard unwieldy yoke
For wark and want but ill agree wi a hinging toom meal pock
And sing, Oh waes me
The Toom Meal Pock, John Robertson, from 'Radical Renfrew'

The poorly paid 19th Century broadside ballad scribblers waxed very eloquent on the hardships and evils of poverty. 'Remember the poor' begins "*Cold winter has come with its cold frosty breath, And the leaves fall fast from the tree"*. 'The pauper and the minister' is satirically cheerier – "*I'm living on the parish now, as happy as a king, From morn to night I've nought to do but whistle dance and sing.*" In 'Scotland's Stagnation' is "*The oldest person in the world, on land or on the water, Never saw such times before since Sampson killed his daughter*".

The Hungry Thirties produced a music hall comment on a pantomime villain, the 'Means Test Man' who assessed an unemployed worker's right to claim financial benefit.

Ah'm no the factor or the gas man, Napoleon or Ronald Coleman
When you hear me rat tat tat upon your door, 'Have you money in the bank or money in the store?'
You better look out or else ah'll get ye, try and dodge me if you can
For ah'm neither Santa Claus or Doug-a-las Fairbanks, I am the Means Test Man

A newer song by actor Duncan Macrae based on the mawkish 'My Ain Folk', appears in the Second Rebels Ceilidh Song Book.

They'll never be forgotten, the days that we lived through
When we hung aboot the Gorbals an we sterved on the Buroo
Wi the lassies playin peever, an the laddies sclimmin dykes
An the weemin gaun thir duster an the polis gaun their bikes
Ma Ain Close, tune My Ain Folk, words Duncan Macrae

And the smallest of squibs, hardly a sparkler, can be preserved in family memory. The author's Auntie May often sang two lines from the popular song 'Ain't We Got Fun?' with one word changed.

There's nothing surer
The rich get rich and the poor get - children

Songs From All Directions

I'm dreaming of a Labour victory, just like the ones we used to know
When the votes were counted, and the press surmounted
And to the ministries we'd go
I'm dreaming of a Gannex raincoat, the one that Harold used to wear
When government appointments were a matter of convenience
And party members didn't care
I'm dreaming of a Labour victory, like 1964 again
May we all get back to Number Ten, and will someone shut up Tony Benn
Tune White Christmas

Bobby Moore collects another trophy, Jimmy Saville plays another song
Barbara Castle clashes with the unions, Jim Callaghan says Barbara's got it wrong
The white hot heat would conquer all our problems, Lord George Brown reveals his National Plan
Hillman Imps and high-rise council houses, Sergeant Pepper's Lonely Hearts Club Band

Those were the days my friend, we thought they'd never end
We'd rule the country in the Labour way
We'd do the things we'd choose, we'd fight and never lose
Cause we had power, oh yes, those were the days
Tune Those Were The Days
Lyrics from The Red Review 1983

In the 1970s the riptide of folk club action began to recede, and festivals, concerts and recording became more prominent. While political folk song grew gradually less visible in professional performer repertoires it became more prominent in 1980s and 1990s protest demos and campaign support concerts, and was documented on recordings and in publications. In 1999 one of Robert Burns' political songs had pride of place at the reopening after 200 years of the Scottish Parliament.

After the 1979 Scottish Parliament electoral victory that was deemed a defeat, support for the SNP waned for the time being, and less use of campaign songs was made. But there had been a 52% vote in favour of devolution. In 1980 Scottish Labour Party supporters took the political song fight to their enemy. Scotland had for many years been a Labour fiefdom; the SNP threatened that situation. 'The Red Review' 1983 songbook tells us that in 1980 the Review was formed by "a group of young Labour Party members based

A song lyric rewritten

At the turning of the century I was a boy of five
Me father went to fight the Boers and never came back alive
Me mother was left to bring us up, no charity she'd seek
So she washed and scrubbed and scraped along on seven and six a week

In '26 the General Strike found me out on the streets
Though I'd a wife and kids by then and their needs I had to meet
For a brave new world was coming and the brotherhood of man
But when the strike was over we were back where we began

The Old Man's Song, Ian Campbell

At the turning of the century when I was just a boy
And Lenin wrote his master plan he was the workers' choice
Before I learned to read and write I learned the line up well
And at the tender age of four I joined the YCL

In '26 it was revealed that Stalin was the man
He'd written Lenin's speeches and indeed the master plan
He'd won the revolution, now traitors he would purge
Show trials were the business, he was never one to fudge

From Red Review Songs 1985

in Glasgow University Labour Club and active in Constituency Labour Parties in the west of Scotland.

"They first performed at conferences, then to a wider audience including election campaigns... The Review writes all its own material," and the 34 songs in their book include recent songs and 'the best' of previous shows. The songs are a step further from traditional Scots or American idioms, the tunes used and songs parodied include four from the film 'White Christmas', and many others from current pop songs. They do not concentrate all their fire on the SNP, but spray buckshot at the new SDP 'Gang of Three', the Tories, and personalities within their own party.

Their 'Red Songs 1985' booklet is "the fourth edition since we started". This time they include under the term 'Something Old' ten staple political folk songs. Seven of these – four international favourites, two from Hamish Henderson, one from Eric Bogle - are considered elsewhere in this book, the exceptions are 'Rosa Luxemburg', 'Bread and Roses', and 'Blackleg Miner'. They also borrow without acknowledgement the tune, shape and many lines from the 'Old Man's Song', made by Birmingham based Scot Ian Campbell, for an all-out assault on an old comrade who has stuck to the Communist Party through the years.

Titles from Songs For Scottish National Liberation include
Freedom's Sword
Now, Free Scotland
No More British Soldiers
Scotland Is Waking
London Is Drowning
The Rebel Heart Of Scottish Resistance
You Are Not Conquered Yet, Scotland
By The Saltire
The Lands Of Liberty
Scotland Will Rise Again

Sometime in the 80s a shadowy radical pro-independence group produced a different booklet of old, new and reworked songs, 'Songs For Scottish National Liberation'. No date, publisher or editor is given inside, instead are the slogans, 'Victory to the Scottish Resistance. Forward to National Liberation', and an inspiring quotation from Scot James Connolly that includes "Until the movement is marked by the joyous defiant singing of its own songs it lacks one of the marks of a populist political movement; it is the dogma of a few and not the faith of a multitude." The songbook producers were surely linked to one of the small groups who carried large Saltire Flags on peace demos, supporting the cause of peace abroad while calling for violence at home.

The 35 songs are a mixter-maxter of the usual Burns suspects, songs made by Morris Blythman, Hamish Henderson and Jim McLean and a few crudely polemical ditties. I illustrate how one of Blythman's songs was reworked in this songbook in Chapter 19. The songbook was I assume linked to a couple of 1980s Glasgow folk song clubs where the author and other singers were invited as guest performers, and found that the resident club singers had a fund of obnoxiously unattractive ultra-nationalist songs.

At this same time fine Revival singers and performers like Davey Steele, Iain Mackintosh, Brian MacNeill and Ian Walker began to develop songwriting skills. Walker in particular created songs of such high quality and character that other singers seized on them.

Left wing politically committed Glasgow continued to identify itself with folk song, in that the only substantial Glasgow folk club to last from the 80s right to the present day in other premises, was the Star Club, which singer Arthur Johnstone of the Laggan group had started in the late '70s in the Communist Party's Carlton Place

Ian Walker lyrics

As I was walking down the road
I saw my brother with a heavy load
I said to him "What have you seen?"
He said to me "I have a dream
In 1960 I thought I'd died
In Sharpeville's bloody town
But I got up, I walked on tall
Nobody's gonna put me down"
Hawks And Eagle Fly Like Doves

Proud lancers, guides and grenadiers
Paraded for the grand show
All waiting with their flags and fears
Remember Solferino
Like tigers that have tasted blood
Hand to hand, no quarter
Savage maddened butchery
Remember Solferino

But one man was witness
Dunant was his name, he cried
"Never, never again"
For he heard the cries of the wounded
He turned his face to the sound
And high above his head
He raised a cross of red
He heard the cries of the wounded
Remember Solferino

home. Johnstone, a dedicated singer of politically committed songs, also became a fixture at the annual Mayday march to and celebrations on Glasgow Green. One Mayday Dick Gaughan and Billy Bragg duetted on that stage, singing 'The Red Flag' to the original 'White Cockade' tune.

As well as performance of songs it was becoming financially easier to create short-run cassettes of new songs. John Greig tells about his work in Edinburgh creating 'Songs From Under the Bed', a cassette recording label whose name arose because the cassettes featured newer political songs that had been made, but the makers did not know what to do with them since there were few places or demos at which to sing them, and no chapbook style publications in which to get them printed. So the lyric manuscripts were stored under the maker's bed. Greig felt they should be brought out into the light.

"Morris Blythman was again working on creating the Republic. I would be taken along, to sing 'Sky-High Joe' or 'Bonnie Wee Prince Chairlie'. They're quite funny, they work OK. I met people writing at miners' benefits, I was running a folk club and people were writing songs and singing them about what was going on, the fall of the Berlin Wall, necklacing in South Africa. Ukes Against Nukes and Nancy Nicolson were writing and performing songs.

"I began to build up the 'Songs Under the Bed' idea. Thatcherism was coming in, things were turning nasty. I got cheesed off with people's attitudes, some avoiding getting involved in miners' support gigs. I decided at some point to start collecting songs and recording them, then put a tape together. Artist Fred Crayk, originally from Inverness, did a drawing depicting a song from each tape as a cover design. I thought, I'll go for it, do it once, others will copy me and do it themselves. Quite the opposite, I became the shit the flies wanted to land on, people felt I should be doing it for them. So there were huge time gaps between each cassette. I didn't make money, and it cost a lot - £500 to get 100 cassettes together with all the technicalities involved. It costs so much less now. I felt pleased with what I was doing. The Folk Club was very satisfying, we had no policy, we let

anyone on. Morris had died before that, in 1981. I felt that gap, he was a great encouragement, he made things happen.
"'Songs From Under The Bed 1' had Ukes Against Nukes, Tony McManus (the singer and poet not the guitar player), Jim Ferguson, Nancy Nicolson, Eileen Penman and myself. I liked 'What Ever You Do Do Nothing' by The Nukes (the title says it all) and Tony's 'Song For The Miner',

You who would not applaud with them
All those upstanding women and men
The well intentioned, the full of grace
Were laughing like fools in my face

and of course all of Nancy's songs, particularly 'Maggie's Pit Ponies' which is a bit of a classic!
"I think Hamish Henderson took some notice of the first cassette. He'd come across it or I'd shown it to him and he'd sent it to a couple of people who managed to get reviews done of it. So I think when he saw the reviews, he thought "Oh aye, this could be quite good" because he'd never really recorded much of his stuff at all. It appealed to him at two levels I think. One was that it was quite small and wasn't going to get involved in big sales and the other was that he had total control over what was going on. I had just said "Do what you want to do." So that's the reason he did it. I think too the idea was to try and lend his name to the whole business. But mostly if the truth be known, it was Hamish seeing an opportunity to do it the way he wanted to do it and not have to deal with BBC producers or whoever who wanted him to go on about the War or something.
"So he went on the cassette, but this didn't work out too well in many ways. He kind of blew the face off it. People started looking at it as something other than it was. 'Songs From Under The Bed 2' had Eileen Penman, Hamish Henderson, Ray Ross, Lucy Johnstone, Allan Dickson, the Allan Johnston Band (aka Seddy) and Sheila Douglas. I think Hamish overshadowed most people on this one but that is only to be expected and no shame to the rest. I think he said this was the

first time he knowingly recorded 'Free Mandela'. I liked 'Glasclune and Drumlochie', a cautionary tale from Scottish history reflecting the madness of the arms race. It is a three verse poem that describes the same tale as Akira Kurosawo took three hours of cinema to tell and it ends with a chorus which is sung,

Then shame, black shame, ay, shame on the bluidy Blairs!
Shame on the Blairs, an sic wuddifu races .
They think nae sin when they pit the boot in
In the eyes of all ceevilised fouk tae disgrace us.

"It also seems quite a good description of Tony Blair's foreign policy. There was a dreadful review of it in 'Chapman' that compared Hamish Henderson to everybody else and everyone else was shite and Hamish Henderson was great. Ugh, slash my wrists, you know? I told Joy [editor Joy Hendry], 'Look, Joy, I can't ask people to do this if you publish things like that about them. These aren't people on the make, they're not looking for publicity, they're people who are trying to put out what they're doing. We're trying to encourage them, no cut their heids aff.'

"It made me think twice about the whole business. And then I decided to do another one because it made me so annoyed. 'I'll do one more anyway, just because I'm seek to death of that attitude.' And it happened. Fred, the artist from Inverness, he was keen on doing one, I was going to put some stuff of Freddie Anderson's on it, because he's indestructible in those sort of circumstances. And you [the author] were on that one. The point was to get people who would come back at anybody who wrote like that about them. And that's what I did.

"'Songs From Under The Bed 3' had Freddie Anderson, Steven Shellard, Ewan McVicar, John Milligan and Jim Ferguson. I liked your own 'Ga's Song' and Stephen Shellard's 'Dog Man', it is a bit like a latter day Tom Joad. John Milligan has to be congratulated for rhyming 'Evening News' with 'screws'. The bit I would like to quote is from Freddie Anderson's 'Blackberry Man'.

The children, while fearing God nor Man
Find the World on the rim of a blackberry can.

"All the cassettes are still sitting up in a drawer because by the time I'd done all that, I just didn't have it in me to go and sell them. As we've said before, we can do everything else about recording but selling them takes a different attitude. Maybe today they would sell, but I just put them away and went 'Right, get on wi your life in some other way.'

"Having said that about the whole thing, Hamish must have read that review. What he took out of it as far as I could see, not immediately, but pretty quickly after that, was to produce a whole tape of himself, through Tim Neat. It was a virtual copy of what I did with no reference at all to my work. I'm not asking for the world, but it was my idea to start off with.

"The problem you've always got is how to do these things without actually becoming a control freak, and looking for money out of it and saying it's got to be commercial, got to be this, got to be that. And the only way I canut of it.

"My view was, look in the other direction, never mind about the critics, look at how many people are doing it. Get all these people down. Because there was no record of it. Martin Carthy for example was going round saying there were no songs being

In March of 1984 the gauntlet was thrown down
When MacGregor told the NUM "These pits are closing down"
"Get on your bike, MacGregor", the miners' answer came
"We fought the Board in '74, and we'll fight you once again"
From South Wales across to Yorkshire, from Scotland down to Kent
The miners showed the NCB that what they said, they meant
Except the scabs who sold their future out to Thatcher and her gang
And turned traitor to their class, their names forever damned
The Ballad of 1984, Dick Gaughan

written about the Poll Tax campaign. Obviously there were no songs down there about it. And up here there were – we did them." *John Greig*

The fear of defying the law overcomes them
But others have broken the law years before them
Peasants, tenants, miners, suffragettes
They all said NO
Poll Tax Dodgers, tune The Black Bear, words Eileen Penman

And if you want to have a vote
You've got to hand over a bundle o notes
It's no use just bein born a Scot
A vote is something to be bought
Poll Tax Rap, words Stuart McHardy

In 1986 Dick Gaughan recorded an album for the STUC as "truly a labour of love", 'True and Bold, Songs of the Scottish Miners'. In fact four of the songs are from England, one is from the USA, and Ewan MacColl's 'Schooldays' End' ranges over Scotland, England and Wales. Two of the songs (Norman Buchan's 1959 'Auchengeich Disaster' and 'The Blantyre Explosion) are about Scottish pit disasters, and one ('Collier Laddie') is a love song that Robert Burns collected a version of. Gaughan himself rewrote an angry US miners' strike song, "Which Side Are You On?' and made the defiant 'The Ballad of 1984'. Gaughan is undoubtedly Scotland's best known interpreter of political song, as well as a superb performer and musician.

The Scottish peace movement had drifted into the doldrums for some years, until in the 1980s it was invigorated by fresh blood, in part sparked by the failure of the Labour government to stop the British Polaris project. In part through the 1982 establishment of the Faslane Peace Camp, and in part by outrage over the US bombing of Libya in 1986.

Scottish CND gathered new strength, supporting the Faslane Peace Camp and creating a need for up-to-date songs to support action in demos at Faslane.

Then SCND rather over-reached itself financially by organising lossmaking largescale events and was in financial trouble.

Doon in the shelter, underneath the stair,
Everybody's dirty; everybody's bare;
We huvnae got much culture; we huvnae got much hair;
Doon in the shelter, underneath the stair.
Tune Doon In The Wee Room, words John Gahagan and Ian Davison

ঙ

You've got to give your life,
For Maggie-the-Knife, the-Knife, the-Knife,
If she says 'Jump in the sea'.
She has to act tough, she has to fight rough,
And blow us all up, for Victory.
Tune Lily-the-Pink, words Ian Davison

ঙ

Underneath the table, hiding from the Bomb,
There I met a stranger, he said his name was Ron.
O, how he sang so sweet to me,
That he would see he kept us free.
My cowboy from the White House,
My cowboy from the West.
Tune Lili Marlene, words 'An English peacenik'

A fresh coalition of street-focussed songwriters had gathered together by now. Singer and songwriter Ian Davison was a SCND committee member and had already created a raft of new protest lyrics to old tunes. His cyclostyled 'Parodies For Peace' gathered in lyrics and choruses for 29 songs, of which only three had originated with the 'Eskimos'. Ian remembers that he and the author shared a seat in the back of a bus coming back from Faslane, and agreed on the need for a strong singing movement.

At a song-developing workshop organised by Ian in a tent in George Square, Glasgow, I shared a couple of verses of a lyric I had developed for a parody of 'The Hokey Cokey'.

It takes your left leg off, it takes your right leg off,
Your eyes fall out and the dust makes you cough.
You feel the radiation turn you inside out,
That's what the bomb's about - kick it out!

It knocks your house down, my house down,
The whole town down and fifty miles around.

Then you get the fever from the Old Fall Out!
That's what the bomb's about - kick it out!

A singer in the workshop, who I never saw again, and whose name I have forgotten, came up with a chorus hook of *'Oh, goin up in smokey'*, so the chorus became

Oh, goin up in smokey, oh, goin up in smokey,
Oh, goin up in smokey, that's what the bomb's about - kick it out!

Ian Davison was Secretary of SCND, and as one strand of the effort to improve the organisation's finances the Scottish CND Buskers were formed, a motley band of musicians and singer-songwriters - Harry Bickerstaff, Nancy Dangerfield, Ian Davison, the author, Pat and Joe Plunkett, and Carol Sweeney. They performed widely, and eventually recorded and sold a songbook and cassette, *Gies Peace*, with 20 songs, half of them written after *Parodies For Peace* had been put together. When a 'Blowup Songbook' version was published in 1989, it held 41 songs. The object was to raise money, and raise morale, "Plus you always hanker after converting or enthusing someone about ideas or about using music and song in this way. That's the third, secret, motive, about your own achievement." *Ian Davison*
Many of the songs performed by the Buskers were Davison's own product, but at least eight other songwriters were represented. One of them, Pat Plunkett, had herself been a resident of the Peace Camp. Others like Nancy Dangerfield were peace activists and supporters, none of them seeking personal glory as song writers. The songs continued the Eskimo theme of the absurdity

Hey, Mr Younger, come and get your banner,
CND is the one to be with.
Join the peace movement, it is a winner,
CND is the one to be with.
Tune The Banana Boat Song, words Pat Plunkett

O, the bogey man's coming, and he steals your pup.
He takes your teddy and he eats it up.
He drinks your blood in an iron cup,
But I kill him with the nuclear - weapons.
Tune The Tennessee Wig-Walk, words Ian Davison

of nuclear weaponry.
A few lyric songs yearned for peace, to original tunes.

We can reach our rocking rhythms into every city and street,
We can mix the mood of the music for a billion dancing feet.
We can save the dying children with our pictures from the sky,
We can make ourselves take action, and we only have to try.
Yes we are the human miracle, with our magic in the sky.
We can save ourselves, and save the world, and we only have to try.
Ian Davison

Time and time we told you so, time and time you answered 'No',
Peace will rain, sing it again, time for peace to rain.
Ewan McVicar

Other songs included 'We can't live in a Trident Submarine', 'Reagan's fine men are at it again in Grenada', 'If Maggie wants to die, fair enough', and 'Will ye go, Maggie, go?'
When the SCND Buskers formed in the 1980s, the 1961 lyric of 'Glasgow Eskimos' was too much of its time for the Buskers' needs, so the author updated it to consider our current foes.

That old cowpoke gave orders out - Gaddafi must be killed.
The generals and CIA were absolutely thrilled.
'Well get the Europeans to back up all our plans',
But Maggie was the only one to give the boys a hand.
Yippee-aye-ay, yippee-aye-oh
Old Reagan's raring to go.
Ghostbusters In Disguise, tune Ghost Riders in the Sky, words Pat Plunkett

ꕤ

Everybody's taking about
Thatcherism, Fascism, Goodism, Badism
Don't-you-wish-you-hadism
Just-a-passing-fadism, politics is madism
All we are saying is give peace a chance.
Give Peace a Chance, new words Ewan McVicar

We'll gaff that nyaff ca'd Lanin, we'll spear him where he blows
became
We're no husky Russkies, like Maggie might suppose
but I retained the central image of the peaceful purposeful Eskis, urging the passerby to
join the Eski movement, see some Eski sense.
Would that they had.

"The Buskers have performed on street corners, bandstands, opentop buses and concert platforms, combating the lunacy of the Bomb, and the absurd attitudes adopted by politicians. They believe that peace can be fun. Their songs are written to "work on the street", where a few lines must contain the message, and a well-known tune helps catch the ear.

"Some of the Buskers songs cannot be recorded because the tunes are copyright. Some were written in the 1960s for the Clydeside Anti-Polaris demos, and have been updated. Politicians come and go, but the Bomb keeps its grip on our collective throat."
From the 'Gies Peace' cassette insert, 1988

As with the Eskimos, the energy that had fuelled the Buskers dissipated once

Ukes Against Nukes lyrics

In 1945, with not many left alive, the Germans they did surrender
And down in a bunker with his brain in a canker, old Adolf ended his bender
And now forty years on from this European con we're asked to respect and remember
You can try to forget, but on one thing you can bet, this peace time so-called is slender
There's a Berlin Wall, and Chancellor Kohl, Ronnie Reagan and Margaret Thatcher
There's Cruise missiles, economic turnstiles, and a VE day to remember
V.E. Blues

☙

I'm a marine infantry officer, I've got a green beret
I don't need no university professor to tell me to shred it all away
I started a war up in Chile, put the slammas into their lammas day by day
They wrote the cheque on the back of my neck and it bounced in that funky Caribbean way
I'm a marine infantry officer, the man with the briefcase demands
That at the end of all my operations it's trains leaving downtown stations
I'm a marine infantry officer
The Ballad Of Colonel Oliver North

SCND's finances returned to a more even keel.
They could have carried on raking in the cash far longer, just by endlessly singing the line 'All we are saying is give peace a chance' on Glasgow's Argyle Street on a Saturday, but other actions and activities beckoned.
There is an East-West divide of Scottish political song – Glasgow's deliberately simplistic demotic communalism versus Edinburgh's poetic anarchic individual expressionism. This is neatly demonstrated by the two peace and political song groups that were formed in the 1980s, Glasgow's SCND Buskers and Edinburgh-based Ukes Against Nukes. The Buskers disbanded, but Ukes Against Nukes continues to issue communiques in the form of not-for-sale CDs and hand-corrected songbooks.
Their spasmodic performances are a riot of ukelele, kazoo, bodhran beaten with a wallpaper brush, and a welter of complex declaimed lyrics. The whole approach assaults expectations. The notes for their 2005 CD, titled 'Mmmmmmm. That Great Event, twenty years of uproar', tell us "First appearances during miner workers' strike of 1984-5 at benefits in Cumnock and Edinburgh, and at the Glenelg Hotel and Southsider *volkbars*.
"Later, at the all-Edinburgh-ukeleles-cabaret (Café Grafitti) and briefly, on the Royal Mile, opposite the access point for the secret service on the night of the Duke of Edinburgh's visit to the Tattoo.

Long distance information, won't you listen to my plea
I'm stuck between a hard place and a soft core in Dounrea
The foreman's left a message that he wrote upon the wall
"I've met my match and blown the thatch. Cheerio", that's all

Long distance information, what d'you think this message means?
Is it some nuclear poopy that's been left behind the scenes?
I need to have your answer quick, ma dentures goin yella
Ma semmit's mingin, the scones are singin and tomorrow is the gala
Tomorrow Is The Gala, tune Memphis Tennessee, words Ukes Against Nukes

(Cameron's Knitwear) Where are they now?
"Went on to demolish the 1990 Folk Festival at the Teviot Union downstairs (Sportsman's) bar during a recording for the School of Scottish Studies. Less impact (several attempts) on the main gates of the nuclear submarine base at Faslane on the Clyde. Good gigs at the Not The Burns Suppers, Anti-Nazi league and ANC benefits.
"But unfortunately torpedoed the Save The Whale rally in George Square, Glasgow. These days it's mostly street corners." *Ukes Against Nukes*
In their 2009 songbook accompanying the CD 'Blues My Decommission Gives to Me', they add "But the work goes on, gulfenised by this country's terrorist invasions of Afghanistan and Iraq. And, right now, by the ever increasing hazard and cock-ups associated with decommissioning the nuclear power plant at Dounreay. George Gunn is a poet and playwright and now Artistic Director of the Grey Coast Theatre Group in Thurso. Bob Macauley lives in Edinburgh and has worked in more mortuaries than most people have had hot dinners. They write the songs together on wine soaked memo pads. The tunes are filched from George Formby, the Scottish hymnary, pop, folk, 'trad' jazz, and skiffle. Digitised hooting, tooting, dub (and over-dub etc) takes place at the kitschen sink in Bob's Fountainbridge bunker." *Ukes Against Nukes*
The Ukes tune sources echo Morris Blythman's account of 'Ding Dong Dollar' references, and the melodies used and abused by the SCND Buskers. Their song titles tell of their topics. In 1984-90 the 'Boak On Ma Semmit' album included 'Ukelele Malvinas',

Oh see, say see, ought to be with Maggie, from the Falkland Isles

'If You Knew Cruisey'

Like I know Cruisey, In the words of Nietzsche, it's a wow

Blood, Soweto and Tears' which forecasts that

The blacks are going to light a flame under the Bruderbond
Burn all the Old Testaments in the Transkei'

and

Whatever you do, do nothing, living on the Welfare State.

The title 'Semmit' track complains about the unadventurous backwards-looking fare offered in folk clubs, and invokes

The ghost of Rabbie Burns with a big tambourine

demanding we sing about the present day.

On their next offering, from 1990-2000, is

Bones flesh and gristle is what you get from a friendly missile

and the tune 'The Sash' is grasped for

I searched through all the poetry books for a rhyme with East Kilbride.

Their most recent two CDs include 'We'll re-mortgage your nosebag',

O little town of Beslan, how deep we see the lie

and

We found your man down a spider hole, Praying to Allah for gun control.

Gunn and Macauley's periodic unleashing of flash flood thoughts expressed in manic musical formats began as many all around them were also beginning to write and perform their own songs, at first as occasional flourishes in parodic rhyme, but growing to a mighty tide of new songwriting and songwriters which by the 21st Century swirled and lapped around the venues that had formerly presented traditional music. The technical quality of the songmaking and performing increased just as the opportunities to present the new work faded away in number and variety. Folk clubs diminished, folk festivals multiplied then gradually the energy leached out of them too, as the age group audience who had fuelled the 1960s Revival grew older.

Some of the numerically much smaller intake of new performing blood sang only their own new songs, and if they had exceptional creative and performance skills became labelled singer-songwriters. They presented in concert and on disc their own work, drawing in various degrees on traditional song models and forms. Other professional or

Ah'm a friend of Maggie Thatcher
If ye don't believe me go and ask her
When she puts another million on the broo
I get the wire sayin "Over to you"
I get out ma calculator, to see how many I can ban
So you'd better be polite, or you'll no be treated right
For I am the Means Test Man
Tune Means Test Man, words Ewan McVicar

semi-professional performers presented programmes that mixed traditional songs and the work of other songmakers with their own compositions.

Rising standards of instrumental skills led to the formation of groups combining traditional and electronic instruments and featured singers and songs in the mix. These singers had the outlet and need for new songs on the succession of new albums – on LP, cassette, then CD – the groups needed to produce for income and promotion purposes.

The economic process of recording and pressing LPs required a minimum quantity of sales, typically 500 or 1000 copies, cassettes could be recorded and duplicated on the home recording machines that were becoming increasingly available and affordable, so a cassette release met production costs on a run of a dozen. When CDs replaced the older media, they were initially only issued by the record companies, but gradually the use of the PC, and the development of small recording studios and inexpensive duplication facilities have meant that songmakers and groups can create and distribute their own recordings, selling them at performances as a major part of their performing income.

As the skills of and opportunities for occasional or

Lyrics from 'Flames On The Water' album

Who pays the piper, who pays the piper
Who pays the piper, who calls the tune?
Who pays the piper, what is the fee?
Flames on the water, death on the sea

And the tune is old and has often told
How the great, brave and bold they do flourish
How bravely they gamble with other men's lives
And profit as other men perish

Who Pays The Piper, Nancy Nicolson

☙

Leave the fishing trade laddie, there's money to be made
The hand-line and the Shetland yawl are from a bygone age
Come to Aberdeen laddie, sights you've never seen
Be a welder on the pipeline or a fitter on Nigg Bay
But when the job is over and my boat rots on the shore
How will I feed my family when the companies move away?

Men O Worth, Archie Fisher

frequent songmakers increased, their compositions reflected their interests, knowledge, priorities and the influences and models they drew on.

Most makers included a few songs of social and political comment in their output and performances. Some who were strongly politically committed. Eric Bogle, Nancy Nicolson, Jim Brown, Davey Steele, Brian MacNeill, Iain Macintosh, became known for such songs. A few performers e.g. Dick Gaughan, Alistair Hulett, Ian Davison, featured political song so strongly they became identified with the genre.

The creation of new songs and their performance on stage and on CD was a continuing process, not so the explosive events that generated demos, marches and support events. As I have commented above, the 1984/5 Miners Strike generated oddly few new songs, and I know of none about the 1986 bombing of Libya by the USA. In 1991 John Greig supported the resistance to the Poll Tax with a cassette, 'Songs from Under the Poll Tax'. It included a blues and a 'Dodgers' song from Eileen Penman, a rap from Stuart McHardy and a

First Gulf War lyrics

Oh Mary love, oh Mary, the countdown has begun
And waves of planes have set us here, beneath the blazing sun
The Proud have lost their patience now, and set the slaughter date
And marked us down for death, my love, in the deserts of Kuwait

The arms investors, politicians, generals and the rest
They'll have the thrill, in armchairs, as we're put to the test
The Press will sell your bitter tears, as we come home in crates
As victims of the war, my love, from the deserts of Kuwait

The Deserts Of Kuwait, Ian Davison

Everybody knows about
Guernica, Hiroshima, Nagasaki, Clydebank
Coventry, Bikini, My Lai, Tienamin
All we are saying is Give Peace A Chance

Everybody knows about
Vietnam, Afghanistan, Cambodia, Algeria
Uganda, Nicaragua, Korea, Biafra
All we are saying is Give Peace A Chance

Give Peace A Chance, New words Ewan McVicar

tango from Aidan McCorry.

Nancy Nicolson responded to the 1988 Piper Alpha oil rig disaster in the North Sea with her song 'Who Pays The Piper'.

The McCalmans group drew on her lyric for the title of a 1990 album, 'Flames On The Water'. "The McCalmans surprised everyone with a completely contemporary album." *John Barrow*

Six of the songs are explicitly political in tone, topics including nuclear power, devolution, whaling, peace and war and the oil industry.

'Flames on the Water', on Ian Green's Greentrax record label, was a commercially released LP, but from a record label and a group deeply committed to supporting, celebrating and spreading the word about Scotland's traditional song and music.

Posters and fliers announced and detailed peace-seeking events that united poetry, song and speeches. A programme sheet for 'Vigil For Peace St Andrew's Night 1990' in Glasgow's George Square includes songs from Ian Davison, John McCreadie and the author alongside readings from Liz Lochhead, Tom Leonard, Cathy Galloway and Hindu and Muslim groups.

A 1991 printed flyer during the gallop up to the First Gulf War announced a Friday night vigil in George Square. "5-30pm – 6pm, War is not inevitable but time is running out. Come and show that you want a peaceful settlement in the GULF. Organised by the Ad-Hoc Committee for Peace in the Gulf." On several Fridays up to thirty people gathered and sang a mixture of Scots and American songs of peace together in a circle, holding a heavy rope to signify group identity and unity. 'Blowing in the Wind', 'Peace Will Come', 'If I Had A

From Ewan McVicar's squibs

If you see Major Major, tell him what you want,
All together, tell him what you want.
If you want some peace! Now! Tell him what you want.

Tune: Jesus Is On That Mainline

As we were walking down the street
We met a Scottish soldier.
We said, 'Hey, Jock, it's time to stop,
The time for battle's over.
Stop the War. You know what for.
We don't care who began it.
Stop the War. You know what for.
We've got to save our planet.

Tune: We're No Awa Tae Bide Awa

Hammer', 'The Freedom Come-All-Ye' and others.

Every other Saturday a march down the hill from Glasgow's Blythwood Square to a meeting in George Square would be led off singing by Eurydice, the Glasgow Women's Socialist Choir. On the George Square stage the group Diggery Venn featuring John McCreadie welcomed the march in song, and would be joined by the author to introduce my latest squib, already taught to Eurydice.

Singer Gordeanna McCulloch, then leader of the Eurydice women's choir, was a key presence in both the Friday night and Saturday morning events. "I remember the [First] Gulf War Saturday demos hazily, and a couple of the songs - 'Major Major' and the one I really liked 'You Know What For'. I also remember the Friday nights, the nights were dark and dreich but everyone sung their hearts out - and we made a noise." *Gordeanna McCulloch*

These squib lyrics, and the more considered lyrics of Ian Davison and other more established favourite peace songs, were included in a 'Old And New Stop The War Songs' lyric sheet. The other songmakers included on the songsheet were Pete Seeger, Bob Dylan, Moyna Gardner and Paula of SCND, and H Chapman.

This was a modern B4 double-sided broadsheet of old favourites and new squibs, anthemic or angry, elegaic or energetic, one of several that were produced for peace marches and demos and sold for the penny or tuppence that covered printing costs.

The 'Flames on the Water' album was the modern equivalent of a song anthology, a selection of the newest "popular and fashionable songs".

The SCND Buskers cassette and songbook 'Gies Peace' was the modern equivalent of the slim volumes of poetry printed and sold by the makers to their friends to raise money.

The 'Songs From Under', the Ukes Against Nukes cassettes, and the other cassettes or lyric sheets of new songs sent hot from the creating by the makers to other makers or singers, were the new version of the self-published not-for-profit slim volume that was a report on the maker's work, to be presented to one's friends and to the newssheets seeking appreciation and reviews.

Substantial books that addressed aspects of Scottish political song and the Folk Revival began to appear in the 1980s and 90s. The first, 'The People's Past', was edited in 1980 by academic historian Edward Cowan from talks delivered at the 'academic fringe' of the 1979 Edinburgh Folk Festival, on "various aspects of Folk as well as a day conference on the subject of 'The People's Past', designed to investigate the place of Scottish Folk in Scottish History". Many aspects of Scots political song were discussed in this volume.
In 1984 came a general account of 'The Folk Music Revival in Scotland', updated in 1996 as 'The Democratic Muse', written by musicologist Ailie Munro.
In 1989 a weekend event hosted by the London-based Political Song Network brought together song activists in Glasgow, and in 1990 issue 9 of 'Political Song News' was a Scottish edition.
'Radical Renfrew', edited by poet Tom Leonard, appeared in 1990, and in 1992 came 'Alias MacAlias' a collection of the writings of Hamish Henderson on Scots song and singers.
In June 1994 a concerted exercise in political song nostalgia put over 20 singers on the stage of Glasgow's Tron Theatre for a show titled 'The Eskimo Republic'. Most of the performers had been active in various political campaigns over the years of the Revival, and the audience was also of comfortable years. The singing Folk Revival had run its race and was settling into a mood of reflecting upon old glories. The professional and semi-professional performers were beginning to retire from the stage.
Some protests that might have been expected to produce songs did not do so. From 1992 to 1997 there was an ongoing vigil for a Scottish Parliament. Stuart McHardy wrote a political song for the Vigil. "It's on a tape somewhere. I wrote it in the Doric. I have it on file,

The buzzing bee can fly for miles,
Spread GM pollen all the while.
No containment for the trial,
Is this their very purpose?

Hey Jamie Grant have you cashed yer cheque,
Or is yer conscience prickin yet?
Accept your GM? Will we heck!
We'll be its terminator.
Munlochy Vigil, tune Johnnie Cope, words Rob Gibson

but once the issue has gone the song has no need to be remembered. I used it for an awfy lot of events on Calton Hill." Stuart McHardy

From 1995 on there was a protest campaign about tolls on the new Skye Bridge protest which occasioned a fund raising CD, but the tracks were all 'donated' by performers from their previous recordings, and the author has been told of only one new made song about the protest.

I tell elsewhere in this book about some post 1999 elements of Scots political folk song, e.g. the Glasgow South Side Baths campaign, the GM crops vigil, the creation of the Political Song Archive. But the chronological account part of this book began with the lifting of the Stone of Destiny at Christmas 1950, and the resulting returning assertion of pride in Scottish identity and nationhood, expressed and celebrated in songs new and old. This part of the narrative should end with an event that most of those 1951 'Sangs o the Stane' poet songmakers would have greeted with jubilation if they had lived to see it.

Winnie Ewing became a Member of the reconvened Scottish Parliament. She wrote that at its formal opening on 1st July 1999 "the highlight, however, was Sheena Wellington's singing of 'A Man's a Man', during which she encouraged the MSPs to stand and join in the final verse. It was a sensational moment of unity and plain Scottish speaking which typified the best things of our country. I have to say that the Duke of Edinburgh looked most uncomfortable, particularly at the verse which goes 'A prince can mak etc'. *Winnie Ewing*

Burns, as he often did, based his 'A Man's a Man' song on an older one called 'For a' That and a' That'. Burns' song was first published anonymously, minus the now well known first verse, in 'The Glasgow Magazine' in August 1795, then in October reprinted in the radical Belfast-based 'The Northern Star'. Burns' name was first attached to it when on 2nd June 1796, just before his death, it appeared in the pro-government London 'Oracle'. The 'Canongate Burns' says, "There can be little doubt that the governmental spy network would have taken notice of the song and judged it as seditious," and that Burns "must have known about this named publication which could have had him arrested at any moment from 2nd June 1796 onward and charged with sedition".

Here is irony. Robert Burns died probably worrying that publication of this new plain speaking political song founded on an older folk song could lose him his job, or even have him transported to New South Wales. 200 years later the singing of it personified a moment in his nation's rebirth.

Is there for honest poverty, that hangs his head an aa that
The coward slave, we pass him by, we dare be poor for aa that
For aa that an aa that, our toils obscure an aa that
The rank is but the guinea's stamp, the man's the gowd for aa that

What tho on hamely fare we dine, wear hoddin grey, an aa that
Gie fools their silks, and knaves their wine, a man's a man for aa that
For aa that an aa that, their tinsel show an aa that
The honest man, tho e'er sae poor, is king o men for aa that

Ye see yon birkie ca'd a lord, wha struts an stares an aa that
Tho hundreds worship at his word, he's but a coof for aa that
For aa that an aa that, his ribband, star an aa that
The man o independent mind, he looks an laughs at aa that

A prince can mak a belted knight, a marquis, duke and aa that
But an honest man's abune his might, guid faith, he mauna fa that
For aa that, an aa that, their dignities an aa that
The pith o sense and pride o worth are higher rank than aa that

Is There For Honest Poverty, Robert Burns

Aspects of Political Song

Organisers, songmakers and singers tell about how they became involved with song, their influences, and their thoughts on the songs of others.

BEGINNINGS

"I discovered what a folk song was when I came to Edinburgh University, aged 18. I began to learn songs, and in summer went home to my local folk club with my new guitar and songs. I found much later my mother knew Geordie songs, though she was a card carrying member of the Tory party, because she taught English country dancing, and she'd used the songs in her teaching work. I must have learned the songs in quite a different way from her. She'd never thought to teach me about what she knew, she'd restrained herself from handing it on." *John Barrow*

☙

"I was immersed in politics from an early age, and prior to the folk song revival, because my parents were political, and because of the quasi-religious attitudes of the Socialist Sunday School movement I went to. There was a kind of utopianism in the songs, the building of the New Jerusalem. Quite a lot of the songs related to the need for working class people in the cities to get out into the country. There was an element of what later became the Woodcraft Folk.

"My father and mother were both cultural socialists as much as economic and political socialists. They were involved in the arts. They were interested in choral singing. My father was interested in commercial popular entertaining. And they were both actors, interested in drama. I was conscious of the use of political songs parallel to the use by religious groups of songs which were ideological.

My first awareness of deliberately political songs was 'The Red Flag' and the 'Internationale', and 'The Very Fat Man that Waters the Workers' Beer'." *Ian Davison*

ꕤ

"I'd always written songs. I started with poetry as a child, and I wanted to be a writer. I joined the Perth Folk Club in about 1960, and I used to sing every week. I got that I just wrote a song to sing. Some of the first ones were dreadful. But one of the first songs was for John Walton, who was killed, he was a pillion passenger and fell off. *"When a young man dies without any warning, The sky is dark."* I started off being influenced by American songs and singers - Phil Ochs and Bob Dylan were examples for me, and Joan Baez. I always heard Scots, my father was a real 'man of independent mind'." *Sheila Douglas*

INFLUENCES

"I just missed the skiffle phenomenon. I listened but I bypassed it into solo guitar. The folk stuff started coming at me from every angle. My father sang cowboy songs, my mother sang Burns songs, I was meeting people like Norman Buchan who had ideas about more modern songs. I started to formulate my own anti-antiquarian ideas. I was keen to see what was modern in folk song and in songs written in folk song style. I was worried even at that time that the wonderful work that MacColl and Seeger were doing could turn quite antiquarian. I was conscious that a lot of their songs were about ways of life that were already disappearing. A lot of folk song material was being valued just because it was old.

"A Tory could value these older songs just as much as a left winger. They could be an antiquarian hobby, and that happened. Strange alliances developed, clubs which stayed ethnic and accepted the attitude that you should perform in your own ethnic tradition. Some people spotted right away that one of the attractions of folk song as it emerged from the song carriers was a dangerous one of the exotic." *Ian Davison*

ꕤ

"I had been involved in the 'Folk scene' from my school days in Inverness. There was a guy called Duncan MacLennan ran the folk club in Inverness. Duncan had been to University in Aberdeen, where he met people like Jeannie Robertson. He was a great traditional singer. One of the people I liked a lot was Hamish Grant who had a tremendous voice for bothy ballads and for big ballads. He studied as a doctor in Aberdeen and knew Andy Hunter and knew Jeannie Robertson's songs. Dylan's first LP came out about 1963 and I heard his songs through covers by Peter, Paul and Mary. The Corries were touring at this time and always filled the local music hall. I liked them as a trio with Paddy Bell. The Ian Campbell Group with Dave Swarbrick also played Inverness and they were my favourites at the time.

I came down to Edinburgh and the whole place was really awash with music. There was the Crown, the folk club of the University, which had different names and moved through lots of lifetimes. There was the Triangle; in Randolph Place at the West End and a club in the chaplaincy centre in George Square that I think became the Edinburgh folk club." *John Greig*

ꕤ

"My greatest influences are Karl Marx, Groucho Marx, Flann O'Brien, Bert Jansch, Betty Frieden, John Lennon, Vladimir Illych Lenin, Hugh MacDiarmid, Tim Berners-Lee, Davy Graham, Doc Watson, Hank Williams, Jeannie Robertson, Ewan MacColl, Somerled, Bertolt Brecht, my mother (my mother, not Brecht's), my father (likewise), my grandparents, Calgacus, Dolina MacLennan, Crazy Horse, Sandy Denny, Martin Carthy, Clarence White, Sean O'Riada, Jack Mitchell, John Maclean, Big Bill Broonzy, Hamish Henderson, Robert Burns and everybody else I ever met, read, saw, heard or spoke with." *Dick Gaughan*

☙

"I try my best these days to only be influenced by styles of music and not by individual writers or singers. But here's a list of names of various people, only some and far from all, that I regard as playing some kind of a role in my formative process...in no particular order...

"Bob Dylan, Woody Guthrie, Leadbelly, Lightnin' Hopkins, Joan Baez, Robert Johnson, Jeannie Robertson, Joni Mitchell, Sleepy John Estes, Elvis Costello, Rolling Stones, The Clash, Pogues, Sex Pistols, Patti Smith, Ewan MacColl and Peggy Seeger, Leon Rosselson, Roy Bailey, Robb Johnson, Martin Carthy and Dave Swarbrick, Ray Fisher, Luke Kelly, Belle Stewart, Ry Cooder, The Exiles, The Clutha, Dick Gaughan, Hank Williams, Lucinda Williams, Robert Burns, Dylan Thomas, Leonard Cohen, Bertolt Brecht, Arthur Rimbaud, Marianne Faithfull, Lou Reed and a host of others too numerous and unnecessary to mention. Recent fave listens include Gillian Welch, Old Crow Medicine Show, Alasdair Roberts, Madeleine Peyreoux and Levon Helm (an old fave recently rediscovered). Yeah. I think I'm done." *Alistair Hulett*

☙

"Hamish Imlach would add things when singing political songs. He was a master of that, I wish he had written songs. He was one of my heroes, he truly believed in the left wing principles, and he did it in quite a gentle and thoughtful way. He was a sensitive and thinking man. I was in bits at his funeral. There was no more gentle singer of political songs than Iain Mackintosh, but he got them out there. Another of my heroes is Pete Seeger. I was lucky enough to play with him in Tonder. Mr Seeger has written a lot of incredible songs, but also he has done the biz, he put his liberty on the line, done more than the rest of us singing at a safe distance.

"Norman Buchan was another hero, '101 Scottish Songs', me and my brothers and I would learn each song, whatever it was, in his Weekly Scotsman column, and sing it together. He was political, but most of the songs he printed were traditional. I came up through that rather than in a family full of protesting people, then Dylan came along and influenced a lot of Scots who didn't think about the protest nature of songs so much." *Ian McCalman*

ᘓ

"I grew up with protest, very much at grass roots level. My first involvement was with my parents, in a Communist Party theatre group, there were a couple of songs written then. That led straight on to CND, and I was running up against political song there as well. Hand in glove wi that in oor hoose went an interest in jazz, matched by an interest in blues. We had recordings of Sonny Terry and Brownie McGhee, Big Bill Broonzy, Josh White. From the point of view of understanding the blues, being an expression of people - not necessarily downtrodden, that's not the way we saw it - but expressing their own position in life.

"In terms of political song, I got it with my mother's milk, and it's never changed. And every so often you have to write things yourself, because whatever issues you get involved wi, there's a requirement for a song, so you do it when you need it. It seems as natural to me as breathin." *Stuart McHardy*

ᘓ

"Dick Gaughan is an inspirational performer for me. I saw him thirty years ago at a CND concert in Stirling, and I always recall he said you've got to get up and do something. I signed up. I didn't know him, but he taught me a lesson that someone charismatic on a stage can influence people." *Ian Walker*

THOUGHTS ON POLITICAL SONG AND PARTICULAR SONGS

"Karine Polwart's 'Where Do You Lie, My Father?' is about Srebrenitsa, but also about anywhere! I have raved about it, and some other people don't get it. Half of the people on the folk scene just want to be listened to. Belle Stewart told me that there were two kinds of singer, one says 'Listen to this voice', and the other says, 'Listen to me'."

"I went to Methil Folk Club. Jim and Maureen knew I had this song, re the Michael Colliery Disaster, they said 'Don't sing the song just now, it's too soon, too near what happened. The colliers had been afraid to go down below the ground, there was a fire had been burning down there for years.

"The next Xmas they asked me to sing it there. I was introduced, 'She's going to sing The Michael song'. I was standing there singing to people that it had happened to, and I didn't like it at all. One of the men had been going to go down, and he had a cold. I said I felt awful about the song, and he said, "Don't worry, if it hadn't been a good song it would not have moved me." You are showing a bit of yourself to an audience.

"Political songs are to express what you think about a particular situation. Not necessarily right, in fact, they're very biased, but for the listener in a 'protesting' audience to say, "Oh yes, I agree with that". Tunes people would know, because they wanted people to join in."

Sheila Douglas

৩

I've never heard anyone singing a Whig Jacobite song, though there are plenty of them. We love a loser. I said to Mick Broderick 'You're a bizarre guy, like a lot of the rest of us you're a left wing Jacobite Marxist Socialist conservative Presbyterian. How many people who sing J songs know the slightest thing about the Stuart monarchy. People who are republicans sing J songs. I think they are singing about an ideal of somebody who was popular, singing about something good that might have happened, though BPC was not universally popular in Scotland. And of course people can be attracted to the tune, and the language and images are brilliant in some of the songs. They are sung now for different reasons, sometimes from a basis of ignorance.

Geordie McIntyre

৩

"I see political song as part of a continuum, at one extreme there are songs which have a political implication without anything explicit in them at all, what I call communitarian songs, songs that have a social setting in or implied in them, without any expression of ideology. That's at one extreme. At the other extreme there are simply slogan songs, which are meant to be overt propaganda and are not reluctant to show that. Songs that contain within them very often slogans as part of the actual song.

"In between there is a terrific spectrum of openness, or deviousness running right through these songs. Some are intended for general consumption, and some are intended for an occasional limited use with less political audiences, but they have a certain amount of fairly clear politics in them.

"I think there's a terrific spectrum within political song. The best definition of it is to do with the authors or composers of the songs, rather than the actual songs. It's a political consciousness in the singer, it means that almost every song that's written will have a political implication, no matter how disguised it may be. It is not easy to give a neat definition that covers all that, because it's a huge spectrum." *Ian Davison*

ꝏ

"All songs are political in one sense. You can write a song about politics, or a political issue, or an incident. Songwriting can be a piece of journalism, or a piece of history, datestamping an incident. Political song in terms of performance and writing songs, you'd be hard pressed to find no political line in most songs. Many [old] ballads are political, they contain things that are instructions or are acknowledging the political temperature of the day. I prefer things in songs to be personalised. Not so much having a hidden meaning, but use of the writer's skill, layering something so it's not too overt.

"The longer lasting political songs have those layers inside them, so the true meaning is not specific. An example, re the use of humour, is 'Twa Recruiting Sergeants', a favourite of mine. Examination shows there's a great skill of wit, irony, juxtaposition of the powerful and the

ridiculous, hyperbolising the situation. Underpinning that is a very serious anti-war motive, in the rejection of the urging that he should go to war. That is not explicit in the lyric, but all the apparently ridiculous events going wrong that are suggested to him are just everyday occurrences to the plough boy. He rejects the advances, the game is up for the recruiters, he sees through their guile and outsmarts them. That is the narrative I find around the song. The writer uses their skill, and they acknowledge that the audience has skills too, of understanding and relating to the song. The surrounding narrative can change over time. That's all right. "'What's so wrong about being misunderstood?' The new interpretation and perception is probably far stronger, will last far longer than what was intended originally.
"'Protest song' is a horrible weak description. Slogan songs have purpose. 'Maggie Maggie Maggie' is a song, hugely effective, it makes no bones, you sing it on the march. When you get to the concert at the end of the march, you expect songs to have more depth. It has to do with functionality.
"The carrier of a song is the melody. In the Scottish tradition tunes are often up for grabs, the lyric is what's first. Sometimes writers are clever enough to refer to the originals they work from. Ian Campbell's 'Old Man's Song' used the tune of 'Nicky Tams' – a slightly ridiculous music hall and bothy ballad song that has just lovely images, it is not scared to poke fun, it has a buxom woman and a comic scene in church for instance.
"Ian hangs on it a terrifically poignant song, with great sense of period throughout. He chose a tune which does not refer to that, or has a sense of carrying that kind of density." *Rab Noakes*

☙

"In Tim Neat's account of how the song 'The Seven Men of Knoydart' evolved, Hamish Henderson was at a protest meeting in Glasgow, and then wrote the song overnight on the boat to Belfast, inspired by what he heard at that meeting.
"As I understand it, that meeting was after the land raid event. A major issue in the politics of the time was land for returning ex-

servicemen. Clann na h'Alba in Glasgow had the same idea, with support from some lordly figures. Elsewhere, for example, at Scoraig, the laird allowed them to resettle amicably.
"Lord Brocket was an extremely hateful figure, his Nazi leanings would not be lost on a post-war world. Hamish was writing raw material, not anti-English at all, but the 'wa wa' tendency in land ownership was the target. English people were on our side in these struggles. The problem is perhaps Henderson's use of the word 'Sassenach', which means 'Saxon'. The song is raw and funny, and hits at behaviour of landowners. James Hunter writes in 'The Claim of Crofting', about the land raid at Balelone, that that action was successful in the end.
"I had heard Archie Fisher sing a short version of a song, 'Kincardine Lads'. I learned it came from Kincardine in Easter Ross. I found a full set of words, from Davie Ross of Dounie, it tells of setting up a still and avoiding the gaugers. The gaugers were based at Dalmore Distillery in Alness, I've found out who wrote it, the father of an SNP activist, it has thirteen or fourteen verses, and names local people.
"Singer songwriter Jim Hunter who lives at Lochailort, he's a blues rock singer. One of his first songs was about a failed attempt to get land back in that area. Their priest who accompanied his flock to North America led these MacDonalds to try to buy the land back once they were a bit better off. Unsuccessfully! The song is 'The Way of the White Cloud'. People come to songs that have a political message, that may celebrate a far gone event as an argument that other people should remember these injustices. Land issues are a major source of song. Munlochy is a story of land use. Before we had our own Parliament, the iconic motif of Scotland and change. Losing your land is fundamental to losing everything else.
"My friend Willie Mackay of Reay on the North Coast, is the village bard, he would recite a poem at the Hogmanay dance re the doings of the last twelve months. He came to our first festival in Dingwall, and after the festival wrote a little poem, contrasting between the festival and the bus tours arriving at the hotel the next day, the tourists' normal expectations versus the heightened ones of our own musical activities. Sometimes these things are best as poems, but some of his

poems were put to tunes by a friend of his from the North Coast, so they became songs." *Rob Gibson*

☙

"How is the political sense activated? When Alistair Hulett was out in Australia, he wrote a song called 'He Fades Away', which is a straightforward narration of a man dying from asbestos poisoning from the blue asbestos mines in Australia, and the effect that has on his wife and family and so on. It's a story with no overt political content but it's very political. It outrages by the content and could motivate people to political action.

"On the subject of warfare and the generalisation of experience, God knows how often I've listened to a good Dubliners' version of Eric Bogle's 'The Band Played Waltzing Matilda'. I think this is a very powerful, very strong song about a specific phase in a war involving Australians. But it's so easy to generalise to a universal, political situation.

"Related to but different from the idea of generalisation is the power of association of songs. What makes a song political can be just associative. So where groups of people are engaging in political or "political" activity, via a sub-culture like for example the punk sub-culture, there may be some overtly political songs attached to it like 'Anarchy In The UK', but then the whole of the music, the whole song becomes political because it is an identifier for the sub-culture group. So in some ways, you can call anything political.

"Talking about differences between Scottish and English political song, I think nowadays there is more of an international element to the Scottish songs. Scots are always reaching out to identify or support or link to political causes in other areas. Maybe it's because they feel that they've been put through the mill politically and socially by the English and the English don't feel that – I don't know. But certainly the evidence of Scottish support in song for the Anti-apartheid Movement or for Chilean refugees for example is much greater than in England. The Spanish Civil War is another good case. More people went to the Spanish Civil War from Scotland than any other country.

"I think there's as much political song activity as there's ever been. A constant question you'd hear, especially after the 2003 invasion of Iraq, was "Where are all the political songs? People are not writing political songs any more." They are! Simple Minds in their hey-day probably had a fairly straightforward method of disseminating their songs by performance or via a record company. Now there's a much wider spectrum for dissemination. Now anyone can just record and put it up on Face Book or My Space – interesting because they can escape the censorship of the record company, of the multi-national organisations, of Government – unless they're somewhere like China. So I think there's still as much political song, still as much political activity, but it is very different.

"Apartheid doesn't exist any more, but there are still songs being written about the situation in South Africa, about the HIV crisis, about the fact that black economic empowerment has maybe gone a little awry, and that the real grass-roots proletariat are not benefiting in the way they should have done. There's still the songs there, but shifted, and it's more complicated than just saying "Apartheid is wrong, bang!" That's easy, but it's when you say "Ah, but there's difficulties about black economic empowerment" – it's more complex.

"When we're doing workshops in the Centre, I put up on the board what I've called the three 'A's. Appropriation – you take an existing tune. Adaptation – you change the words. Association – the song gains power by being associated with the original. Now there's your song – you can go and sing it! A standard example of that is one of Alistair's Govanhill Pool songs, 'We'll Swim Again for All That'. Obviously it's based on 'A Man's A Man'. It uses that tune, it uses some of the original's words, it's a fairly trite, comical song about welly boots – but the power is there because of the association with the original. And I can listen to that song and it makes the hairs on the back of my neck stand up, this ridiculous song about welly boots and things. It's because it's got the power of the original. Now the only question is, how does that affect people who may not know the original?

"And another really interesting question, how does being exposed to that kind of song, with its associations, how can that radicalise people into general activism? Can the guy who might go along to the meeting to protest about the closing of the Govanhill Pool become generally imbued with a sense of activism? In a song in the same album, Alistair uses the first two verses of the Joe Hill song and it's only in the 3rd verse that the Govanhill Pool comes in – at which point it's become a world cause and the spirit of Joe Hill is there, fighting for Govanhill Pool, and it's incredible. And that's the power of the three 'A's, and that's why people do it. And there's nothing wrong in that." *John Powles*

☙

"'We'll Have A Mayday' began to seem like a sad song in latter years, when Tony Blair came in. It was a good song because it did not overstretch itself. It said, 'This is what we've come from. Some of our parents had bloody miserable lives, and we deserve better. And the only way we can get better is by putting people in that will make a change the way we want to see the change, and keeping them on their toes.'

"Therefore it was quite straightforward, not at all abstruse. It reminds you that the bosses have their hands in your pockets as often as they can, emptying them as quickly as they can and you'd better watch out for them. In that sense it wasn't a sophisticated song, but it was a song to say to people 'Remember where we're from, and remember how we can operate if we operate together.'" *Ann Neilson*

☙

We will sing in a few days at the MacIntyre Clan Gathering in Oban, our last song will be 'Come by the Hills', written by W Gordon Smith in the 60s.

The first verse is reflective of the love of the land. The second verse begins "Come by the hills to the land where life is a song". You can't get more romantic than that verse - life isn't a song. "And even the

wind sings in tune". Taken out of context, MacGonagall couldn't have done better.
Then his last verse has

Come by the hills to the land where legend remains
Where stories of old fill the heart and may yet come again

And here's the line that gives it a political slant.

Where the past has been lost and the future has yet to be won

That line, and almost the whole song, made me think about how so much Scottish history has been excised by omission. There was only one school history book of the 1960s that mentioned The Crofters' War, it had been airbrushed out of history, we could have been the Soviet Union, reshaping history by selection or omission.
The past hasn't been lost, but some people would like elements of our past to be lost. That is one of the strengths of the retroactive song. We sing that great song 'The Seven Men Of Knoydart', about land ownership, "The sacred rights of property shall never be laid low". Very little has changed in the Highlands. These people are still behind their big wall in their big estates, and can pay for anonymity. That's still a reality. So these are songs that are valuable to sing.
They're good songs in themselves - in structure, poetically and musically, but they also have a story to tell. Whether they lead to action is another issue. When I hear people say they do not sing political songs I groan, because I think they do not think enough about what they do sing. *Geordie McIntyre*

☙

"One of the songs I sing is an American one, 'Bread and Roses'. It's an inspiration, about women millworkers so long ago in the USA, striking and marching at a time it was really hard to march. The song is not just about money, though money was so important, but about roses. We need to struggle for money to feed our kids and put a roof over our heads, but if we don't have roses, you don't have a rich life. It's about quality of life. One of the lines in the song is "*Hearts starve as well as bodies, give us bread but give us roses*". People need to grow up with hope, and the good things about them, not material things but enjoying where they are, enjoying music, having education – that's the roses." *Cathie Peattie, Singer, MSP, Grangemouth*

❧

"Songs like the 'Wee Magic Stane' throw ridicule and poke fun in a light hearted way. Politicians are not lighthearted. Music lifts the consciousness in a different way. The fun and cleverness of ridicule is there in Nancy Nicolson's songs, the warmth and humanity in them, but also the sharp edge that says "Look at this". Without alienating people it invites them to come into the song.

"I'd always been interested in folk song, since in the 1950s I saw Dolina MacLennan in the Waverley Bar, Archie Fisher, Jean Redpath, these were motivated singers putting a point of view. That sort of couthiness and laconicness, and catchiness, the sense that it's a wee bit of fun, and that you can join in, I think it does marshall a kind of conscious solidarity of opinion after a while. It enters the bloodstream of people's thinking when they sing these songs. So a campaign that is making songs is an amazing thing.

"It is related to the idea that in all cultures when people do things like going to war they have done so with pipes blaring and drums beating. You can align a regiment behind you with music. 'Onward Christian Soldiers' marching as if to war, because they are for peace.

"It is unavoidable that people will be angry, and express their anger. Not all political songs are in harness to idealism for the good. Sometimes the rancour and sense of being a victim is not enlightened in a benign way. There can be a war in words, enflamed and exasperated by differences between classes. We're all blood and bones and heart, and brought up by mum and dad, and struggling to find our way in the world.

"I was just looking at Tannahill's 'Braes o Gleniffer' song, such a beautiful poem song, and also political, Johnnie is marched away to war, breaking the heart of a woman. When you invite people's affection for the places of beauty in the land of their birth, holding them precious and beautiful, is a deep kind of statement of relationship we have to land. The respecting all living creatures is in a wide sense to do with the politics of living.

"When people have to speak, in song or otherwise, to give a voice to something, then you must be heeding the zeitgeist. It's an expression of the soul of the age, singers and musicians who are moved by songs, expressing something that invites itself to be expressed about the age. It should and must be heeded. It is a very primitive thing – if somebody is hurt or moved, and you have a kind of congregation of voices moved or inspired, then just as slaves in the USA sang to hearten themselves and bring them together, it is deeply significant. Things are expressed in novel or song. But song enters the consciousness. When songs are sung they become more available, more universal, like a mantra entering the consciousness because of the music and the rhythm.

"Part of its significance is that it brings people into contact with each other. Now, people are separated by being glued to the solitary confinement of screens. When voices are joined in song, something actually happens, it's hard to define, they are psychic emotional realities." *David Campbell, storyteller*

'WHAT DOES POLITICAL SONG MEAN TO YOU?'

Answers to this question were gathered quickly at a Glasgow Council reception for Scottish C.N.D, at singing weekends in Fife and Aberdeenshire Cullerlie, and in the course of detailed interviews.

Political song is the voice of the people, not the voice of the media or the establishment. In a lot of societies political songs were banned, and the songwriters were shot – the ultimate compliment you can pay a songwriter – shoot him! Like all social or political comment or songs they act as a banner for people to rally behind. *Eric Bogle, songmaker, Australia*

☙

Basically it is about songs concerning the subjects that are controversial, that are thrown up by every-day life, that pose people problems, that throw up a response of various sorts. Responses either of protest, and / or of attempted solutions to problems, to encourage people, to make them feel they can do something in a world that seems unequal. There are many ways of looking at politics, but political song is about giving people the spirit to resist and / or change the world. *Rob Gibson, musician and MSP, Easter Ross*

☙

What it means to me is a song that comments on people's way of life, ordinary people's way of life quite simply. It's not a soapbox thing, an aggressive thing. It's just simply a comment on the price of bread, or that people arny workin, women's position in society for example - and men's position.
One song last night, a new one by a chap from the North East, about unemployment. Or there's a lot of old ancient political songs, about women being pregnant and not knowing what to do about it, or

raped. About women's position in society, and depending on whether the chap's gonna come across with some support or not. *Ellen Mitchell, singer, Glasgow*

☙

Political song is a reflection of political culture. I think it is essential to know yourself, know your country, know what it is that you're campaigning for.There has to be a cultural connection with the politics. It's not just about ideas, it's not just about campaigns, it's about a sense of who you are, where you are, what you bring to make sure you're well grounded in what you want to achieve.

The obvious song is 'The Freedom Come-All-Ye', which has always been magical to me in many ways. It's one of the few modern songs that said to me Scotland is an international country, that being a nationalist means being an internationalist, and it also has the social values of caring for humanity that are part and parcel of Scotland. Sometimes songs can stand up and reflect who you are, but sometimes they can stretch you.

The wee Rebel Ceilidh book is part and parcel of the SNP's heritage and culture. It was a different generation from mine, but it was extremely creative. Now we've got Facebook, political song was maybe the equivalent of that in the 1970s. Humour is one of the best ways to prick at authority. At an anti-war demo I was at it was the older people who had the songs.

How can we make sure that political song is not just about the past? The next generation of political song is yet to be discovered. I think it will come though the internet. *Fiona Hyslop, MSP for Lothians, SNP, Culture Minister*

☙

Initially I think of the anti-nuclear stance. But in fact I think even the older songs, especially bothy ballads, had quite a political slant to them, because they were quite anti, they were protesting in their own way about the conditions on the farms at the time. The hard conditions then. Even some of the ballads. Have you ever heard a ballad that hasn't got a toff, it's almost all toffs, or workers trying to get to become toffs or to marry a toff. I think almost every folk song's a political song. *Jimmy Hutcheson, singer, Fife*

☙

Ah was brocht up on a fairm, an politics didny mean an awfy lot. My auld man used tae vote Tory, an that wis aa politics meant to me. And of course ah consciously learned aa these bothy ballads, which ye ken on reflection is just full a political statement - and of course aa the songs, they aa look intae this cry oot for help, or there was some statement bein made aboot the conditions an 'at.
Ah dinna ken if that affected what I thought of as my politics. Ah wis just brocht up on the fairm, ma faither, he wis maybe the bad employer, as the fairmer. But I was part of that system, which ah didny really recognise. I mean, I had to work as hard as the rest of them - my work ethic, when I then got a job it just came natural, you just got stuck in owre there and worked away with the rest o them. I wis nivver aware until ye start readin things and ye became aware of how the system was set up. But when ye're growin up wi it, it's just how things are. *Geordie Murison, singer, Aberdeenshire*

☙

I have difficulty in separating politics frae life, I canna see a separation. The way of life is involved in aa the struggles, ye look to social and economic side of things, ye canna separate. There was an element in the folk scene that was against the influences the Communist Party had, and MacColl. They had a mission, not just about song, but others felt you shouldn't sing political songs in folkclubs. *Danny Couper, singer, Aberdeen*

☙

'A Man's a Man For Aa That' - I think that there is nothing that has been written subsequently that is any better than that. I think the principle of universality, and everybody's right to be an equal member of a society, is the socialist principle that we're all looking to do. And while there's been great songs written subsequently, I don't think anything has the power of that song. *Davey Stewart, singer, Kirkcaldy*

☙

If you took an extreme Marxist viewpoint, you could argue that everything - all songs - reflect political realities directly - some are more overt than others, some are layered, but there's a political component. A song like 'The Dowie Dens of Yarrow', where the lord becomes a ploughman, it's egalitarian, it's about class. People today pretend class doesn't exist - it's sort of non-U to talk about class. I don't know what they substitute for it, but it's a reality still, and divisions between the status levels. So we can have that very wide definition.

But there are the songs which have a very specific overt bias, saying a direct unequivocal message. It can be done very seriously, like a song I remember Pete Seeger singing 'The Little Child of Hiroshima', which is emotional, sentimental to the extent that it is designed to arrest your attention and try to reflect, in so far as any song can reflect reality, the horror of being engulfed in a nuclear holocaust.

And then there are songs like the one you wrote yourself, which always comes to mind, 'Goin Up in Smokey'. That's something I don't do much in my own songwriting, using that humour which is - OK it's black humour, but it's effective. Although it's a CND song if you like, an anti-nuclear war song, it goes beyond its context, it goes beyond its period.

But there's a narrower definition of these agit-prop songs, which are very very specific, and *do* date. 'Ye'll No Sit Here'. 'Doon at Ardnadam' is out of date. A song, unlike a poem, goes out there and it has an immediate effect. If you sang something like 'Ye'll No Sit Here' without knowing the background and the context, it's lost. But there are songs like 'The Man With The Dreadful Knob' by Enoch Kent, a reworking of 'The Man That Waters the Workers' Beer', which is brilliant, it can transcend its period and live on. They cease to be agit-props just because of their structure.

And then there are those squibs that are only written for the occasion, and they date.
I wrote an agit-prop one in the sixties, inspired by information I was receiving from Helen Fuller, who was a trained scientist. I knew nothing about ecology, and she gave me the first copy of 'The Ecologist', published I think in 1964. I'd no idea, ecology wasn't part of the language, of the general knowledge. I wrote this wee song called 'The Weekend Song', which was very specific, it was based on things that she'd told me. How hedgerows were being removed and biological controls of pests were no longer operating. I was not aware of this at all. She talked about acid lakes. We saw this more recently in Chernobyl, where air contamination and pollution is no respecter of class or creed or wealth or status. It applies to all.
That body of information encouraged me to write the song, and I linked it up to people going away for the weekend into the countryside, escaping the smoke of the city, and yet the countryside is contaminated. Peggy Seeger said to me the song should really have a hard-hitting conclusion. I said, "No, I'll leave it open". I deliberately left it open. But the interesting thing is, it's not an agit-prop song, because sadly it's actually still relevant. The last verse goes "Where else can we run to? The answer none can tell. If acid rain drips down, and poison wind blows snell. When will this weary winter pass? What will the future bring? Will our children see a cornflower grow, or hear a robin sing?"
At the time, in the 1960s, there was an article in 'The Scots Magazine' by the late Tom Weir, asking where have so many of the species of birds gone. The quantity of birds had diminished dramatically even then, and that was a background to the song. I didn't say, "I am going to write a political song". I just had to express that, asking the listener, "What are you going to do about it, are you going to be passive, or active? Are you going to be concerned?"
At the same time, the songwriter who concentrates on political songwriting, they want to engage an audience, they want to entertain at the same time. There's a balance to be struck. If it's too didactic, too heavy handed, maybe they should leave that to prose. A song has

to be really well crafted to get a particular message over. But it's actually designed, at least in theory, to try and change people's behaviour or outlook, so to that extent they're biased, there's a point of view being presented. *Geordie McIntyre, singer and songwriter, Glasgow*

ꟹ

I wouldn't think right away of political song as a separate category of song, because my first experience of getting directly involved in real folk and popular song was not until the 70s.

I felt that it was all political, recovering the old ballads for example in the voices and language of the culture they belonged to, and allowing that to be heard was a hugely important political thing. *Donald Smith, storyteller and organizer, Edinburgh*

ꟹ

It seems to me to come from people who were outraged by the fact that people are still incapable of solving things by any means other than bombs and bullets. Particularly, from people fighting for justice, who saw enormous injustices perpetrated in their name. The big example in my experience was Vietnam, the way that song could help turn the tide, with Joan Baez and many others.

Political song is not just to do with war, but with the voice of people, epitomised by the bard expressing that, trying to make a difference both to the consciousness of the world, and the opinion of politicians. It's a way of shifting consciousness, and doing it through the heart. When the heart feels something, it can creep into the mind and generate an action.

Political song for me means that galvanising way that people who feel deeply want to shift and improve the world. There are the other enormities, the rich getting richer and the poor getting poorer, the world is ruled by a crazy acquisitive capitalism, a perpetual grab and growth and greed that is a downhill road to nowhere.

Political song is nearly always motivated by a kind of vision, by heart and by idealism, sometimes by religious belief, but frequently by a great sense of humanity. In our country it was epitomised very vividly by Robert Burns. He felt the enormity of betrayal in 'Parcel of Rogues', but still this positive sense of the reaching out of hands to one another in 'A Man's a Man'. *David Campbell, storyteller, Edinburgh*

Ꞓ

Political song is a way of bringing people together. It's quite strange, I imagine it happens in other political organisations, in the SNP at the end of the night everyone coming together and spontaneously bursting into song. Nobody has a control over it, it just happens. That's a good thing. There are songs that belong to a movement, to organisations. It's part of each party or organisation's politics. It brings people together.

In the SNP it can be any number of songs - 'Scots Wha Hae', 'Flower of Scotland', 'The Freedom Come-All-Ye'. There's always somebody, a couple of people, know the words to something and can lead it in, kick it off, and everyone joins in and then it gets passed down. Somewhere in the SNP songs have always been passed down in that way.

I don't know why, it's kind of part of the heritage of the whole thing, the history, it's a lesson in some cases, a need to know the things, the history, to take you forward. It lets you reflect on what's been before. You go home and reflect, if you don't know the songs you look into the history of the song. *Councillor Alison Thewliss, SNP, Calton Ward, Glasgow*

Ꞓ

Political songs mean for me songs of resistance, of struggle, of injustice. Songs from anywhere, songs of solidarity are very important to me. *Eileen Penman, singer, Edinburgh*

Ꞓ

I was part of a group called Local Heroes, part of Ploughshares, not part of a song group, but definitely a supporter around affinity groups, and ad hoc actions at Faslane, primarily anti-Trident. There was no singing in our particular actions, but I have joined singing groups that have turned up at Faslane. There's one called Raised Voices in Edinburgh. One musical thing I did do at Faslane was an anti-Trident oratorio. [It was] performed first at the High Courts in Edinburgh. We all kind of dressed up as lawyers, and managed to get into the building by stealth, and take over a hall and sing it, about three years ago, when the ruling on Trident came out. It had gone up to the High Court, whether our Law Lords deemed whether it was legitimate, whether there was a case in international law to fight against nuclear weapons.

What does [political song] mean to me? Strengthening my faith, and if I'm involved in something. [Her young son Shonny then interjected "Goodness to me', and she responded "It means goodness to Shonny"]. It's a way of getting through bad times and dark times as well. And because it comes from the voices of people, quite often people who have gone before, and you know that song has been sung by people before you, and hopefully by people after you, it is part of that historical continuum that's really important in terms of social justice, and movement for social change. *Babs [Barbara] McGregor singer, of Stornaway, now living in Glasgow*

☙

It takes me back to [an Eden] time, when possibly I was just coming up into the folk scene, and I got tapes from people, recordings of people. Things like the campaign down on Clydeside, songs like 'Ding Dong Dollar', all that sort of stuff, that immediately rings a bell, that was to me the ultimate time of protest songs. Then you have the American side, songs about Vietnam, *"All the years of growing up are wasted now and done*". About the young girl that was killed on a Vietnam demonstration. These songs, they don't let us ever forget that the impact of a song, it can make a difference, because people heard about this girl that was shot. Also, it helps the situation where political pressure can downplay an incident or an event, and somebody writes a song about it. Even a generation later, I hear it and say, "What the hell was all that about? I never heard about that. My god, did that happen?" It's probably still happening today, because there's suppression of free speech all around the world, and on our doorsteps still. I don't think that the writers are around now with quite the same power as there used to be in think that generation, the Vietnam war, anti-nuclear demonstrations, which you [the author] were very much a part of. You had your hand in it. *Dougie MacKenzie, singer, Inverness*

☙

I think there's maybe three strands of this for me.
One of them is I think people sing political songs as a declaration of what team they belong to. "This is me and my beliefs." It's a kind of alignment and a belonging thing.
It's about somewhere to put your rage. What else can you do? You can go and you can sing the song. Maybe it's an extension of that old thing about flyting.
And it's also, if you're somebody who doesn't live too easily with powerlessness, as I don't, then there's maybe an illusion of being less powerless.
The one that gets me impassioned the most is one I've been singing a long time. 'I didn't raise my son to be a soldier'. Unfortunately it continually becomes relevant, and I have three sons. The whole idea of any of them ever putting themselves and me through all of that just would be appalling, so that would be the biggie for me.
Another thing, it's not just a declaration of the tribe that you belong to, to the people who are in the same tribe, it's to the people who are not. But there's also something that's just an extension of what I think singing is about. I think singing - you could use the word communication and that's as clear as anything - I used to say 'Me too' because - I like songs about pain anyway - I've been there, I've got that T shirt, and so there's a sense of less isolation, an emotional thing. And now I would express it as, "Let's you and I talk, let's say 'Who are you, who am I?'" And of course the other person isn't talking - but they are in their response.

Whether it's about the conversation they come up and have with you, or the look or body language or anything else. We're talking. So, the political song is that kind of conversation.
There's two that are important for me. There's the one about the pain, which might not be about politics, might be about abandonment, rejection, those kind of things. And the political one is about *all* the things that make you angry about the world that you live in, you think are unfair, and "Do you think that too?" *Chris Miles, singer, Fife*

☙

I think the most political songs I know are songs where people have a really rum do in employment, if you understand me. They don't necessarily mention trade unions, they don't mention labour history, they mention how they've been done wrong in their job.
I was thinking of one about a navvy, just five minutes ago. He ended up killing his ganger, and the ganger's name was Green, and it's 1840/41, on the New Western Railway in Glasgow - Bishopbriggs. He murdered his boss because his boss charged him four and fourpence for breaking a wheelbarrow, so the song goes.
That's the sort of labour song that I think about. I also think about soldiers' songs in that bracket as well, the sort of soldiers' songs that took the mickey out of their bosses, like "*Bless em all, the long and the short and the tall*", and 'When This Bloody War Is Over', and this sort of thing. They're sort of linked in with labour songs, although we named our son after a labour song, because his name is Joe, named after Joe in the labour song 'The Ballad of Joe Hill'. Hillstrom was his proper name. "*I dreamed I saw*" - that's associated with him, although Joe Hill's actual song was a parody of 'The Sweet Bye and Bye' - "*We'll get pie in the sky when we die*". But the song people associated with Joe Hill was "*I dreamed I saw Joe Hill last night.*" *Ian Russell, Director of Elphinstone Institute, Aberdeen*

☙

I would differentiate between songs of protest and political songs. Songs of protest are aimed at all politicians and political songs are either for or against a political party or ideal. *Archie Fisher, singer and songmaker*

☙

Much political song is a form of activism. The recorded history of activism as such is very much missing, because the people who would be best capable of doing it, and most motivated to doing it, are the activists themselves. And most of them are too busy being engaged in these activities to be involved in recording about it. It's not an unknown problem. Activists often do discuss the absence of that.

I don't really distinguish between political song and any form of art. I think there is danger of seeing these things in a category, some of the greatest politics is about survival, and most great art is about survival or existence in one way or another. I see some great political songs as not having anything overtly about politics in them. That would be a danger to say that songs have to be issue related, I don't see it in that sense at all.

A song like 'Joe Hill' has an obvious political sense to it, but there's something else going on besides that, maybe a function of who is singing it. Joan Baez at her best, or Paul Robeson, will do something different singing it, but at the same time the aesthetic quality is not absent from the song. It's not just a song to try and motivate a political struggle, it's also about the life of a man gone who was a really committed human being.

Some songs are very much of their period and time, made for immediate use and using existing melodies. But Freddie Anderson [an Irish writer who lived in Glasgow] for example was capable of both making lyrics for the event, and of showing a great sensitivity in some of his really fine poems.

There are some great Gaelic songs. I don't even know the words but I would regard the very act of singing them as political because it's a language that has been proscribed. What if it's a Kurdish song? People have been executed in Turkey for singing a song in Kurdish. So that the very act of singing in a forbidden language is a political act. It

might be the equivalent of 'To A Daffodil' by Wordsworth in translation, but the very act of doing it is political.
The opinions people have about it are obviously to do with the people themselves, where they are coming from. Those who tend to put [songs] into boxes maybe have options, a choice in their lives. Other people don't have a choice, it's almost like the very act of survival is a political act.
That would be the case of people working in prohibited languages for example, like the use of Gaelic. You can bring that argument to songs being sung in a Glasgow voice, that in itself is a political act, because you'll be punished for it, when a child does that, it doesn't matter if they're singing 'Eeny Meaney Minie Mo', that in itself becomes a political act. For people to dismiss that as non-political indicates that they don't have that experience in their personal background. They've never seen their children belted by a teacher because they've spoke in their own voice. That categorisation is really a function of one's own often economic and cultural background. *Jim Kelman, novelist*

☙

I remember singing many years ago at a Morning Star concert. It was the first political gig I had done. Dick Gaughan was the main attraction. I sat down and had a cuppa with him before our performances and told him I was a tad nervous - I was shaking. He asked why and I said that I really didn't know any political songs. He came straight back at me and said "Listen hen, they're aa political." That made me stop and think. From that day to this I've looked for the political connections in the songs I sing and the connections are there whether overtly political or at a more personal level. Politics to me is integral to folk song - no matter what culture it comes from. *Gordeanna McCulloch, singer*

☙

I must admit when you first mentioned it I was thinking of Billy Bragg and that vein of political song, which I've got a lot of sympathy with. [Then] songs about people's situations in the working class, their lives.

Like "*Shift and spin, warp and twine*", that's a political song, in a way. And Mary Brooksbanks' song 'Oh Dear Me', about women's politics. *Mary Russell, organizer, Aberdeen*

☙

I think it's a way of telling a story, it's much easier for people to listen to, to encourage people to reflect on the words and their own views, it's a really good way of getting a message across. *Cathie Peattie, Singer, MSP, Grangemouth*

☙

A lot of things. There is the argument that the personal is political, and the political is personal. The first thing to come to mind is the notion of a song that aspires to make a difference, either by alerting people to something they didn't know, or by gathering them to fight something they did know but put them together as a unit, a group.
But I think you could also say that these amazing recordings that Alan Lomax did on US prison farms, where the singer is doing a wordless moan, and all his heart is in it, that cannot but be political, when you hear it and you're not in that situation. So political song can be direct, it can be very indirect, it can be very personal. *Ann Neilson, Singer, Rutherglen*

☙

It's one of those questions that can have two meanings, because I would contend that songs being by and about people, then they're all political. But if you mean in a more precise sense, I suppose it means generally songs that tell me what I know already. For that reason really, since I was about thirty I suppose, I've been less and less interested in them. In my teens and twenties I loved that stuff. I have a sort of theory that probably Bob Dylan was responsible for the opening of many more folk clubs than a lot of people realise. I certainly know that when I heard the second Dylan record I'd learned all the songs within a fortnight, and wanted nothing else than to sing them with and to people who had also learned them and enjoyed

them. In the local folk club. And if there wasn't one, which there usually wasn't in the early or mid 60s, you started one. You started one yourself in the local pub, and it was where people came together and sang the songs they were desperate to sing, because presumably there was something that was inside you and needed expression, and you hadn't had any way of doing that before, really.
[Bob Dylan is a political songwriter] because most of his songs address political issues, albeit obliquely. I know there are a lot of what I consider his better songs didn't. He wrote some wonderful ballads, but a lot of the popular ones, the protest songs, address political issues, and yes, are political songs.
In my experience most overtly political songs in the 60s were telling me to believe something I already believed. ['The Freedom Come-All-Ye'] is still relevant, and will be as long as there are people on the planet I should think. But most of the CND songs that were in fashion then were incredibly simplistic and naive. Even quite a lot of Leon Rosselson's songs, who I feel is one of the best of that sort of writer, there are exceptions but so many of them are incredibly naive and simplistic, and for me don't stand the test of time. [They were] simplistic in their approach to the problem. The 'Freedom Come-All-Ye' is a simple song, but immensely rich, deep, call it what you want.
Rod Stradling, Editor, Musical Traditions web magazine, London

☙

Political song is anti-establishment and anti-war. It depends what you're fighting against. There is a wonderful anti-war song in Gaelic, 'Gillein Uibhist, the Men of Uist', it is anti the last war. It speaks of Hitler and Himmler and Goebbels and all, and the boys of Uist striking them with iron rods to their death. Oh, it's the most powerful anti-war song in any language I know. *Dolina MacLennan, singer, Edinburgh*

☙

I could interpret that question in two different ways, so I will - and answer them both.

'What do I mean by political song' first of all. Well, in the field of music that I work in, folk music, for me it means a song that interprets society as structured along class-based lines and in some way comments on that society and sometimes, though not always, seeks ways to reshape it. If we understand folk music as the musical and poetic expression of the labouring classes, ie.'the folk', then there is a real sense in which all folk music is political. It is the music of a certain class and reflects how that class perceives itself in relation to the rest of society.

Many of our ballads, the Muckle Sangs, are intensely class conscious. We often find the ploughboy laddie or the serving man, the collier, weaver or whatever, pitting his wits or locking in struggle against the masters. I'm thinking here of our 'big songs' like 'The Dowie Dens Of Yarrow', 'MacPherson's Rant' etc. and also the later lyrical compositions such as 'The Collier Laddie', 'The Four Loom Weaver' and so on.

Other times it can be women who are defending themselves as best they can in a male dominated society. 'The Knight and The Shepherd's Daughter' or 'Bruton Town' for instance. Even bawdy ballads such as 'The Broomfield Wager' or 'Home Boys Home' are political in this sense. These are all political songs to me, as are the ballads of poachers, sailors taken by press gangs, recruited colliers, female highwaymen and drummer girls.

Even our bothy ballads are filled with a very partisan class-consciousness, pro-labourer and anti-farmer. I've often thought you could do a set of entirely traditional ballads and songs, and by contextualising the songs in this way, it would be a highly political statement. Then, of course, there is the outright political repertoire, both traditional and contemporary we would all instantly recognise. Irish rebel songs, Jacobite songs and the industrial-era strike and disaster songs.

Okay, so what do these songs mean to me, personally? Why is the political nature of folk song important in the modern age? Well, for a start, these songs of antiquity remind us that inequality and oppression have been around for as long as class society itself. The world that gave rise to them may seem on the surface to be greatly altered nowadays, but when we look closer, we see that the same social relations still persist today. Even if the social conditions we live in at the lower end of the economic spectrum are far less deplorable than they once were, the level of inequality between the classes remains as great, if not greater than before. And the cruel wars that slay the young men in our folksongs are far more lethal now than in the days of muskets and cannons. For me, folk songs are political because by singing them with understanding, we develop our class consciousness and that increases our political awareness and reinforces the need to reshape our society. *Alistair Hulett, songmaker, Glasgow*

SONGMAKERS AND SINGERS, SONG MAKING AND SINGING

Some readers may expect this chapter to concentrate on the well known professional performing interpreters of Scottish political song, but this book's business is more with the makers and making of the songs, the groupings and the settings where the songs were made and sung. The preceding chapters have told in part a chronological story up until 1999, in part the background and history of various kinds of Scots political song. This chapter goes into more detail, often in their own words, about many of the key people and their approaches and values.

ARTHUR ARGO

"Arthur's biggest contribution was I think that he understood that the folk songs of the North East were gold. They weren't just about the North East, there was a global context. He understood that songs [American] Jean Ritchie sang were a direct link back to Scotland, none of us knew that. Arthur went to America, I think he met Dylan. He brought over Doc Watson, Brownie and Sonnie. He understood the different threads and the international links. [Englishman] Bert Lloyd also understood this, but it was great to have Arthur, one of our ain loons, who understood this. He started an agency, he got Aly Bain doon frae Shetland. Politically, he was left when he talked to me but because he was a journalist, for the Press and Journal, he stepped back." *Danny Couper*

MORRIS BLYTHMAN

"It's a simple fact that Morris Blythman was one of the people who changed the whole course of my life, and it's no exaggeration to say that Scottish music would not be the same without the influence he exerted. His work lives and continues to change and grow." *Jimmie Macgregor*

☙

The author's own interest in Scots political song originates in the coincidence that at the age of 14 I encountered Morris Blythman as a schoolteacher. In issue 32 of 'Chapman' magazine, in his long and excellently illustrated article 'Songs For A Scottish Republic', Adam McNaughtan analyses Blythman's songmaking closely. He notes that Blythman, other than 'occasional' songs for social events, wrote only three non-political songs.

"The songs are ephemeral and were never regarded otherwise by their author. My pleasure [in the 'Sangs o' the Stane'] depends not solely on the songwriter's art but also on my familiarity with the events and people dealt with. And it is here that the songs remain important even when they cease to be sung. For they express opinions and attitudes which are satisfactorily recorded nowhere else; they convey better than any other source the moods of the time: the Scottish glee at English discomfiture over the Stane; the exuberance of the Anti-Polaris campaigners. In the songs of Morris Blythman we can hear the voice of the people." *Adam McNaughtan*

ERIC BOGLE

My first political stirrings were back in the CND days, we all went on the marches. The Eskimo songs made us feel more unified. That's the purpose they serve, and the context. I started off in Peebles, which wasn't a terribly political hotbed. But like a lot of young Scots when the Yanks put Polaris submarines in the Holy Loch I began to take more notice of what was going on. 'We Shall Overcome' - we owned those songs because we all sang them together.

The people I met through the songs, not so much the songs themselves, helped develop my political thinking and awareness. The songs themselves, a few lines make you think, but the discussions with people and the books that people recommend, they really get you thinking. The songs led me to the people.

People always seem to shove labels on everything. I've always thought of myself as a songwriter, not left, right, centrist, Scottish, Irish, Venusian. That people feel a sense of possession is a compliment in a way, that it speaks to them on a few levels, so they feel a sense of ownership.

When I've written the songs and sent them out into the wide world, I've never felt greatly possessive about them. Generally I don't mind how people arrange them. Every version is valid within its own musical genre. The first impetuses to write songs were political and social, other influences came in later on. The bulk of my thrust is still, if not overtly political comment, certainly some social comment contained in a lot of them.

But I've tried not to be the haranguing type of songwriter, who hits people over the heid with the same message in every verse. I aim to leave enough room for people to make up their own minds. I write narrative songs. I'm not that good on descriptive ones. I can get into the skin of a thing better in narrative form. What I say is important to me. Whether it becomes important to anybody else is another point. Often the songs are a way of trying to explain to myself what is happening.

I never think of myself in terms of whether I write country, folk, whatever. My first love was of political song, not traditional Scottish song which I had dismissed holus bolus because it was shoved down our throat at school.

I never made a conscious attempt to develop my own style, I wrote songs about what I felt strongly about, or what amused me. Life is about timing. My songs came along at the right time, at some other time they probably would not have had the effect they have. There was a hiatus between the rise of pop music that swamped everything else, and was good fun, then became big business and pissed people off, hence punk. Lots of folk turned from that to songs like mine with some sort of social comment and some sort of conscience. They were saying things that people wanted to say at that time, it was a matter of timing and luck. I'm not downgrading the quality of some of my songs.

This genre of music has no room for stars. The people who have gone before, the wealth of history and knowledge they have gifted to us is worth shouting about. We are just vessels, it's a cliché, but the banner

has been passed to us. We are keepers, trying to keep the flame alive, the banner aloft, some sense of bloody justice alive in the world, and add it on for the next generation. We write political songs, one of thousands who do it, just like the thousands before us who did it. We should be happy and proud to be part of that tradition
Australia is a very young country, we're still forming our ethos, I am part of the forming process, of the bardic process, I'm contributing a bit and I like that, it's a reward. *Eric Bogle*

"I heard Eric Bogle's 'Waltzing Matilda' song sung by June Tabor at Inverness Festival, and there wasn't a dry eye in the place. Here we were all weeping about something we had never been part of. And I said to her, 'Where did you get that song?' She said 'I got it from a friend of the chap that wrote it'. And she never mentioned his name! I couldn't understand that." *Sheila Douglas*

NORMAN AND JANEY BUCHAN

Norman Buchan was another of the three architects of the Scottish Folk Revival. Buchan's writing of a song column in the 'Weekly Scotsman', then his editing of the books '101 Scottish Songs' and 'The Scottish Folksinger', fuelled the repertoires of singers. Eventually Norman became an M.P. and Shadow Minister for the Arts, and Janey became an M.E.P. In 2001 Janey sponsored the creation of the Centre for Political Song in Glasgow Caledonian University.
The Buchans kept open house in Peel Street, Partick, Glasgow, for a stream of young singers seeking to learn songs from recordings and books. These included Archie Fisher, the author, and Ann Neilson.
"Norman Buchan was our English teacher. In about 1957 he put up notices saying he was going to have this Ballads Club, come along. I didn't go to the first one, I had this terrible feeling he would fall flat on his face. He had sung in class, 'The Dowie Dens of Yarrow', which has a weird tune and we weren't sure if it was right.
Next day I asked the others in my class "What was it like?" "Oh, it was great, you should have been there!" "Yes, but what was it like?" "Oh, it was great, you should have been there!" So I had to go.

"We were given sheets with three songs on it. The first song on the first week was a ghastly American one, 'Lollie Toodum'. *"As I went out one morning to take the pleasant air"*. I think the others were 'Rothesay O', and perhaps 'The Worried Man Blues', skiffle was going at the time, some of the others played guitars enough that we could access this material. We learned two or three new songs each week. Norman must have sung some of them to us. We had access to Room 16 every lunchtime, and practised there, sometimes Norman would play LPs or tapes to us. Eventually we put on a concert every Friday lunchtime, and occasionally Norman would take us out to a concert in a Women's Guild or a literary society or something. Anybody who wanted to could come. In the early stages he would construct the programme, and introduce us, and through listening to the introductions we learned about the songs.

"Eventually we leaned how to construct a concert programme ourselves. Anybody who wanted to sing, sang. If they were not a good or competent singer they were encouraged into a small group to sing in unison. Everybody was valued, it was a very supportive and sharing community, we would roar our way through songs all lunch time, well away from the staffroom. Other staff would come in and do their special interests, Old Time Music Hall and others. Some of us went into Glasgow, to Collets, and bought the Rebel Ceilidh Song Books.

"We sang Sangs O The Stane and Holy Loch songs in Room 16, but not in concerts, we made a distinction. Gordeanna McCulloch came in to the Ballads Club later than me, she was in Fourth Year when I was in Sixth Year. Brian Miller was another Club member who is still singing.

After Norman left to go into Parliament, the Ballads Club was taken on by Ian Davison, then Adam McNaughtan, who came as English teachers. Neither of them were pupils of Norman's.

Janey was immensely supportive of Norman, and very hospitable when hordes of us were invited to descend on their house in Peel Street in Partick, or when I went to their house to listen to records and copy down lyrics.She never seemed to mind folk taking up residence in her front room.

"Later, she was very generous with her time and her money, keeping an eye out for something somebody would be interested in, buying books and not telling Norman how much they cost, and giving them to singers who would benefit from them. And she did most of the organising of many of the Glasgow 1950s Ballads and Blues concerts. She and Norman were a partnership, they each worked for the other." *Ann Neilson*

ꟹ

"The Centre for Political Song, to give it its full title, started in 2001. It was really the idea of Janey Buchan. We started to have contact with Janey in 1994 when after the death of her husband Norman, she contacted us about putting some of their books and records etc into the University, and that really started us on what became research collections.

"Janey's was the first special collection we had. Being Janey and Norman, it was a very eclectic collection, but obviously centred on left-wing politics, activism, human rights, culture and song, mostly to do with the Left. Research collections then developed given that lead, and like attracts like. We soon built up a considerable collection of archives and books.

"Then in 2001 Janey, with whom we were working very closely over this period, came up with the idea of starting a centre for political song. She always said that she had become aware that the archives and libraries she visited everywhere she went, all had examples of political song being collected in one form or another. But there was no collection of political song per se and certainly no centre to promote research or particularly focus on political song." *John Powles*

ꟹ

In August 2002, a sequence of eight concerts was devised by Janey Buchan, Adam McNaughtan and Anne Neilson, part of the Edinburgh International Festival, 'Them and Us, Scottish Political Song'. The themes included Scabrous Song, Jacobites, Land, All Faiths And None, Freedom, McGinn, MacColl and Henderson, and Campaigns and Causes.

ROBERT BURNS

"By [the 1860s] a moving force in drawing crowds to events celebrating Burns appears to have been Burns-inspired Scottish nationalism... Thus in Glasgow in January 1877, when the waiting crowd gathering in sleet-showered George Square for the unveiling of the new Burns statue was entertained by what was described as 'a party of vocalists' who from a warehouse sang Burns' songs, with the loudest cheers accorded to an anonymous woman who, at the top of her voice, sang 'Scots Wha Hae'. Equally telling testimony to the same sentiment was the presence in 1896 in a procession in Dumfries of the centenary of Burns' death, of an old Chartist flag, with the inscription 'Scotland shall be free', while another banner carried the uncompromising words, 'Now's the Time and Now's the Hour'."
Professor Christopher A Whatley, in a book in preparation

DAVID CAMPBELL

The BBC tried to be even-handed, at the same time it took a very Presbyterian moral stance. Duncan Williamson said that some verses of his camping grounds song the BBC would not broadcast. The BBC is always interested in balance, I would see the balance being put is by making programmes with different voices, to indicate phenomenon. I remember talking to Hamish Henderson a long time ago, when I was working in BBC, he attacked me vigorously because the BBC consistently in Scotland ignored Scottish song – as if the whole of the Revival did not exist.

I got into trouble about choosing newsreaders who spoke entirely in RP. I said so in children's educational radio, I criticised that voice. I was doing a schools programme called Scottish Magazine, for twelve year olds. There was a huge stramash. People responded with 'don't invade us with gutter English' when dealing with a Scots dialect. It was a BBC attitude, are we being parochial and couthy and kailyard? There was a timidity, and a sense of inferiority. Burns was the token exception, twice a year – Burns Night and Hogmanay. You didn't hear Hamish Henderson, a giant.

Stuart McGregor was a very passionate patriot, very politically aligned to Scotland's culture and independence, a nationalist. He really initiated the Heretics idea. He talked to me in Milne's Bar and asked me to come along, I read from 'Scots Quair'. His idea was to give a voice to Scotland, its big poets, its developing ones, its singers and musicians, a cultural voice. Politics to me is to do with the people. It should not be aligned to parties, should be how you try to look after the people. Songs and stories re heart, all one family.
There were from time to time people with strong political views, Sorley MacLean had strong views, the Spanish Civil War occupied him hugely, he was a strong socialist. Largely speaking it was more the artistry, and to give a Scottish voice, which is a political statement. There were monthly meetings promoting Scottish voices, in the New Town Hotel. We would have a leading Scottish poet and an established musician, say Billy Connolly or Aly Bain, plus the ducklings – Liz Lochhead, Bernard McLaverty. We also ran Festival themes shows. Then often a ceilidh back at my flat. They ran from the beginning of the '70s. *David Campbell*

DANNY COUPER

An interesting thing, in the 80s the folk festivals was starting tae blossom, bands starting up, [older singers like] Willie Scott and Belle Stewart were not getting gigs. I was in Shetland wi Archie Fisher who was running Edinburgh Folk Festival. I said I'll sponsor a concert, form a small committee, choose all unaccompanied singers. We'll call it the Arthur Argo Memorial Concert. We ran it for ten years, people like Jane Turriff, English singers, singers from Ireland. Suddenly I got a feeling that some Revival performers wernae speekin tae me – what have ah done? It was all got to do with I'd not invited them to sing or play. I didn't get a chance tae explain to them that this is what Arthur would have wanted, he was a collector as well as a singer and organiser. He would have wanted people to go up and just be able to sing. Professional folk performers, they do weekends and get big money for it, these unaccompanied singers do not, you surely canny

get annoyed about it? Now the unaccompanied format happens at all festivals, though the old source singers have passed on.
Arthur Argo and Hamish Henderson made me aware about unaccompanied singing. Not just the singing. You can get songs out a book, words, melody, and anyone can sing a folk song, but ye canny get the style. That's what Arthur appreciated. I remember talking to him aboot it. He explained it something like the visual arts and the performing arts. Visual arts you can go back a thousand years and see the work of artists, with the oral tradition you can not. Except for the travellers, because they have continuity and integrity in how they sing. So I tried to get as many travellers as possible singing in the Arthur Argo Memorial concerts. In the performance arts you can only go back so far. In workshops I say to singers "Go back as far as you can, and listen."
At Whitby I heard a young Irish gypsy guy, his singing was a cross between Joe Heaney and Margaret Barry. I sang 'Doomsday in the Afternoon', and told the story of John McCreadie making the song after hearing Belle Stewart's answer to how long the travellers would be with us – "Til doomsday in the afternoon". The Irish guy said 'I've never heard that song". I asked had he heard 'Yella on the Broom', and sang it to him.
These communities are still alive. His uncles and them in Ireland, it's natural for them to sing like this. [Fife-based singer and collector] Pete Shepheard went into a pub in Appleby during the Horse Fair there, he took a chance and sang a really old ballad. A listener, an English traveller, named the family Pete had got it from. A lot of hope there yet. *Danny Couper*

IAN DAVISON

In 1957 I wrote my first song, and kept writing songs over a long period of time. Only a small number, although the years were so many that two or three songs a year becomes quite a lot of songs. That was part of a lifestyle for me that included song all the time, and also included politics all the time. I suppose in many ways I was integral to the folk movement, not as a famous personality, because I

was involved in all the relevant ways. Some of them I valued more than others. For instance, the antiquarian thing always worried me, and I tried not to become an academic. I did a lot of studying, I always felt you should have that up your sleeve, so that people wouldn't talk down to you, and they would have to take seriously what you were saying, you could say it in their language if necessary. I was very political all through and very proselytizing. So what profession would I go into? A teacher or a lecturer. It seems very organic to me, I didn't have a moment when someone converted me to folk music, a question of osmosis more than intent.
The reason why I never emerged as someone who could be fitted in one, I was in them all.
I always hankered after doing only the political work I found enjoyable, it's a way of involving people, you can express and enjoy your politics, find new and creative ways of operating your political commitment. I was born and bred a political animal, born and bred a musical animal, and born at the time when a folk song revival or something like it was desperately required.
We didn't start writing songs enough at the right time, and we didn't start a proper dance movement. If we had had the ceilidhing revival at that time, and a lot more songwriting we would have had a movement that would have been virtually unstoppable, like in Chile.
On one hand I was accumulating and collecting political songs, and using a lot of them in school English lessons, and singing in concerts, at the level that I sang with my group.
There was also a trickle of songs I had written myself, in response to need. I first did that about 1971, ten years after the Polaris ships came into the Holy Loch, we decided to mark that important and unfortunate anniversary, and look for new ways to mark it. I started to write a few songs then. In the middle 70s I started writing again, because the focus came off Aldermaston as a march, and there was the first one to Faslane. I wrote and updated songs, as we did again in the 1980s. Because nobody else was doing it in the 1970s. In the 1980s you and I did it because there was a need for it. The peak of the peace movement was 1982, after that we were keeping it

together, morale was important. If you don't change the world in three years, you can feel it's a waste of time.
I had retired from the Revival to be a political animal, but in the 80s I began writing songs hand over fist. The SCND Buskers had two purposes, fundraising and raising morale for people at marches and demonstrations. *Ian Davison*

BOB DYLAN

"He understood power of song, he was raised in an environment that meant he saw what popular song could be, how rock could be used. Before, pop song was just entertainment, but he saw it could be protest." *Stuart McHardy*

☙

"I admire him still, he's documented something over the years that no-one else has. An erudite, bright, informed person, never 'the voice of a generation', but a terrific gatekeeper for me. You entered the door he opened, and there was a cornucopia of things you'd not come across before, and also things you had come across before that took on additional provenance for you. There is something really generous in his artistry. His songs are full of references, reworkings of folk music melodies and sometimes references to the original meanings of original lyrics also. He is still writing prescient stuff, his take on things now as 68 years old, not 'trapped in a haircut' like some older artists.
"Dylan is not always a great craftsman, but art is the human being's saving grace, when it flies. Without art the human being has not achieved a great deal. We have to be open to the art, to enabling and allowing the art to happen. But the craft still prevails, you must go back and tidy up, make it as strong as you can.
I think that rules are appropriate in the craft, but utterly inappropriate in the art. There is nothing wrong with applying the rules you know and letting the art fly. When the art flies, the impetus is there, you often don't know where it's going to go.
"If you've got a list of things you want to achieve and hear, and you've worked out your four or six line format, and the list of things

you want to get in by hook or by crook, that's an excellent piece of craft, but there's probably not much art in it.
If it has art, it will touch people emotionally. And if politics means anything it's an emotional as much as a pedantic response." *Rab Noakes*

EURYDICE

"Eurydice will have been going for 21 years in 2010. The idea behind it initially was a night when women, (most of whom were involved, to a greater or lesser extent, in politics) could get away from the home and family and learn the songs they had often heard on demos etc. The songs sung covered a number of genres, more political in the earlier years than in the last six or so. Over the years Eurydice has lent its voice to, raised funds for and awareness of a number of causes - Oxfam, Amnesty International, Anti-Apartheid, Chernobyl - the list goes on.
"A lot of the stalwarts left, moved away, had other things happening in their lives etc. Recently the choir has been considerably involved with Asylum Seekers and singing at concerts to raise awareness. Work is also still done for the cause of peace and there's usually a gig every year for Amnesty.
"The choir had a broad range of material drawn from the Scots, English, Irish and American traditions, but also sang songs for fun - eg. "Sisters", Cole Porter's "Don't Fence Me In". The range of songs and traditions covered came from the fact that choir members came from "a' airts an' pairts" and we tried to encompass songs from as many cultures, places, traditions as we could. By far the most favourite song, in my opinion, was "Nkose Sikelele", particularly since the choir sang for Mandela that very wet day in George Square and in the concert hall afterwards. A memorable day indeed for everyone involved. Another song lustily sung was and still is of course Hamish's "Freedom Come-All-Ye"." *Gordeanna McCulloch*

ℭ

"They started as the Glasgow Socialist Women's Choir – they have enough vocal power to raise the [Glasgow Green] Mayday marquee off its moorings. The name came about because they felt, 'Well, we're no the Orpheus Choir'." *From 'One Singer One Song' by Ewan McVicar.*

ARCHIE FISHER

My induction into political song in the late 50's was through blues and protest songs on American issues. At the time, I was not aware of any current British or Scottish material that would have been classed under the term of current protest. Jacobite ballads were going through their second retrospective phase ... the first being when they were written in a romantic hindsight and then when they were rediscovered in the early stages of a new Scottish National awareness. It was hard in the atmosphere of the swinging 60s to find parallels to some of the extreme issues in the American songs and although many of the singers on the folksong Revival circuit sang British industrial ballads of mining, weaving and other industries, they too had a retro 'bad old days' context.

The retrieval of the Stone of Destiny spawned a batch of satirical and humorous ditties that amused our audiences and conjured up wry smiles but they were not the kind of stuff to set them all marching. The Polaris base on the Clyde was the tipping point for active and song protest ...I nearly said 'musical protest' ... but music was a mere carrier of the message as practically all of the songs were either parodies or set to familiar melodies to make them more easily remembered. Several highly reputable poets and writers became 'jingle bards' and kept us supplied with a steady flow of catchy and witty material.

The other wave of 'wee songs', mostly with a short shelf life, came in the 60's, many with an anti-royalty tone and what nowadays might be described as a xenophobic attitude towards our southern neighbours who always took it on the chin ...and why not ... we were the ones complaining.

I've never been an 'in your face' political singer and anything I've written, either industrial or personal, would probably fit more into the description of songs of what is broadly called 'the human condition',

perhaps better described as 'the shared experience of a culture, society, or community'. Are they political with a small 'p' ?
Specifically environmental songs had yet to emerge and the laconic remark from the late Alex Campbell about 'never singing about the rain forest with 'a chunk of mahogany and ebony round his neck' rings true of the time. There's a narrow line to walk in writing political songs. Some issues just won't sing and they are obvious to most sensitive people.
There were in the past, many examples of folksingers who could move between a traditional ballad about a battle to a contemporary antiwar song, or sing a whaling shanty followed by a 'save the planet' lyric without a flutter, but that was before political correctness overcorrected us all into a self conscious skid.
The death of the protest song has been regularly heralded over the last six decades and perhaps the fact that we are all much better informed politically may contribute to some songwriters' reticence. The 'canon' of Scottish Political song had a silencer on it for a while. Notable exceptions are the new works of past and present members of Battlefield Band Brian McNeill and Alan Reid who look to the newsreels as well as the archives. *Archie Fisher*

DICK GAUGHAN
"He is from Leith near Edinburgh, and was brought up immersed in the musical traditions and culture of the Gaels, both Scots and Irish, which naturally, therefore, provide the foundation for everything he does. He has been a professional musician and singer since Jan 1970, and made his first solo album in 1971. Working mainly in the areas now known as 'Folk' or 'Celtic' music, he has recorded quite extensively since then in many countries and in various combinations. Has also worked as a session musician in a wide variety of musical styles.
"He was an early member of the band 'Boys of the Lough', made three ablums with the band, 'Five Hand Reel' and in the 1990s he founded and produced the short-lived but quite extraordinary ensemble Clan Alba. His natural instrument, and perhaps what he is

happiest playing, is acoustic guitar. His greatest musical love is for the ancient traditional Scots ballads, and over the years he has recorded and performed many of these *"Muckle Sangs"*, The great Scots Ballads are mostly of very great antiquity with some of the themes and motifs being traceable back thousands of years." *Dick Gaughan's website*

☙

"During my tenure at Edinburgh University Folksong Club Dick Gaughan was an apprentice plumber, and I don't think he had it in mind to be a professional singer. He was a superb ballad singer and was a frequent and welcome guest at Folk Soc and my house. Apparently I had some happy influence getting him paid and first recorded." *Abby Sale*

☙

"Dick was not really doing what he is doing now in the late 1960s. He says it was not until Allende in Chile that he realised what he should be doing. Though he had a very short distance to travel. Dick asks why should he be that particular person who is identified as the political singer? It's because he does it so well. He doesn't do guitar workshops now, because others won't stand up with him, it's just a cheap concert. Nowadays people are in awe of him, probably a pity, the show businessisation." *John Barrow*

☙

"He is uncompromising in those areas where people need to be uncompromising. He never went seeking popularity, but because he was right he has become extremely popular. As a performer and as a writer I could sit and listen to him all night and be ready for more. His song 'Do You Think that the Russians Want War?' is a distillation, distilled into the title, which is the absolute, utter core." *Nancy Nicolson*

☙

"Some people say they are not sure about Dick, but he's one of the few political singers around, talking straight. Some people are uncomfortable about that." *Eileen Penman*

ROB GIBSON

During the period [of the 1950s] Gaelic and Scots stood alongside, in poetry books as well as the 'Ceilidh Song Books'. Willie Kellock encapsulated the idea of merging both cultures. Activism was related to a much more direct culture of songs passed on by word of mouth, songs were a much greater part of demonstrations, meetings or afterwards in the pub. It was the pre-Television era, people got a greater understanding of the songs, by hearing them. The 'Rebel Ceilidh Song Books' and Buchan's '101 Scottish Songs', they set things in train, we went through an activist phase in the 50s and 60s, when we were singing Blythman's and Jim McLean's songs, and the Corries were spreading a similar range of Scottish song.

At Munlochy, what became a ten month vigil in a yurt and a small caravan was at a layby that had not been declassified outside a farm on which there were GM trials in 2000 and 2001. After the first trial and knowing where the second one would take place, the attempt to focus energies across the country onto this area by having this vigil brought a whole lot of different responses, some were the kind of people who wanted to cut the crops down, which some of them did eventually. There were others who got involved in the issue of how to stop by legal means the expansion of such crops in our country.

In order that we popularised these things, part of the process was that the local radio was involved, that people were writing letters and preparing for a conference eventually on the subject. In that process the object of poems and songs and logos for the vigil which were represented by the bumblebee, that can "*fly for miles and spread GM pollen all the while*", to take a line from my song, we decided we would have some fundraising. At that, people started to write songs for the fundraising events.

Strange Fruits, around the time of Hallowe'en, was one of the first of those events. Local radio journalists were great at covering some of the music, so we decided to record some songs. We got together an EP with five songs to help raise money, called 'Oil Seed Raped', with the help of a recording studio at Auldearn who gave their services free as long as we paid for the discs. We sold several hundreds of them. It got

to the stage that at Christmas the Inverness Courier newspaper said it was in the local Top Twenty.
It was great because the music was the basic traditional material, with some more modern twists added by some of the artists. We used traditional tunes, as I did with 'Johnnie Cope', and put new modern words aimed at the farmer Jamie Grant, who was planting the crops, no doubt for a well paid fee. I think that was the traditional and modern response, it inspires people, makes them laugh perhaps, brings in satire, and a message that things can be different.
Because the fact that this was very much a Parliamentary response, by the then Labour Lib Dem executive, they were obviously 'looking at the precautionary principle' by allowing these field trials to take place. I know that Robin Harper, Green MP, and others were playing the CD in places where they might be heard by people in power. This is one way to get through, beyond singing to a live audience, and also some tracks were played on Moray Firth Radio. We wrote the words for the 'Munlochy Oil Seed Rape' song, and used the tune 'Johnnie Cope'. You can write new tunes, but sometimes the old ones are the best.
Andy Mitchell, now living in Portree, wrote an anti-nuclear song in the 1980s based on 'Grannie's Heilan Home'. His grannie lived on the seaboard at Balintore, Easter Ross. 'Grannie's Heilan Hame' was at Embo just across the Firth. He used the tune to have a go about the fallout from Chernobyl but also the fallout from Dounreay. A very funny song that became a theme song for the campaign against nuclear dumping. "*The heather bells are blowing a bonny bright yellow green*". It has a very pithy verse at the end, the council finally start to listen, the local MP gets down off his fence. I put the choruses onto a big card, and when we had an informal ceilidh we'd put up the card so people could sing the choruses. *Rob Gibson*

JOHN GREIG
In 1979 I lived in Frankfurt a.m. for about six months. It was there I heard the news that the Referendum had been lost. People I met all asked me how there could be a majority for the vote and it was lost? I had to admit that I did not understand that myself other than there

had been a motion in the Westminster parliament that became known as the sixty percent rule. This 'threw up' questions for the UK constitutional democracy. When is a majority not a majority? If law underpins democracy, which law should apply, Scots or English? The questions cascaded down at the time and the one question that remained unanswered until years later was who proposed the sixty percent rule? Well it turned out to be surprise, surprise Robin Cook, Scottish Labour Party minister. Sic a parcel o rogues in a nation!

A few weeks later I wandered into a radical book shop/ record store in Frankfurt (called '2001') and found a copy of a vinyl record on the American Folkways label called 'Ding Dong Dollar'. This was a collection of songs written and sung by amongst others the said Morris Blythman. I had heard these songs while still at school and they were protesting against the then new American submarine base at Faslane on the Clyde. I cheered myself up with this album from the post referendum blues. I had never seen this record for sale in a shop in Scotland.

I returned from Frankfurt to find that the unthinkable was on the cards; the Tories were going to win the next election due to something called the Winter of Discontent (winter? It was a whole fifteen years). The English middleclass had had enough of the strikes and were going to vote in someone called Mrs Thatcher. Who? I thought.

In the mid 70s I met Raymond Ross. He was just starting to involve himself in the literature of the Scottish left. He set up a literature magazine called 'Cencrastus' that ran for twenty-five plus years. Raymond was lodging with Morris Blythman, who talked and lived and breathed politics and that was how I met him. Raymond used to be always thinking up spurious reasons to run events in support of the magazine – like Sorley MacLean's birthday. I always ended up singing at them. At this point Ray and Morris were actively encouraging me. I knew the 'Ding Dong Dollar' repertoire. Morris would have us across in Glasgow at Harry McShane's 90th birthday, singing to the tune of a Leadbelly song – "Harry will be 90 on the 7th of May". The whole place would sing this like idiots – Morris had us all standing doing it!

He loved Leadbelly tunes. Morris was always working on creating the Republic. *John Greig*

HAMISH HENDERSON

"Thinking back, I guess we all knew Hamish's politics, interests, personality flaws and genius. He was an overwhelming feller and I don't know of anyone who vaguely thought the less of him for any flaws. What we felt right up front were things like extreme generosity with his time and knowledge. Nearly anyone collecting in Scotland consulted him and he always came through with names, addresses, background, and in several cases I know of, basic glossary of Gaelic and Tinker Cant. In at least one case the beneficiary baldly claimed to have researched these things himself.

"Hamish would never again speak to someone who lied about these things or who stole credit for himself. Hamish didn't care overmuch about receiving credit, he just wouldn't tolerate someone stealing it. I think Hamish was the most painstakingly honest person I ever met. The generosity and honesty (in folk music but also in life) were the influence he had on me more than his politics. I can't speak for others." *Abby Sale*

☙

"Hamish is a wonderful figure to me, but not the propagandist that Morris Blythman or Norman Buchan were. He would not compromise re Scots linguistic difficulties, but the aesthetic results were wonderful - a joy to sing if you understand references – a coterie appeal, farfetched, making poetic demands on the listener." *Ian Davison*

☙

"I'm always surprised at Hamish's 'Men of Knoydart', it takes a racist anti-English line. 'The John Maclean March' is too international. His structure is beautiful in 'The Banks of Sicily', but general as far as Scotland is concerned, people can read their own thing into it, it's not specific enough for me. Was he Sky High Joe? I don't believe it, knowing him and talking with him. There were few songs from him in those days, never felt he had that oomph, I didn't see it. His songs require quality singing, his language is tremendous. I'm surprised he wrote so few, and so general. He was generous, 'Knoydart' is the only one that is quite strong." *Jim McLean*

☙

"To hear Arthur Johnstone sing totally unaccompanied the 'Freedom Come-All-Ye', can just about move me to tears, no problem. It's the conviction that the singer has." *John Powles*

☙

"Hamish to me is the huge figure that epitomised that idealism, making things more fair. The enormity of John Maclean going to prison and being force fed, but then the voice of people, "*Great John Maclean has come back*" and the streets of Glasgow are filled, huge rejoicing though he was tragically depleted by his treatment. Hamish's great anthem of the 'Freedom Come-All-Ye' – stretching hands over the world very much like Burns. These songs have a quickening effect on people's consciousness – can't think they don't shift people's opinions." *David Campbell*

ALISTAIR HULETT

I left Scotland for New Zealand with my family when I was nearly sixteen. We went there on the assisted passage scheme. I had discovered folk music a couple of years previously. First it was Dylan and the 'Folk Boom' protest thing, then I heard the Dubliners and that set me off in pursuit of a repertoire of songs from my own culture rather than adopting the American version of folk culture. By the time I got to New Zealand I was singing mainly Scots, Irish and English traditional folk songs, some American stuff, blues and country and also contemporary stuff by Dylan and MacColl, people like that. Really, anything that took my fancy, although I was still adopting different voices and styles of delivery for the different songs I sang, rather than making them my own, as I try to do now. At that time, nearly every folk singer I admired, both in Britain and in New Zealand, was either a Communist Party member or a fellow traveller. It seemed that way to me, anyway. Folk song and the folk scene was my introduction to socialist politics. I never actually joined a political party back then but politics and political campaigns were part and parcel of

the scene in those days. You couldn't be in the folk circle and not be somehow drawn into the political nature of those times. Later, after my two years in New Zealand were up, that being one of the imposed conditions of assisted passage, I went over to Australia and it was exactly the same there. To be a folk singer was a political position in and of itself back in those days.
I lived in England for nearly two years when I got back from Oz in '96. I'd recorded an album in '95 with Dave Swarbrick and we came back together. My first taste of the folk scene here was down in England, and my strongest impression was how de-politicised the scene had become. In Australia I was playing with a very loud and abrasive punk folk band called Roaring Jack and I was used to expressing myself onstage in quite a politically strident way. Audiences in England seemed rather taken aback by it, I thought. Swarb always encouraged me to really go for it but I did begin toning my way of putting it across down a fair bit. You do when you can hear that sharp intake of breath all around you. Even so, it seems I was still much more politically outspoken than some of these audiences were accustomed to or thought was decent. I met a few kindred souls gigging round on the folk scene, Roy Bailey, Robb Johnson, people like that, but openly political, left wing folk music definitely was rather thin on the ground around the English folk clubs and festivals. That's not a criticism, just an observation. I love a lot of what I hear in England and don't for a second want to suggest that folk singers have a duty to be political or of the left. I do notice, though, that whereas it was once commonplace for most performers to be politically engaged, that is not the case at all nowadays. There are the notable exceptions of course, old timers with the fire still burning in their bellies and new kids coming through with the fire in their eyes. I just wish there were more of them.
In '98 I moved back up to Glasgow where I originally set out from and instantly fell in with a great crowd of politically engaged and motivated folk artists who were pretty much in the mould of the folk singers that first inpired me back in the sixties. I don't mean overtly political zealots, just your honest folk artists with a varied repertoire

but a way of seeing traditional music that is rooted in a class analysis of society. People who stand in the tradition of the likes of Hamish Henderson, Ewan MacColl, Gordeanna McCulloch, The Exiles, Matt McGinn, Ray and Archie Fisher, Dick Gaughan, oh I could go on forever. I would rather listen these days to a traditional singer or a contemporary song that understands the social relations, the centuries of inequality and exploitation, that gave rise to this music, than to a left wing sermon set to music. Although I'll admit I've given a sermon or two in my time, but that's how I feel about it now. Of course, this is not the 1960s and 70s, it's not a comparable time of social upheaval and political unrest, but politics seems still to be part of the warp and weft of the folk scene here in Scotland in a way it's not down south right now.

I got involved in songwriting through necessity really. I was on the hippie trail back in the mid-seventies, living in the far north of Queensland, Australia. I was beachcombing, doing itinerant farm work and living in makeshift shelters. There wasn't any electricity and no canned music, so if we wanted new songs to sing we needed to make them up ourselves. I began writing a lot then. I'd had a few goes at it previously but this was my first real burst of sustained songmaking. Other musicians began doing my songs around the campfire network we had going and that really encouraged me to keep writing. It continued in much the same way when I went around India for a couple of years, before I got back to OZ just in time for the Punk War in the very late 70s and early 80s. I got a band going in '85 called Roaring Jack that was basically a punk version of the 60s folk groups I used to listen to. All the other guys involved were from a similar background and the folk music we knew and loved was political and class conscious. I really began songwriting in earnest then and many of the songs from that period are still in my repertoire today.

IAN MCCALMAN

It's a misconception that groups who sing together have the same beliefs. Since I was fifteen I started thinking about inequalities in politics and how people were treated. Some great memorable songs that might look quite simple [may have been] written for a march, but they have lived on through their simplicity, and being catchy can have much more import than what I write. I'm much more social comment, the wagging finger. Hamish Henderson was the 'Sandy Bell's Man'. He was always there, we'd see a lot of him and we'd all join in, an element of 'who the hell is Mandela' but you'd find out.

We dealt with images, because we performed more in foreign countries. Inspired songs deal in images. I've heard quite a few songs with too much information, so the message gets confused.

We don't preach just to the converted. We have to accept that our particular scene is dying. Youngsters who are going into rock are doing more with political song than the guys doing half full folk clubs. The McCalmans have built up our audience, and they have not yet died, and they'll accept songs. We were singing a new song about family members not talking because of what happened in the miners' strike in 1984. I can explain it to a Denmark or German audience, about old arguments in families. These songs are generally understood. I hear more new political songs in clubs than in the recording studio I run. I think, "That's a good song, but we can't, don't need to sing them." I write songs myself. If I write a song for a purpose, for someone else, I'm going to fail. I write songs for myself, as a therapy. I have a lot to write about.

Can songs change opinions? That is more likely to happen through me than through Dick Gaughan - he sings to like-minded people all the time. People come to hear us sing songs they know, then we give them something new. Some of my songs use the sugar-coated pill to draw people in.

Others do not. 'The Lying Truth' is a song of mine that says people have their own truth, it can be obscene, political, religious, but because they have their own truth they cannot accept others' truth. It was written out of sheer anger, about torture in Iraq. People say 'We do this because it is right'. The song is vicious, it pulls no punches. *Ian McCalman*

EWAN MACCOLL

Some would expect me to consider Ewan MacColl a Scottish political songwriter and examine his work in detail. He was certainly a gifted and committed political songwriter, and through his Scottish parentage would have been eligible to play sports for Scotland, but he was born and raised in Salford, and his work was on the national British stage – both theatrical, folk song singing, song making, teaching and developing the skills of younger singers. He sang many older Scottish songs with great power and a convincing accent.

Of his politically explicit songs I can think of only one that has any Scots language or reference – 'Jamie Foyers', where like Burns he took the first verse of an old song and made something glorious and new from it. MacColl and Peggy Seeger, together with BBC programme maker Charles Parker, created the radio series of 'Radio Ballads'. His recorded work and collections of songs were very influential for young Scots singers. Ewan MacColl was his nom-de-plume, he was born Jimmy Miller.

𝕮𝕲

"He thought somewhere in his head he was Scottish. He wrote mounds of stuff, a lot became very popular but it's the singer songwriter, because people borrow his persona, rather than taking the song on. People took on his nanny goat voice. He was a fantastic writer, but I'm not a fan of his singing. He was very generalist, communist in approach. I sat and talked with him for two hours, when aged 21. He's talking, Peggy crocheting. He'd lose the point of what he was saying, she'd dig him in the ribs and tell him, he'd leap up to get a book down to make his point.

"I was a Scottish Nationalist Republican, I had a tartan tie on, McLean tartan. He got annoyed, 'Look at this tartan', I said 'It is McLean tartan - Mr Miller'. Peggy had to hold him back. He stopped at the Jacobites re Scotland, wouldn't have anything to do with Republicanism." *Jim McLean*

MATT MCGINN

"I took to Matt very quickly, when I met him in the Iona Community. He had straightforward songs like 'Mambo', but it struck me then his forté was humorous. I picked up gradually how serious he could be. I didn't realise he was writing quite soulful songs as well as very useful political songs." *Ian Davison*

☙

"I met Pete Seeger at Tonder [in Denmark], he was asking after Jeanetta McGinn, Matt's wife. He knew and admired Matt. That's hard for people to believe, but this god, Pete Seeger, looked up to Matt McGinn! We don't know the strength of who we have in Scotland." *Ian McCalman*

☙

"Politics seemed to seep out of Matt McGinn, there was no way you can say he wasn't political, he was the one guy in the 1960s I'd call a political songwriter and singer." *John Barrow*

STUART MCHARDY

I played about with [writing songs] back in the CND days, bits and pieces. You don't think about them beyond what you're doing, they're for that period. You use them to attract people to meetings, as a social bond. Don't hold on to them. I wrote ' The Poll Tax Rap' for the 'Songs From Under the Poll Tax' cassette. I would need the text to perform it now. "We all know what's going on, Just another Tory con etc", with an electronic drum backing. That was not written for a march or event, but using a recording to get the word out, and 'drum up support'. But all such schemes fall down when it comes to marketing, they become more a memento.

Another purpose of political song is as a form of education. 'The Freedom Come-All-Ye' - people say they don't understand words, then I explain a bit, and they say "I'm beginning to get it". Hamish Henderson's 'D Day Dodgers' kept cropping up in the 60s, it's a good song. History is propaganda, spin, the party line. Popular song has taken the place of story.

How important was Bob Dylan? How long have you got? He understood the power of song, he was raised in an environment that meant he saw what popular song could be. He saw that rock could be protest. Before him pop song was entertainment. Dylan had ability, drive, genius. Is he still not political? He still comments on social conditions.
In Scotland we have the problem of inheritance of empire. There is pretence that Scottish history is like English history. In fact communitarianism defines your life, and it survives here, these ideas develop and are accepted here. Songs are one way of identifying our tribal element!
Burns is known as a songwriter here, to the rest of the world he is known as a poet - other than 'Auld Lang Syne'. He accessed the voice and shared experience of people, the common thread of humanity that is close to our surface, so he was the antithesis of high poetry.
I was excited about CND, thousands of people marched in Glasgow, a few dozen of us did in Dundee. There were massive Glasgow marches against the Iraq war – not the same in Dundee. Marches are not organised by posters now, mobile phones etc are used. Community now has different forms, through the Internet songs can be swapped, videos shared. *Stuart McHardy*

GEORDIE MCINTYRE

I don't write a lot of songs, I'm not disciplined. When I went to the Glasgow Folk Club, there was no way I would write songs. Adam McNaughtan, Ian Davison and Dominic Behan were writing songs. But I read an argument in the press that The Pill was anti-life. Someone said "What's wrong with coitus interruptus?" I wasn't quite sure what that was, but when I did find out, I knew that the popular phrase for it was "Jumping off at Paisley".
Matt McGinn had written a song about The Pill. I knocked off a few verses, pro the contraceptive pill, 'Don't jump off at Paisley', and sang it in the club. Hamish Imlach heard it, and recorded it on an album called 'Murdered Ballads'. That was my first song. It was a wee political song, one line was "Remember your conscience is the boss",

very weak, but too much analysis leads to paralysis. Some songs need to be broken down line by line, and the more you look at a text the more you are likely to do it justice.

We are all trying to say the same thing differently. War is bad, peace is good - there are a million ways to express that. You can draw motifs and phrases from older songs. Some songs take three days, some three months, some thirty years. Songs on current issues must be got out, and so have to be squibs, for the occasion and the issue. I am one of the singers who write songs, I'm not a singer-songwriter - they only sing their own songs.

We sing songs that have to be listened to, not part of a percussive pulse for dancing to - those don't need to have any poetic merit, they're part of a sound package. 'The Seven Men Of Knoydart', The Peatbog Soldiers', these are not knees-up songs. Having said that, when the Glasgow Song Guild was in its heyday, they wrote songs that were so clever, thoughtful and perceptive. They said, we want these songs to go out, we'll use good familiar tunes, whether for marching or concerts.

In about 2005 we were singing at Girvan Folk Festival. Just before we finished one song, this bloke stood up in the middle of a packed audience and said, "What the hell good are these songs you're singing? They've done nothing to improve the human condition, they've not prevented any wars."

I could not ignore it, or say, "Caw canny, Jimmy, I'm in the middle of a song."

I stopped and winged it, and said, "It's perfectly true that so many political songs are by their nature idealistic. Maybe the writer would see themselves as part of the practical solution, but they are often dealing with ideals. Ideals very often come from dreamers. Hamish Henderson was a dreamer. The 'Brotherhood of Man' is a dream. Freddie Anderson was a dreamer. Without the dreamers, where would we be?"

The anti-war tribe is a tribe I happen to applaud. The songs are transparent, openly saying "This is the way I see it and how I hope you'll consider or reconsider seeing it". I began to hear these songs when I was a radio mechanic. It was through folk song that I eventually went to University, expanding my horizons. I could see the songs in a wider perspective. They opened my eyes to many aspects of life. *Geordie McIntyre*

JIM MCLEAN

All my songs are political. Even the poetry I wrote way back as a child, in some SNP paper, when 15 or 16, was making the point that I wanted to make. I don't think I've written something that isn't political. People talk about my 'Glencoe' song. I like to make my point there that King William signed that order, so there is a point there too. Then when I used to do themed albums, with Alastair McDonald, I would write a song about Culloden. In my liner notes I would say this is not in praise of Bonnie Prince Charlie, he chose the graveyard for himself.

When I heard Morris Blythman's 'Coronation Coronach', the words and tune hit me. And the Scottish language. I'm from Paisley, Glasgow has idioms, Paisley has language. In Glasgow they'd say "My belly's hurtin", in Paisley "Ah've a pain in ma wame". We sang Irish political songs [in early days] because we'd nothing for ourselves. My initial songs used Scots tunes - 'Maggie's Waddin', 'NAB for Royalty'. I did this because few folkies could read music and I didn't sing. I sometimes used American tunes. I liked Guthrie's songs, I first heard them through Josh McRae's singing. They were strong, fighting the establishment. Josh and Nigel Denver were the two front singers on the 'Ding Dong Dollar' album. Josh was a lovely man, very honest, but Dylan was the killer for him politically. [*McRae began to sing Dylan's songs rather than his earlier repertoire.*]

I realised what I wanted, a separate Scotland. Labour was always unionist. I wanted to bring out an album, with sleeve notes by MacDiarmid, nobody in Scotland would touch it. I went to Major Minor in London for my first album, in London. Then I began producing, and then started my own Nevis label. Topic was the only big company at the time, Ewan MacColl was recording Jacobite songs,

safe material, nothing more. There was no money in poetry or folk music, no small labels.
My first themed album was 'Scottish Republican Songs' a Republican album, sleeve notes by Hugh MacDiarmid. Winnie Ewing wrote to say it helped her get elected. Then I did a Major Minor album with Hugh MacDiarmid reading his own work, and I edited it. I made other albums after the [1972] UCS album, with Alastair McDonald, then Nigel Denver. A Burns album, then another Republican one.
I think some of Eric Bogle's songs are tremendous. There are very few singer songwriters I can listen to, most are too introverted, telling you what they feel. Dylan is the same. He broke the scene. To me he diverted the movement away in Scotland, people began to write introverted songs.
I knew him, took him to clubs in London. When I first met him we chatted and he asked me if I was Hamish Henderson. I had a long chat with him that night explaining, in my opinion, all Scottish songs were political. This, incidentally, was the first time he sang in London. He visited Martin Carthy who lived across from me. One group [of singers and songwriters] were the pot heads, writing introverted songs. The other group were the drinkers. Lots of singers after Dylan didn't write for the punters, but for themselves. Very few of their songs could be picked up by others.
I'm not surprised fewer of my songs are sung now. They were of the time, but 'Glencoe' has political lines, people don't always notice that. 'Smile in Your Sleep' makes my point, but as a lullaby. I wrote a lot for marches and platforms, later my songs were for albums.
Jim McLean

DOLINA MACLENNAN
There was a lull in song writing in Gaelic until [the group] RunRig. In 1892 Mary McPherson said, "The wheel will turn for you through the hardness of your hand and the strength of your fist." There was a wonderful song writer in Uist, Ho Dan, Uist bard, very famous, dead now. He would write songs about the tinker's horse, but also political

ones. They wouldn't know what a folk song was, but songs were being written all along by village bards, about anything that happened.
[When I met folk song] I had just come down from the Islands. My education didn't start properly till I came to Edinburgh. My father was a Labour man, an election agent, he died when I was twelve. There were local songs about poaching, making fun of bailiff. 'A rod from the wood, a deer from the hill, a fish from the river – three things a Highlander should never be ashamed of.'
I joined the SNP in Dublin while 'Cheviot and Stag' was playing in the Abbey Theatre. A man came up and said "What a nationalist you must be." I answered "I can't equate nationalism with socialism." He said "Remember what Connolly said, 'A nation first of all has to be free to make its own decisions'." I said "Thank you sir", and came back to Scotland and joined the SNP. *Dolina MacLennan*

NANCY NICOLSON

I was writing songs that were political before I'd actually realised I was writing political song. There's quite a lot of thinking it's dangerous to do before you start. Sometimes you've done something and it amounts to more that you thought it was going to amount to.
It can be dangerous to be very unconsciously writing a political song, because you forget what was the impetus that made you do it, and you then think of it being judged from the side as if by a teacher, or a college or something, trying to analyse it. It has to be listened to, and it has to get its home in somebody's head long before they have any right to analyse it, because they'll interfere with the process itself if they're too busy analysing to listen to the heart of it.
There are very few things in the world that are not political, and a song is one of the most effective ways of expressing yourself. So I will probably argue that most songs in the world are political, and I do know that one of the most political songs that I've ever written is 'Listen to the Teacher', which sounds tinky tinky, little girly, you know, skipping along merrily, telling a funny little song, but that song speaks of a bairn going to school and finding that her or his own native language is rejected. Now, if you reject the only way a child speaks,

that's tantamount to rejecting the child themselves, and all that they can do. The first verse, the child goes to school, is scolded for saying 'hoose' instead of 'house'. The second verse has the child not opening his mouth to say a word.
It was very sad. I'd found myself at the age of about five or six being rejected by somebody that I deeply knew should not have had the right to reject me, and the whole culture of that day was so much that you do what teachers tell ye that I didn't even complain to my mother when this teacher gave me the big angry eyes which said that saying 'hoose' was wrong.
I would worry if someone introduced me as a protest singer cos they're often looked upon as people who have a very personal agenda and they're protesting on their own behalf, not on anybody else's.
Nancy Nicolson

RAB NOAKES
I have done some songs with a political purpose, for example 'Won't Let You Do That Again', 'Don't Keep Passing Me By', 'Spin' and 'How Can I Believe You Now?'. Thatcher's re-election put a number of things into focus for me. I looked back on my old man's generation. That was the end of what they had achieved. After the Falklands you knew we were in deep trouble. This was a mean spirited person. I had come across people like that all my life, people who demonstrated disdain for others, feeling intellectual and economic superiority. Was there ever a more pointless exercise than the Cold War? Nobody has ever explained to me what is the desirability of power. Why do people go to extreme levels to expand what they don't even enjoy?
I wrote a couple of songs at that time. My father and many others went to fight World War Two for socialism. Not just to beat Hitler, it was much deeper.
You get some terrific songs sometimes about issues. The 1984/5 miners strike, the UCS struggle, the South Side Baths campaign – that was Alastair Hulett writing the songs - all good projects need a good

project manager, person who can corral people, and mobilise things and abilities.

Some issues fire me up, the lack of public housing just now, and the treatment of our service people post the Iraq conflict. Our services men and women are a highly specialised workforce and should be treated accordingly. There's an urgent state of affairs between our armed forces and our public, the treatment of wounded soldiers. Economic decline pushes people into war. The main reason for war is commerce, and now also for the clean-up economies – that's why we have wars. The best war songs are about the service people, not about the always ludicrous politics. War equates with a flaw in evolution, there is something wrong, that we can think war is a sensible way of conflict resolution.

Scots songwriters see the absurdity of the Bomb, and can demonstrate it through use of tunes and cartoon imagery, and the quick journalistic response to what someone says. If anything, an anti-war message is more successfully carried through drama than song. Songs tend to become date-stamped, and from a wordsmithery viewpoint a lot of the words you have to put in there are a bit lumpy.

I find it hard to empathise with territorial conquest and nationalism, except for nationalism as respect for your own national culture and therefore for others' national culture. But nationalism for nationalism's sake! Which is all there is left, there's very little respect left except for the homogenised global culture that covers us all.

I have worked on accompaniment, I am not a musician as such, I play guitar in behind the song. I've worked hard on that, starting with guitar phrases to make songs. It imbues them with a rhythm and mood, more than a keyboard can.

Burns did not write tunes, but clearly he had an ear for memory, he decided his energy was best expended elsewhere. Why did Elvis not write songs? He did all the things a songwriter does, had skills of interpretation and finding his way into songs, unusual qualities as a singer, his high tenor voice, he had all the necessary elements.

Many of my songs are about relationships, they are interpersonal about what is going on around you, not self-centeredly personal as in mass-produced pop. My songs generally come out of chord sequences, or rhythm, or mood created, out of that comes dummy little things that fit rhythmically, where do the vowels go on the beat? Often a line comes out. Anything to get the thing going, then something sticks. I sometimes use other people's tunes. If it's a lyric idea, maybe try and find an older tune to stick it in, maybe amend. I also like to put in little bits of homage that are hopefully undetectable. *Rab Noakes*

CATHIE PEATTIE

People may not think their songs are important enough, because they themselves are not important. I grew up with music and song, my father sang, and played the mouthie and the bones. Cowboy songs were the pop music of the time, he liked Gene Autrey, but also Scots songs. My grannie was a singer, but she'd never have dreamt of singing at a concert. She had wonderful versions of 'Danny Boy' and 'Dark Lochnagar', my father's lullaby for me was 'Scots Wha Hae'. I don't see that song as a Nationalist dirge, but I'm a socialist, for me it's Burns challenging the society he was living in.

When I was twelve or thirteen my music lesson was about singing opera. Then I heard Donovan and Joan Baez singing, and that was me. I identified with that more than with Puccini. It was different, and it was real, you could sing freely from the heart, and enjoy and understand what you were singing. I particularly identified with the political songs that Joan Baez and Dylan were singing. Then I went back to look at our own stuff. My dad knew Irish Republican songs, he collected songbooks, and he brought in the Bo'ness songbooks from the Lea-Rig.

The 'Ma Maw's an MSP' song that Linda McVicar wrote for me reflects women now, the suggestion that women want it all, you can be a politician but you've still got to live your family life and meet your responsibilities as well. I do a lot of work in schools, I get invited as an MSP, and I teach it to the kids, and discuss with them about what if your mum was a politician, and they love it. It's a funny song, and kids associate with it, and that I'm a woman daft enough to come to school and sing to them. They ask for the words.

The first year of Parliament a group of MSPs decided to do a Fringe concert for Childline. I was the only Labour party member there. When we were sharing the songs we would sing, I had my Eric Bogle songbook with me. Alec Ferguson was excited to see it, and borrowed it, he sang Eric Bogle songs. I was surprised that a Tory was happy to sing these songs. We go through life having opinions about folk, and we can make a mistake thinking that say Tories will not want to sing political songs.
When Hamish Henderson died, I put a motion down in Parliament. When we debated it and discussed his life, I had to get permission to sing in the Scottish Parliament, you're not allowed to do it, it's against Standing Orders, but I was allowed "One verse, no more, and don't expect others to join in". The Glasgow Herald asked why did I not sing more.
In the Labour Party, after branch meetings and AGMs, we sing. Folk in politics enjoy songs, and singing together. If someone starts to sing, it's not about alcohol, people hear and they join in. I remember at a Conference, Neil Kinnock was speaking on the stage, and he spoke, then sang 'We Shall Overcome'. Folk got up and sang it with him, though others were appalled.
Bill Butler, Anniesland MSP, hosted a Parliament anniversary event on the Spanish Civil War. Arthur Johnstone came along and sang. He finished with 'The Freedom Come-All-Ye', I see that song as a song of peace, Arthur saw it as a song of struggle. I grew up hating war, but what do you do about Fascism? *Cathie Peattie*

EILEEN PENMAN

have always sung. My dad sang a bit. He was very active in the NUR, my parents were old lefties of the 30s in the Communist Party, and Labour. We were brought up in a political household, for us it was every day, him working for the union. My older brother, Jack, got me interested in folk song. He discovered Alan Lomax, Pete Seeger, Woody Guthrie, he started bringing American folk music home in the mid to late 50s. He knew about the Howff in Edinburgh, Roy Guest. I saw Martha Schlamme in Edinburgh. I was hooked, the singers I heard at the time had a lot of passion, it came from the gut.

Then I got involved in youth politics, 'Bella Ciao', then the anti-Polaris songs. I got a guitar, and Jack taught me a few chords.

Then I had kids and was away from the scene. At the first Edinburgh Folk Festival, in about 1979 in Chambers Street I saw the very young Cunninghams, they were just magic. I felt I wanted to get involved, went to the Crown Folk Club in Parish St, and saw Dolina MacLennan, Jean Redpath, Brian Miller, Cyril Tawney and Josh McRae there. Then I began to go to Edinburgh Folk Club. I started to sing there, the first song I sang was Hamish's 'Farewell to Sicily', I can't remember what drew me to it.

I went back to work, became heavily involved in the Trade Union movement. In 1984, during the Miners Strike, Left Turns was set up. It was an Edinburgh organisation set up by Dick Gaughan with May Shaw from Ireland, and performed at benefits for Miners, for Lee Jeans, for Nicaragua. I started singing with May, we would end political events with 'Carry it On'. I got involved, organising and putting on singers' workshops with the Crown Folk Club.

I have written some songs. They were made for the time. Dick had adapted the American union song 'Which Side Are You On?', I've carried on adapting it. I sang in a pub with John Greig and Tony McManus. When the Poll Tax campaign on I put my thoughts together and came up with a couple of things. Then I got involved in the 'Women's Right to Choose' campaign.

I wrote a few anti-war songs, but I don't sing them very much. I'm not sure why I don't, I think I'm unsure about ramming my thoughts down someone's throat. I'm quite a direct writer, not subtle. I write when I've something to say. When the war started in Lebanon a few years ago, I felt impotent, I got out a guitar and wrote a song. It's an anti-war song. I sang it on the Long March from Faslane. I've sung that at a few places.

I've written another new song, about an Edinburgh suffragette, because of the 'Guid Cause' march to mark the centenary of the Suffragette Movement. When we are marching people will sing older

songs, we decided to put together a songbook, some of them older and less accessible, some newer. The book is to be called 'The Right to Vote and Aa That', it includes a song written at the time to the tune of 'A Man's A Man'.
Sometimes a line will fire the imagination – 'walking makes the road' was said to me by someone. I was going to South Africa, with the SEAD charity, on an exchange study visit, and decided to write a song for it, on the theme of mutual solidarity. I used the line "*Walking makes the road, when freedom is your goal*'. I used an American style tune, I'm not very good at writing from the Scots tradition, I don't know why that is, you'd think something would come out closer to my own culture. A Somali student was murdered in Edinburgh, and I wrote a song about it. I adapted MacColl's Moving On Song', added new verses re refugees in Scotland.
I am involved in the Protest in Harmony Edinburgh group. It is uplifting to have a big presence of voices. In about 2004 some of the members of an Edinburgh singers' group wanted more songs to sing on demos. Workshops were organised, then monthly workshops. Some songs were written specially, and a book put together. Now song themes themes include climate change and the environment.
I don't often sing for money, mostly for benefits. I am unable to separate my political background from my singing. I assumed when young that folk music was all political, then was surprised that some singers are not. *Eileen Penman*

ABBY SALE

Only the work of Ewan MacColl was available to us. He was a promoter and a good performer. We came to Edinburgh, and went to Edinburgh University Folk Society – Folk Soc. There were people singing, doing harmonies. We said to ourselves, 'Oh, this is what it is supposed to be. This is not people in Harvard Square or Greenwich Village showing off, these are people joining together and doing stuff. And this I like'. We were solid from day one.
I had no sense of an actual political element in the way songs were sung, not in the the sense of Woody Guthrie or Pete Seeger. Songs

would come in, for example those of John Watt, but just as casually as songs of the Copper family or Archie Fisher or the Stewarts of Blair.
Dick Gaughan had not developed as a political singer at that time. Even MacColl did not bring that material in at that time, it was just folk song. You would hear a Mary Brooksbank song, or maybe even be lucky enough to hear her, you would be swayed by it, how she was speaking about conditions. But you would not go out with flags and torches.

Matt McGinn was the one exception. You would get carried away by what he had to say. The one person that you would get involved with the politics of what he had to say, though he would also sing something hysterically funny.

Hamish Henderson came to our house, and I became one of his 100,000 closest friends. Hamish opened other areas to us. His songs were sung and well known, I sat and drank with him, but everybody was in awe of him. He was such a charismatic person, and such a strange person to be charismatic – tall, gawky, funny speaking guy – but totally amazing. You enjoyed being with him, maybe because he was a good writer and thinker, but he was not a preacher like MacGinn. Hamish would write and pull us in. You could be influenced but not preached at. I liked that man.

I appreciated Folk Soc. It needed officers, elections. I'd always wanted to be treasurer of something and was elected. I would suggest ideas, people would agree. I did make some attempt to influence the idea that we actually promote and support folk music. *Abbey Sale*

PEGGY SEEGER

Political song is to me a total necessity. Musicians, we express ourselves in different ways. Being a folk musician, folk music coming from the lowest economic strata, I have always sided with the impoverished majority. Their songs express their hopes and dreams, and sometimes what they're gonna do about it.

So I sometimes feel that just singing hard times songs about the past is kinda like being a museum keeper. That's fine, nothing wrong with

that at all. I made that big step ahead when I went with Ewan MacColl. We decided to be museum keepers and add to the museum.
'Political' is virtually the science of human organisation. People often say political and they mean left wing. Of course political is all strata. Right from Che Guevara to Robert Mugabe to Hitler it's all political. It's action in trying to create an organisational difference, if you like. And sometimes just stating the case can do that. Just going along with the museum, and what there is there, and saying 'This is what happens'. When you do that you can almost predicate, you can almost expand that into saying 'This can happen again'. Singing about your troubles is the first step in political action, defining what there is to fight about.
So I think being political, they say nowadays especially with the ecological thing, and the global warming, you set yourself wherever you feel comfortable, and go a little bit further on issues. You can be political when you recycle your trash, you can be more political when you get other people to do that. You can be even more political when you set up an organisation that will arrange that all of the trash is recycled. You can get even more political when you force government to do this, so protest - you are protesting against something, when it's political you are in a way protesting for something.
I'm not an academic about these things. Protest songs sometimes seem to be what glues the protesters together, and help us to feel that we're not alone, and to help us protest together. Songs sometimes rub up - they're very abrasive for people who aren't in movements. Sometimes they're vulgar, not well expressed, they are for the converted. I feel the converted need a lot of songs myself - we need more than just 'Here we go, here we go, here we go'. Things that will keep us moving. And will also have to suggest how we can speak more to the unconverted.
The strongest Iraq song that I have is the 'Ballad of Jimmy Massey'. It's a song I made out of the words of an Iraq marine. It was Radio Ballads style, make a song out of their words. This song talks about an ordinary boy, comes from the working class. It's his words, [I just helped him along]. It talks about his life. He thought the Marines were

the cat's whiskers, and then how the Marines literally moulded him and sent him to Iraq, where he found himself killing women and children. He left, and he came back, and he now works in the anti-Iraq War body. But it tells it in his words.
To me that's a political song, but it's also a protest song. It's his protest, but I'm retelling it because people can identify with him in a way they can't identify with me. He actually says 'I think the world shouldn't be run by men'. But if I say that ....
I take it back to him, and ask "Is this what you want to be saying?" Which is what we did. I see that as a big difference between political and protest, though the line is shady. *Peggy Seeger*

DONALD SMITH
I was very influenced by Hamish Henderson's approach, that was at the core of everything he was doing. Going right back to the People's Ceilidhs, you had union songs, bothy ballads, protest songs, traditional ballads, all there in the mix.
That connected up for me, at that time I was becoming involved in Scottish theatre. The very same impetus drove that. We were moving toward the Cheviot and Stag. It was tapping into cultural forms that belonged to communities, that should be allowed to own those traditions as their own, to develop them as their own, to contribute to them.
It contributed to that atmosphere of shaking up the sense of who was running Soctland and why, in terms of the culture and the politics together. Folk tradition is not a museum curiosity. Songs are made in particular contexts or adapted for particular reasons just as stories are. And I think that is what is so powerful about the specific political song. We see, as it were, the process of development and creation in a very live and immediate way.
For example, one of the songs we were taught in school was 'The Bonny Earl O Moray' – "*Ye Hielands and ye Lowlands, whaur hae ye been?*" – and I loved that song before I had ever heard a real traditional singer utter it as one of Scotland's great traditional ballads. And of course it was a bit of bloody, political propaganda as I was to

find out later. The Earl of Moray had been murdered and his mother had exhibited his body in the church at Leith, naked with all the stab wounds – somebody had to come along and paint it. It was the equivalent of appearing in The Sun or the Daily Record, and the song appears, not only condemning the murder, but hinting that the reason for it was sexual jealousy, and that the king looked the other way and let Moray be murdered by Huntly.

So that's a song that absolutely picks up on all sorts of traditional elements of folk song, but it's made in the crucible of really, really dark political conflict. I think that's where political song comes into its own because it demonstrates so many really important things about how folk song works, how songs are made and why they're made – the context in which they're made. There's a kind of energy and immediacy in all that. It's a specific and fascinating example, but not different from the way folk song as a whole works.

The influence of song tradition in poetry in Scotland is massive. One of the ways that that continues to come out is the emphasis on public reading of poetry. Now that's much bigger here, relatively, than in England. Of course poets at these events sometimes move between song and poetry, but actually the speaking of poems at public events is still important to Scottish poetry, and it affects the style of poems as well – part of that same sort of cultural mix.

So on the one hand, political song is very specific and immediate, and on the other it's tapping in to universal themes like the struggle for freedom and liberty. Civil Rights, anti-war and anti-nuclear songs – they all tap into international universal values. They communicate across cultures as well, and that's another important aspect.

At the moment, we're in this very individualistic period in our culture and society. It wasn't really until the credit crash that people questioned it. There's been an overwhelming public and political consensus, which is incredibly alarming. When everybody seems to be heading like sheep in the same direction, that's the time to start worrying!

Politics have become very global, and the state of the environment is so critical. At the recent Summit in Edinburgh there were over two

hundred thousand people on the march. It will be interesting to see what will come out of promises to "break the chain of debt."
The contribution of rock music to these big global campaigns has to be a continuing illustration of the power of political song. It's only one aspect, but there it still is, absolutely up front. You can be cynical about the rock stars up there condemning governments, but at the same time, the power of rock music is there to tap into genuinely popular radical protest. *Donald Smith*

IAN WALKER

The funny thing is I don't see myself as a political songwriter. My songs don't come from carrying a banner, they come from personal situations. Other people say my songs are political, they influence people. 'Hawks and Eagles' became an anthem in certain ways, it was even sung when Mandela was in George Square, but I didn't write it that way. 'Roses in December' has been taken up as about Vietnam, 'Some Hae Meat' about poverty. They were not written to advance a political position. 'Don't Turn the Key' now in Penny Stone's CND book, about the bombing of Libya.
I went through a period of years when I seemed to get inspiration [for songs from newspaper stories]. I read about a pilot who bombed Libya. Another time I read about the nuclear key holder who deserted his post, and was praised by the judge. 'Some Hae Meat' came from anger about the millions spent advertising food. Anger that maybe comes from the way I was brought up? It's a Scots trait to rail against the misuse of authority, unearned power and authority of Royalty, etc
The songs are social comment, my response to social situations. They were not written to bang the drum, but they get taken for that purpose. People say "that expresses what I want to say".
I didn't know what I was doing to begin with. I started by writing little parodies. Political parodies, for example one about credit cards, 'You're my best friend' that was about poverty, spending all your money on the card. My first real song was 'Some Hae Meat' to a traditional tune. 'Roses' has a traditional tune, 'Hawks' is to a basic American trad tune that I learned from an American girl busker in

Germany. I'm not a musician as such, I don't know where the tunes are coming from, sometimes I think I'm maybe using the same tune all the time. *Ian Walker*

JOHN WATT

"John has been a prolific writer. In the tradition of the 'people's poets' his subject matter is wide-ranging, taking in all kinds of issues but always with a local flavour and with a streetwise perspective. John is a natural wordsmith and most of the time he has chosen song as the vehicle to bear his words. Traditional song has had a great influence on John and he has had a greater influence on the Scottish folksong revival than most people would appreciate.

"The overriding image of John is of fun, but below the surface lies some sharp political observation and social comment. His subject matter might mitigate against his name being mentioned alongside such luminaries as Sorley MacLean, Norman MacCaig and even Robert Burns, but it would be a grave misjudgement of his talent if he was not recognised at this level." *Pete Heywood, in the sleeve notes for John Watt's 2000 CD of his own songs.*

EWAN MCVICAR

Over the last fifteen years I have worked in many dozens of Scottish schools writing new songs out of old ones with the children. You wonder at times if you have a right to express in song your ideas on what has happened to someone else, and at times you take a risk of hurting or offending those who know more at first hand about what you are using in a song.

Early on I worked with a class in the primary school in Bridgend, beside where the Auchengeich coal pit had been. We made a song about the 1959 pit disaster. We sang our new song during a school concert, then I was asked back to help sing it at a community Christmas concert.

I was told that some of the widows of the men would be there, in the front row, and that there had been a debate in the village as to whether the song should be sung. I said, "It's your community, you should decide". The song was sung, and four women came to me afterwards, tears in their eyes, to thank me and the kids for remembering their loss.

In the 1980s I made several songs to sing with the SCND Buskers, and for demos. My last gasp as a street songmaker came in the long buildup to the First Gulf War in 1991. Every Friday evening there was a singing vigil in Glasgow's George Square, and every other Saturday morning a march from Blythswood Square down through the city to a demo in George Square. The march was headed by Eurydice, the Glasgow Women's Socialist Choir, and the vigil led by the choir's organiser, Gordeanna McCulloch. First thing every other Saturday I sat at my breakfast cooking up a new song, met Eurydice, taught them the song, and we marched off singing it.

The principles of 'contrived banality' and 'creative redundancy' were much employed in the songs. One Saturday we marched round a corner, and a middle-aged woman on the pavement began to have hysterics. I knew she must have a son out there in danger, and thought that we were the Evil Reds intent upon getting him killed. I wanted to stop, to explain and convince, to point out that the next verses said *'Bring the boys all home alive'* and *'Why should any young man die for petrol and for power?'* But the march rolled on, I felt she could not hear what we were singing, only hear the thump of her own anxious heart. Song is only a support for action, not a cure for heartache. *Ewan McVicar*

The Revival of an Auld Sang

Roch the wind in the clear day's dawin
Blaws the cloods heelster gowdie ow'r the bay
But there's mair nor a roch wind blawin
Through the great glen o the warld the day.
It's a thocht that will gar oor rottans
-A' they rogues that gang gallus, fresh and gay -
Tak the road and seek ither loanins
For their ill ploys, tae sport and play.

Nae mair will the bonnie callants
Mairch tae war when oor braggarts crousely craw,
Nor wee weans frae pit-heid and clachan
Mourn the ships sailin doon the Broomielaw.
Broken faimlies in lands we've herriet
Will curse Scotland the Brave nae mair, nae mair;
Black and white, ane til ither mairriet
Mak the vile barracks o their maisters bare.

So come all ye at hame wi Freedom,
Never heed whit the hoodies croak for doom
In your hoose a' the bairns o Adam
Can find breid, barley-bree and painted room.
When MacLean meets wi's freens in Springburn
A' the roses and geans will turn tae bloom,
And a black boy frae yont Nyanga
Dings the fell gallows o the burghers doon.

The Freedom Come-All-Ye, tune The Bloody Fields Of Flanders,
words Hamish Henderson

On 22nd April 1707 the Scottish Parliament was dissolved, and Chancellor Seafield said it was 'an end of an auld sang', but auld sangs continued to be sung and new sangs of Scotland and its politics kept being made. This last chapter considers song types and categories, the use of tunes, the songmakers and singers, and the future.

Hamish Henderson's song 'The Freedom Come-All-Ye' has been mentioned several times in this book. It has repeatedly been urged as a new National Anthem for Scotland, though Henderson himself did not favour this. His strongly Scots poetic lyric is initially difficult and inaccessible for many listeners, yet new hearers feel an urge to learn more about its meanings. The core message is of internationalism and peace, while acknowledging the past celebration of the soldier Jocks. The Maclean of the lyrics is the Socialist hero John Maclean.

The tune Henderson used is 'The Bloody Fields of Flanders', a WW1 pipe tune which Henderson said he first heard played on the WW2 Anzio beachhead by Pipie Tom Smith of the 6th Gordons (Banffshire Battalion). Henderson also used this tune for his song 'The John MacLean March', and Glasgow writer Cliff Hanley used a different setting of the tune for his 'Scotland the Brave', which has been advanced as another candidate for a Scottish National Anthem. In a letter to the author Henderson wrote that the 'Flanders' tune stems from the Perthshire folk song 'Busk Busk Bonnie Lassie' aka 'Bonny Glenshee'.

The 'Come-All-Ye' was probably written at the urging of Morris Blythman, who was soliciting songs on the topics of peace and opposition to the American nuclear submarines coming to the Holy Loch. Henderson said the songs was written 'for the Glasgow peace marchers, May 1960', and it was first recorded on the 1962 'Ding Dong Dollar' album on the American Folkways label. It has been recorded many times since.

The 'Freedom Come-All-Ye' holds many of the threads of Scots political folk song that I have tried to disentangle in this book – protest, Scots language and poetic expression, peace, socialism, past warfare and the Scottish soldier's role in Empire, internationalism, and the reuse and reapplication of older tunes.

SONG TYPES AND CATEGORIES

Themes of identity and the need for action run through the topic of Scots political song. Rich Scots language both rural poetic and urban demotic is often employed, important when the lyrics speak of identity and confrontation with a ruling elite and media who employ a standard slightly Scots inflected English. Although creation and use of the songs are more prominent in left wing and nationalist settings, there are also the songs of the right wingers and unionists. Sometimes songs of right and left, of union and separation contend directly through response, comment and confrontation.

How can we characterise song types? In chapter one I proposed a few basic types - action-based, illustrative, retrospective and supportive. In this book I have described in use some more detailed types.

'Agit Prop', agitation cum propaganda songs, are created to be sung on the march or demo, or played over the loudspeaker mounted on the political campaign van. The songs are immediate, current and simplistic, they utilise Scots vernacular and feature redundancy in their lyrics.

More developed immediate protest songs are sometimes made or adapted for the platform at the end of the march or to sing at the demo, and also for the support concert and recording. Some of these are the individual protest of the singer songwriter, others have strong accessible choruses. The themes are protest, anger and indignation, and vigorous comment. A few of these more developed songs made for immediate purposes, through qualities of poetry, singability, universalism, the persistence in performing them by the maker or by a well-known singer, etc, can transcend the immediate situation that called them forth and join the ongoing corpus of political song, for example 'Such a Parcel of Rogues', 'Hawks and Eagles' and 'Who Pays the Piper?'

This corpus also includes lyric protest songs made not in response to specific events but as pro-active, more general protest and urging of responsive action. For example 'Both Sides the Tweed'. A very few songs transcend the folk song genre to become anthemic 'National Songs', espoused by the whole nation, e.g. 'Scots Wha Hae', 'Flower of Scotland', ' A Man's A Man', 'The Freedom Come-All-Ye'.

To the outright political songs we must add songs of comment, comment and narrative, or straight narrative accounts without comment, that are utilised for political purposes or in political settings. There is social comment within some work songs e.g. bothy ballads or songs of strikes. Many of the old 'big ballads' contain sexual and class social comment, explicit or read into the narrative by the singer. These ballads also carry many narrative accounts of political violent strife and contention, e.g. the Border Ballads of cross-frontier encounters, the North East ballads of battles and smaller clashes.

Many songs use retroactive historical comment, illustrating principles to be promoted and fought for in the present day by telling of past injustices and iniquities. They make present political points by recounting tales of past issues and causes, e.g. the many Jacobite songs written long after the 1745 Rising. So much political song was and is retrospective, creating partisan accounts of past conflicts and issues to use as illumination and support for current attitudes and actions.

For example, Thomas Crawford writes about Alan Ramsay's ballad opera 'The Gentle Shepherd', written in 1729, set in 1660, the time of the Restoration. Crawford quotes from a ballad, to the tune 'Cauld Kail in Aberdeen', that curses those in rebellion against authority, referring explicitly to the Restoration but surely aimed against 1720s Jacobites.

Cauld be the rebel cast, -
Oppressors base and bloody;
I hope we'll see them at the last
Strung a' up in a woody.

Political and comment song descriptive categories could include reportage, comment, parody and squib. They could be illustrative, critical, celebratory, complaining, topical, retrospective, oppositional, modern, substantial and more. Anger and outrage are prominent characteristics of Scots political songs, as is Scots vernacular whether city or poetic, and immediacy e.g the 'Ding Dong Dollar' and Republican songs of the 1960s, and many of Matt McGinn's songs. Even when the subject is deadly serious Scottish political song is often humorous, usually satiric in tone, and this is much more prominent in Scotland than the comparable songs of our Southern cousins. The lyric of the anthem of the English anti-nuclear movement in the 1960s was written by science fiction author John Brunner.

Don't you hear the H Bomb's thunder,
Echo like the crack of doom?
While they rend the skies asunder
Fallout makes the earth a tomb

The equivalent Scots anthem had several hands on it when it was 'workshopped' by the Glasgow Song Guild. It used humour and the vernacular to sharpen its point.

O the Yanks they drapped anchor in Dunoon
An they had a civic welcome frae the toon
As they cam up the measured mile, Bonny Mary o Argyle
Wis wearin spangled drawers below her goon
O ye canny spend a dollar when ye're deid

USE OF TUNES

The tunes used for 'The H Bomb's Thunder' and 'Ding Dong Dollar' lead us into the topic of tune families. The primacy of lyric over melody on political song, up until the recent rise of the singer-songwriter, results in much reuse of older tunes. The term 'parody' is sometimes applied to such use, but unless the new lyric makes substantial use of, or plays directly off, the older lyric then there is no parody, only tune re-employment.

The origin of the tunes used for both the above anti-nuclear tunes is American. Is this using the foe's resources against them, or just pragmatic employment of simple bouncing tunes?

'The H Bomb's Thunder' was brought by Brunner to a group of singers who "were planning the music for the first Aldermaston peace march [in 1958], and asked if we could turn it into a song for the march. After trying all sorts of tunes it was [Karl Dallas] who suggested we use 'Miner's Lifeguard.'" (Dallas 1972). This American trade union song, *"Keep your hand upon your wages and your eye upon the scale"*, was in turn drawn out of a white US spiritual, *"Life's like a mountain railway, sometimes up and sometimes down"*, and writer Karl Dallas says the tune in origin "is derived from the Welsh hymn 'Calon lan'".

The 'Ding Dong Dollar' tune was the Scots children's anthem 'Ye Canny Shove Yer Grannie Aff A Bus', *"Ye canny shove yer grannie cause she's yer mammie's mammie"*. This derived from the American 'She'll Be Coming Round The Mountain When She Comes', which also had a US religious ancestor 'When The Chariot Comes'.

Other US song tunes were turned and employed against the nuclear invaders. 'Yankee Doodle Dandy' became *"Chase the Yankees oot the Clyde an send them hame tae mammy"*. 'We Shall Not Be Moved' was the first to be workshopped, *becoming "Like a tree that's standing by the Holy Loch, I shall not be moved"*, and eventually moving to the football terraces to *become "Like a team that's standing in the FA Cup"*. 'John Brown's Body' transmogrified into *"Ban Polaris - Hallelujah, And send the Yankees hame"*. The tune 'Marching Through Georgia' is an incitement to civil strife on two continents. Whistling it in the USA below the Mason-Dixon Line will get you punched, but so will any use of it on the streets of central Glasgow on a Saturday afternoon as the 'bears' are heading for their football derbies. The SCND Buskers learned this in the 1980s when they had to abandon singing their updated version of 'The Glesca Eskimos'. The tune had been adopted many years earlier by a proud gang of Proddie ruffians, rumoured to tuck open-blade razors behind their lapels ready for use, and provocatively proud of their Bridgeton home in Glasgow's East End and their allegiance to King Billy – William of Orange.

Hullo, hullo, we are the Billy Boys,
Hullo, hullo, we are the Billy Boys.
Up to the knees in Fenian blood, surrender or ye die,
We are the Brigton Billy Boys.

So the SCND Buskers would be challenged by Celtic supporters for using such an offensive tune, and by Rangers supporters for using such a proud tune without authority. Peace lovers cannot win sometimes. The reuse of tunes is not new. Robert Burns wrote no new tunes, though on occasion he would slow down or speed up or change the mood of a tune. Of the first generation of Revival songmakers, neither Blythman, Henderson nor Buchan made new tunes for their songs. Jim McLean and Matt McGinn used many old tunes, but also began to make new ones for their songs. Burns played fiddle,

All these lyrics were written to the tune of 'The Wark o The Weavers'
Our sodgers and our sailors, 'od! we mak' them a' bauld
For gin they hadna claes, faith, they couldna fecht for cauld
The high and low, the rich and puir – a'body, young and auld
Mair or less need the wark o' the weavers
David Shaw, Early 19th C

☙

Sae here's tae George Buchanan, wis first tae gie 't a name
An here's tae William Wallace, and John MacLean
An here's tae Bonnie Scotland - we'll see her free again
Wi Perfervidum Ingenium Scotorum
Morris Blythman1960s

☙

The Welly Boot Song
Tom Buchan / Billy Connolly 1970s

☙

We don't want British rule, we don't want it to stay
We don't want a spirit that fears the break of day
It's not a time for cowardice it's time to break away
With the spirit of the Scottish Resistance
ANON, 1980s

MacLean plays piano. Most of the next generation of songmakers had guitar skills – Ian Davison, Archie Fisher, Dick Gaughan, Robin Laing, Jim Brown. Nancy Nicolson plays melodeon, Ian Walker, Brian MacNeill and Billy Connolly play a number of instruments excellently. All of this grouping use a mixture of old and new tunes for their songs, but the later singer-songwriters tend to use new tunes only, e.g. Rab Noakes, Peter Nardini. Perhaps an increase in instrumental skills leads to greater creation of new tunes?

Morris Blythman often used tunes considered part of the rousing marching repertoire of Ulster Orange flute and accordion bands, and also seized on tunes from Scots and other traditions. On a 1950s family holiday in Brittany he heard the ancient Breton tune 'Al Alarc'h', and realised it could be applied to the old ballad of 'The Twa Corbies', the crows who profit from the slaying of a knight, his body abandoned by the ones he loved.

When, through the Reivers group, Norman Buchan brought the song 'The Wark o the Weavers' into the repertoire, Blythman and others grasped the tune firmly. Blythman's song 'Perfervidum Ingenium Scotorum', begins, "*We're aa met thegither here, but no tae sit an crack*", drawing on the first line of 19th Century weaver David Shaw's lyric. Blythman's chorus makes no lyric link with Shaw's.

Wi Perfervidum Ingenium you hear the ring o bells
Ye watch the wheel o fortune, an see whit it foretells
We'll win our Independence, ay, by takin it oorsels
Wi Perfervidum Ingenium Scotorum

Blythman asserts "*We'll win our independence by takin it oorsels*", and goes on to praise named Scots – George Buchanan, William Wallace and John Maclean. Hector MacMillan quotes two of Blythman's verses for 'Perfervidum Ingenium Scotorum', saying that the last two verses "wittily top-and-tail the whole of our story, from the sixteenth to the twenty-first century." The title Latin phrase works off the phrase 'Scotorum praefervida ingenia, the ardent temper of the

Scots', which was used by 16th Century Robert Buchanan, who was a reformer, historian, scholar, poet and tutor of James VI.
A use of Shaw's song for broader humour came in Tom Buchan's 1970s theatrical event 'The Great Northern Welly Boot Show', which told of a wellington boot factory threatened with closure and resultant worker unemployment. Sung by, and probably written by, Billy Connolly, the 'Welly Boot Song' made use of Shaw's tune and his key chorus line.
Shaw had *written "If it wasny for the weavers, whit wad we do? We wouldna get claith made o oor woo."* The new song said, *"If it wasny for yer wellies, where would ye be?"* In 1983 the 'Red Review' reworked this for *'If it wisnae for the Tories, where would we be? We would have our hospitals and infirmaries'*. Matt McGinn made use of the 'Weavers' song for his 'If it Wasny for the Union', and Blythman's own lyric was mangled for 'The Spirit of Scottish Resistance' in the 'Songs For National Liberation' booklet.
Some tunes change in character as they are reused. I have mentioned the ancient march tune 'Tutti Taiti', used for the drinking song 'Landlady what's the lawin?', then for Burns' 'Scots Wha Hae', usually sung at a dead slow march pace. 'Nicky Tams' is a jovial music hall type bothy ballad, used by Birmingham-based Aberdonian Ian Campbell for his poignant 'Old Man's Song'. The sad German WWII love song 'Lili Marlene' was used by Henderson and other soldiers for the angry 'D Day Dodgers', and by 'an English peacenik' for *"Underneath the table, hiding from the bomb, there I met a stranger, he said his name was Ron."* A British soldier's peacetime song, 'Bless Em All' became widely sung in WWII, then versions emerged used by Scots schoolchildren as a play song, by female factory and office workers when publicly parading a colleague about to be married, and by the Glasgow Song Workshop for 'Boomerang'.
One Scots tune has carried a surprising range of lyrics, political and otherwise. In the 16th Century a nine part pipe tune called 'Gabhaidh Sinn An Rath Mor' ['We Will Take The High Road'] which 'belonged' to the MacIntyres of Cruachan was 'appropriated' by the Stewarts of Appin, who played it when returning from the battle of Pinkie in

1547. After the battle of Inverlochy in 1644 a two part version of the tune acquired a Gaelic lyric. Then in 1715 the Stewarts played it at the battle of Sheriffmuir, after which the tune was known as the 'Sherramuir March'. After the '45 Rising a Jacobite Gaelic lyric was made, drawing on the older words. In 1819-21 James Hogg published (and probably wrote) the Jacobite song 'Will Ye Go To Sheriffmuir' which uses the tune.

Will ye go to Sheriffmuir, bauld John o Innisture?
There to see the noble Mar and his Highland Laddies.
Aa the true men o the north, Angus, Huntly and Seaforth,
Scouring on to cross the Forth, wi their white cockadies.

The tune sank socially over the centuries to become a favourite for children's songs, including 'Katie Bairdie', 'Hard Up Kick The Can', and 'London Bridge Is Falling Down'. And it was used for at least one recent political squib.

Maggie Thatcher's all at sea, Tries tae fool the counterie,
Spoutin rubbish on TV. [Stamp] Maggie Thatcher!

Though she's up tae every dodge, She couldny run a good minoge.
Ought tae fly the Jolly Roger. [Stamp] Maggie Thatcher!

SONGMAKERS AND SINGERS

Who makes the songs? The poets of Scotland make them. For an example from the 14th Century, consider in John Barbour's 'The Bruce' the wonderful 24 lines that begin with *'A! Fredome is a noble thing.'* Then consider Hamish Henderson's 'The Freedom Come-All-Ye', written for the 1960 Holy Loch marchers. Between the two, and since, many and many a Scottish poet has made trenchant and committed comment on their life and times.

Robert Burns' work encompasses the recovering of ballad versions, new songs of the Jacobites, election balladeering, protest at the actions and values of others, social comment and radical universalism.
What has come down to us is weighted towards published poets. As well as known poets whose work can be considered in annotated collections, there are the unknown balladeers. Some such songs are preserved by continuing to be sung because of their worth and relevance. Written or printed records of others are available to us in collections, or inserted into first hand accounts in books or in court proceedings or newspaper accounts of marches and demos.
Collections of printed broadsides of the 19th Century are a wonderful source of political and protest lyric. There are also much earlier broadsides that on occasion tell us of then current political issues and actions. And only a fraction of what was printed has been preserved to be available to us in current collections. The most enduring of what was written goes into the oral sung tradition, then back into book collections. But if it is too topical, it does not endure. If too workaday or flimsy in language or construction, it dies. If written with poetic force and quality, it has a better chance of continued life.
In the early days of the Folk Revival key political songmakers included Morris Blythman, Jim McLean, Hamish Henderson and Matt MacGinn. Only MacGinn was known as a paid public performer. Their work appeared in the Rebel Ceilidh Song Books and Norman Buchan's songbooks.
Nowadays there is a kind of poet called a singer-songwriter who is a professional or semi-professional performer. Roy Williamson, Dick Gaughan, Nancy Nicolson, Ian Davison, Peter Nardini, Brian MacNeill, John McCreadie, Eileen Penman, Ian Walker, Jim Brown, Karine Polwart, and many more have contributed to the fund of Scottish political song. Some of their work may be heard in concert or on recordings, through the efforts of folk club and festival organisers, Greentrax and other record labels. Increasingly these days, individual artistes or groups issue and sell their own recordings.
I have named Blythman, Henderson and Buchan as the three architects of the Revival. In this analogy the songmakers and the professional and

semi-professional singers are the builders who dug the drains and raised and plastered the walls, designed the furniture and plumbed in the electrics. The inhabitants of the building are of course all the above, and they share occupancy with all those who sing or join in or just listen to the songs. In Scotland, political song is part of the key structure of the folk song building, not just living in one room or floor, but from top to bottom, and in the hearts and minds of the inhabitants.

WHAT IS NOT IN THIS BOOK?

Many of the early Jacobite songs were in Gaelic. I have said hardly anything about political song in Gaelic in this book – when you are ignorant, silence is doubly golden. Also, much more could be said and illustrated about sexual or gender politics as handled in Scots song from the old ballads right up to current Scots hip-hop lyrics, rock, alternative country music, and other song genres, and the other kinds of political lyrics they have created.

Lyrics from 'Scheme Songs'
They caged me in a cell
Left me here lonely
I was the pawn in the Police street game
I was guilty, but I know I was framed

☙

All in the one boat together
Shade of skin no difference
We're all the same
Living on day to day

☙

Sixteen today
My feet are sore
Trying to earn some pay
They close their doors and say
Can't exploit you, try another day

Just two examples. First, in Chapter 16 Babs MacGregor tells about the use of a classical choral format for a 'Peace Oratorio', which was first performed without permission in the Scottish Law Courts. Second, in the archives of the Political Song Archive is 'Scheme Songs', a programme for a concert by the socially and politically explicit rock band Scheme, who sprang from and were based in Glasgow's huge Easterhouse public housing scheme. The author heard the band perform when they were tramping the country with an

Unemployment March, playing every night their mix of rock and Caribbean musical influences.

One reasonable response to this book is that it is too parochial in its focus on Scots political song during the lead up to and time of the Scottish Folk Revival. But any folk revival is through its nature strongly parochial – Ireland, Wales, USA, England, Scotland – each had their own version of the Folk Revival, with different key dates and personalities.

Michael Brocken's 2003 book is titled 'The British Folk Revival 1944-2002', but it is about the English Folk Revival. Indeed, at one point he refers to "the equally vigorous folk revival in Scotland". The Scottish performers who are mentioned by him are those who found performance success in London as well as in Scotland, or were involved in one of Ewan MacColl's recording projects, or are the four Scots in Brocken's list of six "folk artists leaving the revival for the sake of commercial success" - Isla St Clair, Billy Connolly, Gerry Rafferty and Barbara Dickson.

The most visible presence of folk music the public and enthusiasts see are the professional and semi-professional folk and formerly folk artists as they tour, perform in concert and record. They are the media part of the story. They are more visible, but in no wise more important, than the lovers (amateurs) of traditional song old or new in its political and non-political forms who sing it and listen to it in its older social contexts.

WHERE DOES IT COME FROM? WHERE DOES IT GO?

We know the names of only a few of the political song makers prior to Burns. Our National Bard is the wonder and the curse of Scots verse, some Scots seem to think that because we have him we need no other. Many traditional songs that he collected, and sometimes edited or added to, are in print wholly ascribed to him. The worst of his verse was sanctified and imitated by the kailyard school of Whistlebinkie poets, his political convictions were glossed over by right wing biographers and commentators. His songs are at times bellowed by tartaned entertainers or demurely simpered by drawing-room belles who seem not to pay any heed to the sense of his lyrics.

Yet the strength and weight of what he achieved resists and survives this mangling. Burns is periodically mined by poets, songmakers and singers. "Lots of Burns songs are performed in concert. Younger singers coming in have almost inverted snobbery, songs that were 'too popular' are not sung any more, e.g. 'The Bonny Lass o Fyvie'. Songwriters have an advantage. Poets are in the same position – 'Who can I tell this to?' Poets have only their own voice, songwriters have the voice of singers too. Folk clubs were of their time. Now there is much more to choose from, a wider spectrum with greater quality, so it is harder for folk music to become popular now." *Ronnie Clark*

Burns collected and edited the work of older songsmiths, after him came Hogg and Nairne and many another. In 1951 Scots poets contributed to the 'Sangs O The Stane' collection, Morris Blythman developed a fine line in anti-royalist songs, then got together a cabal of songwriters of whom the chief luminary was Jim McLean. For the 1960s Anti Polaris demos at the Holy Loch the Glasgow Song Guild produced an abundance of songs. Then their attention turned to campaign songs to support the emerging success of the Scottish National Party. In Edinburgh Hamish Henderson was collecting, writing and encouraging others to sing and to write. Norman Buchan's books provided the traditional song fuel so the Revival wagons could roll and the waggoners could sing their hearts out.

Around the country the folk song clubs, then the festivals sprang up, singers gained confidence and expertise and some became professionals, with many more as semi-professionals. As singers gained confidence in their ability to create as well as sing, the tide of protest song became a flood. Women's rights, the Poll Tax, The Gulf War, the closure of the Glasgow Govanhill Swimming Pool, the struggle for equity in South Africa – when a political issue catches fire, either national or local, of short or long duration, Scottish songmakers are usually to the fore.

Songwriter and organiser Rab Noakes assesses the state of Scots traditional music in 2009. "Currently instrumentally based traditional music is popular, song is in trouble. There is at present a lack of respect for Scottish tradition. There's a perception that it's highly respected, but it has been allowed to be very diluted, till regionality has mostly gone. It all sounds Irish, that happened through the seductive qualities of 1970s Irish music. I empathise with the reasons for that, it is a more seductive and easier sound. Ireland has also suffered from that, there is very little regional fiddling there any more." *Rab Noakes*

Songs are still being made in abundance, but are little heard because of the lack of a mass forum; the occasional radio or TV programmes that feature or discuss Scots political song tend to look to the past, not the present. Journalists and old folkies complain that no-one is writing political songs any more. Writer Stuart McHardy has a positive outlook.

"We used to have chapbooks and ballad sheets, full of political commentary, self supporting media. By the early 60s, technology meant somebody had access to a roneo machine, so could produce leaflets and give them away - individual action rather than rooted in community. Chapbooks were a natural part of the community. Now we are more self sufficient, there's a change there.

"What are the kids using now? The Internet, Facebook and U Tube. At the T In The Park festival, the band Rage Against the Machine's lyrics were absolutely what we have fought for. The band told BBC they could not film them, they said 'We are for the people here'. Some songs are not for the media, but for the people who made them, process is the important thing, the CD is the memento. Does it matter not getting into media? The media are now fragmenting. You can now use viral advertising, make your own list of web contacts, ask people to circulate information, lyrics, recordings. Find your own audience. You can also use the same approach for political purposes. Say a version of 'A Man's a Man' that points at current problems in China? There is a necessary level of professionalism and presentation.

The potential for political song is great. Young folk are doing it already." *Stuart McHardy*

Morris Blythman, Hamish Henderson and Norman Buchan were the key progenitors of the Revival, and all were creators and disseminators of Scottish political song. Among the next generation of songmakers and singers of Scots political song who emerged were Jim McLean, Matt McGinn, Josh McRae, Hamish Imlach, Ian Davison, Nancy Nicolson, Geordie McIntyre, Gordeanna McCulloch, Dick Gaughan, Ian Walker, Brian MacNeill, Alistair Hulitt and Karine Polwart.

The Scottish Folk Revival of this book's time has largely dissipated its energy, the mass chorus singing aspect of it is a withering bloom. Music education courses are training instrumentalists in traditional style whose technical ability is marvellous, but few of them sing, and those that do tend to treat the voice as another musical instrument rather than as a deliverer of narrative and comment. But the Folk Revival is always cyclical – ceilidh and campfire singing leads to folk clubs, then concerts, then festivals, then packs of fiddlers in pubs, then ceilidh dancing, then recordings, feral community choirs, community songmaking by the New Makars Trust, and the rise of storytelling. What will be next?

The impulse to make political songs will be there. The voices of the people, in the songs they choose to make and sing about what matters to them, remind us that, whatever contempt is at times expressed for the ideas and actions of politicians, the ideas and actions of politics are at the core of our lives and our living, and must be sung about.

Is Scotland any closer to creating the Eskimo Republic, and should we be?

Then let us pray that come it may, as come it will for aa that
That sense and worth o'er aa the earth shall bear the gree, an aa that
For aa that, an aa that, it's comin yet for aa that
That man to man, the world o'er, shall brothers be for aa that

APPENDIX ONE

People, groups, organisations, events, places.

ARTHUR ARGO
Aberdeenshire born Argo was a direct descendant of folk song collector Gavin Greig. Singer and collector Arthur Argo was a key activist in the Revival, co-creator of the Aberdeen Folk Club, initiator and editor of Chapbook magazine, and broadcaster.

JOHN BARROW
Tynesider Barrow came to study at Edinburgh University and stayed to organise folk events and run a booking agency for Dick Gaughan and others.

DOMINIC BEHAN
Irish songmaker and singer, brother of playwright Brendan Behan, Dominic Behan moved to Glasgow and wrote and performed in Scotland.

THURSO BERWICK
The literary pseudonym of Morris Blythman.

BOB BLAIR
Glasgow singer, member of the group Stramash, for a time a member of the London-based Critics group.

MARION BLYTHMAN
With her husband Morris an activist in the work of the Glasgow Song Guild, and a member of the Glasgow Eskimos.

MORRIS BLYTHMAN
The Spring 1982 issue of the literary magazine 'Chapman' was 'In memoriam Thurso Berwick', Blythman's pen name. Several chapters

of this book detail aspects of his work - writing, organising others to write and sing, and publishing Scots political song. He was one of the three architects of the Scottish Folk Revival, and was also a considerable poet in Scots. His best known songs include 'Coronation Coronach' aka 'The Scottish Breakaway', 'Sky High Joe' and 'Lucky Wee Prince Chairlie', but through the Glasgow Song Guild he contributed to many other Holy Loch and Republican songs.

ERIC BOGLE

One of the major songmakers of the Revival, Bogle's work includes several songs much sung and respected as part of Scotland's political song repertoire, but Bogle began songmaking after he emigrated to Australia, and his topics reflect the life and history of that country much more than Scotland. His best known political songs are 'And the Band Played Waltzing Matilda' and 'The Green Fields of France'.

THE BO'NESS REBELS LITERARY SOCIETY

From the 1940s to the 1960s the 'Society' organised regular ceilidhs and the publication of songbooks, as detailed in Chapter 2.

MARY BROOKSBANK

Dundee poet, songmaker and mill worker. Her best known songs include 'Oh Dear Me' (aka 'Ten and Nine'), 'Strathmartine Braes', and 'The Spinner's Wedding'.

BROOMHILL BUMS

The Broomhill Bums were a social grouping of singers and friends in 1959-61 who sang together at the Glasgow Folk Club in its first year, and were named after the '19 month party' in Hamish Imlach's house in Broomhill, Glasgow. They included Imlach himself, Ray and Archie Fisher, Mrs Fisher, Josh and Sheila McRae, Jim McLean, Jackie O'Connor and Ewan McVicar.

JIM BROWN
Glasgow born songmaker, singer and shipyard worker Brown moved to live in Cumbernauld and was active in Cumbernauld Little Theatre. There is a chapter on Brown's work in 'Song And Democratic Culture in Britain' by Ian Watson. Brown's best known songs include 'As I Walked On The Road' and 'The Waverley Polka'.

NORMAN AND JANEY BUCHAN
Norman, MP and song book editor, and his wife Janey, MEP, were tireless workers for Scotland's culture, and, through organising concerts and support for young singers, key in the early development of the Revival in Glasgow.

ROBERT BURNS
Scotland's 'National Bard', Burns not only wrote poetry and songs, he collected traditional Scots songs and tunes. He often shore off all the old verses after the first verse and chorus, and wrote new verses for the songs. He wrote many political and social comment songs and poems.

DAVID CAMPBELL
Storyteller, BBC Radio Scotland producer, writer.

WILLIAM CAMPBELL
A contemporary of Robert Burns, Campbell was a right wing Glasgow poet and songwriter who wrote various anti-Jacobin songs but also anti-slavery songs.

THE CENTRE FOR POLITICAL SONG
Based in the Caledonian University, Glasgow, the Centre and its archives are an invaluable resource, and much enriched the making of this book.

CHAPBOOK
Chapbook, 'Scotland's Folk-Life Magazine', was the major periodical of the Scottish Folk Revival, published quarterly, initially in Aberdeen then Edinburgh, from 1963 to 1968, edited by Arthur Argo and co-edited by Ian Philip.

CHAPMAN
Chapman, 'Scotland's Quality Literary Magazine', is still published in Edinburgh.

RONNIE CLARK
Glasgow based singer and folk club organizer. See Chapter 11 for details of his involvement with the Grand Hotel Folk Song and Ballad Club in Glasgow, and 'Chapbook' magazine.

THE CLYDEBANK RENT STRIKE
This 1920s campaign was led by Clydebank women, who resisted the efforts of the private housing owners and their factors to enforce rent increases. A pamphlet on the strike, written by academic Seán Damer, was published in 1982 by Clydebank District Library.

BILLY CONNOLLY
World known Glasgow comedian, actor, songmaker and singer, Connolly began his performing career in Glasgow folk clubs as a member of various groups, including The Humblebums which was first a duo of Connolly with Tam Harvey and later with Gerry Rafferty, then Connolly went solo.

JAMES CONNOLLY
Edinburgh born of Irish parents, Connolly was a union organiser, writer and heroic figure, who was one of the leaders of the 1916 Dublin Easter Rising and was executed. His best known song was 'Rebelsong'.

HARRY CONSTABLE
Bo'ness SNP councillor on Falkirk Council, active in the Bo'ness Rebels Literary Society.

JOE CORRIE
Fife miners' poet and dramatist.

THE CORRIES
This Edinburgh-based folk group was best known as the folk duo Ronnie Browne and Roy Williamson, who recorded many albums. Earlier it was the Corrie Folk Trio, the third member being Bill Smith. The singer Paddie Bell performed and recorded with the Trio.

DANNY COUPER
Aberdeen singer, folk club and concert organiser, and fish merchant.

IAN DAVISON
Davison has throughout the Revival been a well-respected, clever and melodic songwriter, a performer earlier with his own Folk Group and latterly solo, and a developer of the songmaking skills of others. He has written and recorded several CDs of his political and other songs including 'Mandela Danced in the Square'.

BARBARA DICKSON
Fife singer Dickson was a member of the Great Fife Road Show. Her initial recordings were of folk songs, but she achieved national fame as a singer of popular song and as an actress.

SHEILA DOUGLAS
Scone based Douglas has played many important roles in the Revival, as singer, author, collector, club organiser, storyteller. Her books include 'Come Gies A Sang', 'The Sang's The Thing' and 'Last Of The Tinsmiths'.

BOB DYLAN
American, the best known political songmaker of our times after Pete Seeger.

EDINBURGH PEOPLE'S FESTIVAL
One of the early elements of the Edinburgh Festival Fringe, the People's Festival ran from 1951 to 1954, as a left-wing counterbalance to the official Edinburgh Festival. The Friday night ceilidhs each year were seminal in the Scottish Folk Revival.

EURYDICE
Gordeanna MacCulloch was the initiator and for many years the key figure in Eurydice. In Greek myth Eurydice was the wife of harper and singer Orpheus, and the Orpheus Choir was the premier Glasgow choir for many years.

WINNIE EWING
Long term SNP politician, elected to the UK Parliament in 1967 for Hamilton, later a member of the European Parliament and the Scottish Parliament.

FASLANE PEACE CAMP
A long running vigil and protest camp based near an entrance to Faslane Nuclear Submarine base, Helensburgh.

FIANNA NA H'ALBA
Different writers give varying spellings of this 1940 -1950s Glasgow youth organization, sometimes naming it Clann na h-Alba. The association was later renamed The League of Young Scots. The Fianna is referred to in various 'rebel songs' of the time.

ARCHIE FISHER
Fisher has been one of the most praised Scottish traditional song and guitar stylists throughout the Revival. He initially sang in a duo with his

sister Ray and has more recently worked with Irish and Canadian singers, but his major contribution has been as a solo singer, songmaker, broadcaster and an organiser of clubs and festivals.

DICK GAUGHAN
Edinburgh-based singer, musician and the foremost interpreter of politically committed song in the Scottish Revival. Among his best known political works are 'Both Sides The Tweed' and 'Do You Think That The Russians Want War?' The following and earlier material is quoted with permission from his own website and shows his work extends much further and deeper into Scots tradition.

ROB GIBSON
A political and musical activist, Rob Gibson moved from Glasgow to Easter Ross, and is an SNP MSP.

ANNE LORNE GILLIES
Dr Gillies is a distinguished singer of and writer about Gaelic song, a song tutor, an organiser and a project and resource creator.

GLASGOW ESKIMOS
A group of singers active in the 1960s Holy Loch campaign against the siting of an American nuclear submarine base in the Holy Loch on the Firth of Clyde near Dunoon. Members of the Eskimos included Morris and Marion Blythman, Josh McRae, Jim McLean, Jackie O'Connor, Nigel Denver, and Jackie Keir.

THE GLASGOW SONG GUILD
A grouping of songmakers around Morris Blythman. See Chapter 9 for a listing of the songmakers involved and their approach.

GREENTRAX
Scotland's premier folk and traditional music record label, run by former policeman and folk club organiser Ian Green.

JOHN GREIG
Born in Inverness, Edinburgh-based, singer, organiser and activist. His accounts of his political song cassette label, of his involvement in the Edinburgh folk scene, and of Hamish Henderson, are in this book.

WOODY GUTHRIE
Highly influential 1940s American balladeer and songmaker.

OWEN HAND
Edinburgh based singer and songwriter, his best known song is 'My Donald'.

HAMISH HENDERSON
The third architect of the Scottish Folk Revival. Edinburgh-based writer, collector, organiser, enthuser, songmaker, inspirer. His songs include 'The Freedom Come-All-Ye', 'Rivonia' and'Farewell to Sicily', and his books include 'Alias MacAlias, and 'The Armstrong Nose'. A two volume biography of Henderson has been written by Timothy Neat.

JAMES HOGG
18th – 19th Century poet, songmaker and author, 'The Ettrick Shepherd'. His 1819 two volumes of the words and music of 'Jacobite Relics' include many fine songs made or remade by Hogg himself.

ALISTAIR HULETT
Glasgow-based singer, songmaker, activist.

FIONA HYSLOP
Born in Alloway, at the time of interview she was Culture Minister for the Scottish Government. When aged ten her interest in political song was sparked by hearing a recording of The Cheviot The Stag and the Black Black Oil, and by the songs of Burns.

HAMISH IMLACH
Glasgow then Motherwell based, in the 1960s Imlach was the best known young singer and raconteur of the Scottish Revival, and worked and recorded extensively. From the 1970s on he mostly toured abroad. In his autobiography, 'Cod Liver Oil and the Orange Juice', he talks in detail about the political song aspect of his work.

ARTHUR JOHNSTONE
Glasgow left wing powerfully voiced singer Johnstone sang for some years with the Laggan folk group, then as an unaccompanied solo singer. For many years he ran the Star Folk Club, which at the time met in the Communist Party's Glasgow HQ. It later moved to St Andrews In The Square.

WILLIE KELLOCK
A bank manager in Bo'ness and later in Spean Bridge, Kellock was central to the development of the Bo'ness Rebels Literary Society and its songbooks, to the Fianna Na h'Alba and other SNP initiatives.

JIM KELMAN
Glasgow novelist.

DANNY KYLE
Paisley buddie Kyle was a singer, folk club and festival organiser and broadcaster on BBC Scotland's 'Travelling Folk'.

T S LAW
Tom Law, Scottish poet, contributor of 'Reivin Sang' to 'Sangs O The Stane', credited in the 'Second Rebel Ceilidh Song Book' as writer of 'The Glesca Eskimos' and 'Fidel Says No', though it is likely that other members of the Glasgow Song Guild also contributed lines.

TOM LEONARD
Glasgow poet. While he was writer in residence in Paisley Leonard researched and edited the 'Radical Renfrew' collection of radical song and poetry.

ALAN LOMAX
America's most influential collector and consciousness-raiser of folk song and music. In the 1950s Lomax lived in London, and his 1951 collecting trip around Scotland was a spur for the creation of the School of Scottish Studies and the subsequent collecting work of Hamish Henderson.

NORMAN MACCAIG
Eminent Scots poet MacCaig was also a very popular singer of traditioal songs at Bo'ness Rebels ceilidhs.

IAN MACCALMAN
Edinburgh songmaker, recording studio engineer, 'Front man' for the mostly accapella group The MacCalmans.

EWAN MACCOLL
English, of Scots parentage. Singer, songmaker, playwright, actor, teacher, writer, organiser. The single most important figure of the Folk Revival in Britain.

JOHN MCCREADIE
Glasgow singer and songwriter with the group Diggery Venn and solo. His best known song is 'Doomsday In The Afternoon'.

GORDEANNA MCCULLOCH
Introduced to Scots traditional song at school by Norman Buchan, MacCulloch sang with the Glasgow group The Clutha for many years, and became known as one of Scotland's premier solo traditional

singers. She initiated and led Eurydice, the Glasgow Women's Socialist Choir.

HUGH MACDIARMID

The major Scots 20th Century poet, he inspired the Lallans movement in which younger poets began to write in a version of older Scots Language, though McDiarmid himself later moved to write in standard English. He is credited by some with initiating the idea that the Stone of Destiny be 'lifted' and returned to Scotland. Born Christopher Grieve, he took Hugh MacDiarmid as his pen name.

HUGH MACDONALD

An energetic SNP activist and singer since the 1940s, living partly on Islay and partly in Glasgow.

CARL MACDOUGALL

Glasgow writer, editor and folksong enthusiast who was a contributor to 'Chapbook' magazine and one of the organisers of the Grand Hotel Folk Song and Ballad Club in Glasgow.

JOHN MCEVOY

In the early 1950s McEvoy was an actor, and the writer of 'The Wee Magic Stane', the best known song about the Stone of Destiny. McEvoy was celebrated at the Bo'ness ceilidhs as a fine singer with a wide repertoire. He emigrated to Canada in the late 1950s to work in industry, and returned to Scotland in 1987.

ANGUS MCGILLVERAY

A West Lothian based key SNP activist, organising the Alba Pools fundraising scheme, and SNP publications including the Bo'Ness songbooks.

MATT MCGINN

From the 1960s to the 1980s McGinn wrote songs, recorded and performed extensively, and was an extremely popular singer-

songmaker with a distinctive urban Scots voice and a fiercely committed political stance. The book 'McGinn of the Calton' is in part autobiographical, in part a collection of some of his many songs.

JIMMIE MCGREGOR
Glasgow singer, musician and broadcaster. In partnership with singer Robin Hall he made many recordings and TV appearances, and then became very well known as a broadcaster, particularly through his long running BBC Scotland Radio programme 'McGregor's Gathering'.

STUART MCHARDY
Dundonian, Edinburgh-based, writer of many books, braodcaster, musician.

GEORDIE MCINTYRE
Influential Glasgow folk club organizer, singer and songwriter. He has done important work as a collector and resource creator. More recently he and key Revival singer Alison McMorland have performed widely together.

IAN MACKINTOSH
Glasgow singer and musician Mackintosh performed with various groups before turning solo and making several albums that strongly featured contemporary folk song both Scots and American. He became very popular in continental Europe, and at times worked in duos with Hamish Imlach and with Brian MacNeill.

JIM MCLEAN
McLean was Morris Blythman's principal fellow song-writer in the Glasgow Song Guild. McLean moved to London and created several themed albums of his own and other trenchant songs on Scottish Republicanism and other themes, which were recorded under his direction by Alastair McDonald and then Nigel Denver.

JOHN MACLEAN
Left wing political hero Maclean has repeatedly been the subject of or referred to on contemporary Scots folk song, particularly by Hamish Henderson and Morris Blythman. Marxist Maclean was referred to by the author's grandfather as 'the martyr', and suffered greatly in prison because of his opposition to World War One and his urging of reform.

DOLINA MACLENNAN
The first Gaelic singer to become actively involved in the Folk Revival, Uist born MacLennan met Hamish Henderson when she attended Edinburgh University.

ADAM MCNAUGHTAN
Glasgow songmaker and teacher McNaughtan is best known for his authorship of such nostalgic or humorous songs as 'The Glagow I Used To Know', 'Ye Canny Fling Pieces Oot a Twenty Story Flat' (aka 'The Height Starvation Song') and 'Oor Hamlet'. He has also penned several strongly political songs, including 'Thomas Muir Of Huntershill', and 'Blood Upon The Grass' which protests about a Scottish football team agreeing to play in Santigo Stadium where the Chile regime had killed many political opponents. McNaughtan has a central role in the 'Stramash' co-operative group of singers.

BRIAN MACNEILL
Glasgow singer, musician, writer and educationalist. His best known political songs include 'No Gods And Precious Few Heroes' and 'Strong Women Rule Us All With Their Tears'. MacNeill was for many years a member of the Battlefield Band, then a soloist.

JOSH MCRAE
Glasgwegian singer McRae was extremely influential in the early days of the Folk Revival. He was a member of the Reivers group, the foremost singer of the Glasgow Eskimos, and had some Top Twenty success with several songs , ncluding 'Messing About On The River'

and 'Talking Army Blues'. The latter song was satirically critical of conscription.

MICHAEL MARRA

Dundonian songmaker, musician and performer Marra has an idiosyncratic and very attractive approach to songmaking. His songs often contain strong social comment and observation, but his musical approach does not draw on folk influences so his work is outwith the scope of this book.

JOHN MARTYN

Songmaker and musician Glasgwegian Martyn was born Iain McGeachy. His early influences and experiences were in the Glasgow folk scene, he initially learned guitar skills from Hamish Imlach but went on to be a major British stylist on both acoustic and electric guitar.

THOMAS MUIR OF HUNTERSHILL

A contemporary of Robert Burns, Muir was a leading Radical figure who was transported to Australia because of his views, but escaped to Revolutionary France.

MUNLOCHY GM CROPS VIGIL

Earlier in this chapter, see Rob Gibson's account of this 21st Century Black Isle vigil in protest against the test planting of GM crops.

LADY CAROLINE NAIRNE

In the mid 19th Century Carolina Oliphant, Baroness Nairne, was the anonymous maker of many songs on Scots themes, particularly on the Jacobites. She also rewrote many older songs, making them more anodyne.

PETER NARDINI

In the 1980s Largs born art teacher Nardini wrote and recorded songs that were fiercely politically critical. Songs criticising the actions of

Prime Minister Margaret Thatcher included 'Why Sink the Belgrano?' and 'Now That Hitler's Back In Style'. He is now better known as an artist.

NEW MAKARS TRUST

Formed in 1997, the Trust runs community songmaking projects in which groups of adults and schoolchildren work with professional Scots songmakers to write their own songs about their own lives and communities. Large scale projects have been run in Fife and South Lanarkshire, medium size projects have run in many locations around Scotland, and the approach developed by New Makars songmakers has been used in many more places. The key begetter of the Trust is its secretary Gifford Lind, based in Dunfermline.

ANNE NEILSON

A singer from Rutherglen near Glasgow, Neilson was much influenced by her teacher Norman Buchan. She is a member of the Stramash group.

NANCY NICOLSON

Caithness born, Edinburgh based, songmaker, singer, school teacher, children's events organiser for Celtic Connections.

RAB NOAKES

Fife born Glasgow-based Noakes is a 'cult' Scottish songwriter and musician, maker of radio programmes, and record label organiser.

CATHIE PEATTIE

Peattie is a community organizer and singer from Grangemouth who became a Member of the Scottish Parliament, where she is a strong advocate for Scotland's traditional culture.

EILEEN PENMAN

Edinburgh based strongly politically committed singer and occasional songwriter.

PAT PLUNKETT

A former resident of Faslane Peace Camp, Plunkett moved to live in Renton. She was a member of the Scottish CND Buskers, and wrote many songs perfomed by them.

KARINE POLWART

Formerly an Edinburgh based children's rights worker, Polwart in the 21st Century developed an poignant approach to songmaking and has become a much praised professional performer. Her politically commited songs include 'Where Do You Lie My Father' about Srebrenitsa and 'Better Things' which criticises the UK Government's commitment to building a new generation of Trident nuclear missiles.

JOHN POWLES

Librarian Powles is Research Collections Manager for the Glasgow Caledonian University, where his responsibilities include managing Tthe Centre for Political Song.

JEAN REDPATH

One of the best known singers of the Scots Revival, Fifer Redpath moved to sing professionally in the USA in the early 1960s.

THE REIVERS

A group of solo singers assembled by Norman Buchan in the late 1950s to sing on the Scottish Television show 'Jigtime'. The initial members were Rena Swankey, Moyna Flanagan, Josh McRae and Enoch Kent. Flanagan left the group after one year, and McRae and Kent developed solo careers, Kent moving to Canada.

JEANNIE ROBERTSON

Aberdonian majestic Traveller singer whose much admired singing voice and repertoire were very influential for young Revival singers.

SANDY RODGER
19th Century Glasgow Radical poet and weaver.

JIMMY AND SUSAN ROSS
Glasgow based singers and songmakers, active in the Glasgow Song Guild and for many political causes.

ABBY SALE
When Abby Sale came from the USA in 1966 to do graduate work in social anthropology he was already involved in traditional song, studying with ballad authority MacEdward Leach, who introduced his students to Ewan MacColl, A L Lloyd, and Scottish ballads. Sale was learning Scots from the glossary in sleevenotes of the Riverside recording label Ballad collection.

SANDY BELL'S PUB
The bar, in Edinburgh's Forrest Hill Road, was until recent years formally named the Forresthill Bar, but known colloquially as Sandy Bell's after a barman there. It has since the 1960s been the social and musical centre of Edinburgh's traditional song and music scene. Hamish Henderson was an habitual customer.

THE SCND BUSKERS
This 1980s grouping of songmakers (Pat Plunkett, Ian Davison, Nancy Dangerfield, Ewan McVicar) and musicians (Joe Plunkett, Carol Sweeney, Harry Bickerstaff) made new peace songs and remade older Glasgow Eskimo songs, and performed and recorded them.

SCHOOL OF SCOTTISH STUDIES
Formed in 1953 as part of the University of Edinburgh, the School holds Scotland's largest archive of traditional Scottish song, music, story and lore. Hamish Henderson worked there and collected on behalf of the School.

OLD SCOTIA BAR

This pub is on Glasgow's Stockwell Street near the Clyde. It is named for the Scotia Music Hall which was beside it. For many years from the 1960s the bar was a key location for Glasgow's traditional singers and musicians.

SCOTTISH STORYTELLING CENTRE

Situated beside John Knox House on Edinburgh's High Street, the Centre has for several years supported and developed storytelling and allied arts in Scotland. The director is Donald Smith. Storytelling in Scotland has grown to remarkable strength under his leadership and guidance.

PEGGY SEEGER

American singer, musician and political songmaker Seeger was the personal and performing partner of Ewan MacColl, and is still very active in the USA writing and teaching about songmaking.

PETE SEEGER

American half-brother of Peggy Seeger, Pete Seeger is the doyen politically committed songmaker and singer of the American Folk Song Revival, and many Scots singers were inspired by him.

SIR WALTER SCOTT

19th Century Borderer, Scots novelist, poet and right wing songmaker. Scott edited the influential and important ballad collection, 'Scott's Minstrelsy Of The Border - though many of the ballads were specific to Borders life and history, many more had general currency in Scotland and beyond.

DONALD SMITH

Smith is a storyteller and organiser, Director of the Scottish Storytelling Centre and enthusiast for traditional Scottish song and culture.

JOHN MACK SMITH
Smith was a significant contributor of political songs to the Bo'ness songbooks. He is credited with making 'Ding Dong Dollar' because he had the initial idea for the song.

SONGS FROM UNDER THE BED
A cassette recording label of Scottish political songs, initiated and run by John Greig, who tells about it in detail in Chapter 15.

SOUTH SIDE BATHS CAMPAIGN
See singer Alistair Hulett's account in Chapter 10 of this struggle to stop the closure of these Glasgow swimming baths.

STRAMASH
A co-operative group of Glasgow singers and musicians. The members include Adam McNaughtan and Ann Neilson. The group developed and performed a show about the work of Matt McGinn, under the title 'McGinn Of The Calton'.

TRADITIONAL MUSIC AND SONG ASSOCIATION OF SCOTLAND (TMSA)
A national voluntary group which runs festivals and promotes Scotland's non-Gaelic musical traditions.

UKES AGAINST NUKES
The duo George Gunn and Bob Macaulay perform in rather anarchic style their own idiosyncratic highly literate lyrics set to a variety of music forms. Their work is described in Chapter 15.

IAN WALKER
Bo'ness songwriter and singer, his best known political songs include 'Hawks And Eagles Fly Like Doves' and 'Some Hae Meat'.

JOHN WATT
Fifer songmaker and club organiser.

ROY WILLIAMSON
Composer of the song 'Flower of Scotland', member of the Corries Folk Group.

BILLY WOLFE
Wolfe was a former Chairman of the Scottish National Party, and an enthusiast for Scottish song.

EWAN MCVICAR
Born in Inverness, in Glasgow had Morris Blythman as a school teacher. Worked for several years in East Africa and USA, returned to Scotland in 1967 and became active in songmaking. There is a very present author's voice in this book, because I was an active participant in many of the movements and events I describe, and many of the other participants are or were friends and colleagues in songmaking and performing. I have written many political and social comment songs.

FILES ON THE ACCOMPANYING CD

SONG FILES

Tracks 1, 3, 4, 6 and 7 are from *Thurso Berwick, Aa Breenge In,* a tribute cassette and booklet jointly issued by Songs From Under The Bed and Gallus in about 1991

Tracks 2, 8 and 29 were recorded for this disc

Track 5 is from *The Best Of Ian Davison – Volume Two,* Clydetracks 12,13,14

Tracks 9, 23 and 24 are from *Gie's Peace, Scottish CND Buskers,* Gallus GAL 100

Track 10 is from *Heroes*, a Neon/Watt production issued by The Tradition Bearers, LTCD3001, downloadable at www.go2neon.com

Track 11 is from *The Best Of Ian Davison*, Clydetracks Double CD 008/009, see www.iandavisonsongs.co.uk

Track 12 is from *Scotland First*, Nevis NEV LP 108, 1970

Track 13 is from *Scottish Republican Songs*, Major Minor MMLP1, 1966

Tracks 14 and 26 are from *Rhyme And Reason* Gallus GAL 104, 2001

Track 15 is from *Almost New Songs*, Gallus no number, 2005

Track 16 is from *Flying High,* Fellside FE060

Track 17 is from *Crossing The Border Lines,* Fellside FECD88, see www.fellside.com

Track 18 is from *Songs From Under The Bed 1*

Track 19 is from *Songs From Under The Bed 2*

Track 20 is From *Songs From Under The Bed 3*

Tracks 21 and 22 are from *Songs From Under The Poll Tax*, A Songs From Under The Bed Project, 1991

Tracks 25 and 28 are from *Mmmmmm, That Great Event*, Virtual Mary Music no number

Track 27 is from *Oilseed Raped*, Munlochy GM Vigil no number

DATA FILES

A] In place of a book index there is on the CD a fully searchable PDF file of the Eskimo Republic text. Enter in the 'search' box any word or name you wish to locate.
B] Cover images of LPs, cassettes and CDs.
C] Covers of song booklets.
D] Covers and texts of various relevant publications.
E] Song lyrics.
F] Photos and illustrations of various relevant people.